Our Bodies, Ourselves
and the Work of Writing

Our Bodies, Ourselves and the Work of Writing

Susan Wells

Stanford University Press
Stanford, California

Stanford University Press
Stanford, California

Library of Congress Cataloging-in-Publication Data
Wells, Susan, Ph. D.
   Our bodies, ourselves and the work of writing / Susan Wells.
      p. cm.
   Includes bibliographical references and index.
   ISBN 978-0-8047-6308-0 (cloth : alk. paper)--ISBN 978-0-8047-6309-7 (pbk. : alk. paper)
   1. Our bodies, ourselves--Authorship. 2. Boston Women's Health Book Collective. 3. Women--Health and hygiene. 4. Feminist literature--History and criticism. 5. Medical literature--History and criticism. I. Title.
   RA778.W234 2010
   613'.04244--dc22   2009042485

Typeset by Bruce Lundquist in 11/15 Bell MT

To
Lisa Baird
and
Katherine Winkler

One knows the good people by the fact
That they get better
When one knows them.

Bertolt Brecht, "Song About the Good People"

Contents

Figures

Acknowledgments

WRITING THIS BOOK WAS A LONG ROMP, and I have a lot to be grateful for. My deepest appreciation goes to the Boston Women's Health Book Collective for the gift of their archival materials to the Schlesinger Collection at the Radcliffe Institute, Harvard University, and for agreeing to be interviewed by me; those conversations were candid and thoughtful. I am especially grateful to Judith Norsigian, who connected me with people who could help with this project, and to Jane Pincus and to Pamela Berger, who made personal materials available. Jane Pincus also answered many queries in the last stages of revision. Members of the collective helped me correct many errors; those that remain are all my own.

Two pioneering researchers in this field set the standard for my work: Kathy Davis's *The Making of* Our Bodies, Ourselves: *How Feminism Travels Across Borders* (Chapel Hill, NC: Duke University Press, 2007); and Kathryn Flannery's *Feminist Literacies, 1968–75* (Urbana: University of Illinois Press, 2005). I learned from these books and from conversations with both writers.

I am grateful to the staff of the Schlesinger Library at the Radcliffe Institute, Harvard University, especially Sarah Hutcheon, the reference librarian, who guided me to very useful materials, and Diana Carey, the reference librarian for visual resources, who helped with the selection of illustrations. Staff at the Archives and Special Collections at Northeastern University made available the papers of the Cambridge Women's Center. Thomas Whitehead at the Paley Library's Contemporary Culture Collection at Temple University provided valuable aid with photographs.

Temple University sustained me with financial support during this long project. The university gave me time to travel, research, and write: two study leaves, two summer research grants, and a grant in aid of research. A Research Incentive Grant from the Temple College of Liberal Arts allowed me to finish research on the project. The Temple University English Department supported my work with three excellent research assistants: Elizabeth Kimball expertly helped with preparing the manuscript; Tatum Dowling was patient and meticulous with final revisions; and Nathaniel Racine helped with final proofreading. Constance Grady made corrections.

The staff at Stanford University Press is unequalled in its scholarship and expertise. I came to rely on the good judgment of Emily-Jane Cohen, acquisitions editor, and on the advice of Ariane de Pree, contracts and rights manager.

Many friends advised me about large and small problems with this text. I especially appreciate the intellectual support and friendship of Ellen Barton, Eli Goldblatt, Steven Mailloux, Susan Jarratt, Don Bialostosky, Jack Selzer, Bill Overton, Julia Ericksen, Richard Immerman, Ellen Moore, and Michael Sappol.

Audiences who listened to early versions of this work offered valuable questions and comments. I am grateful to those who listened to papers I presented at CCCC, the Penn State Conference on Rhetoric and Composition, the Rhetoric Society of America, the National Library of Medicine, Case Western Reserve University, the University of Virginia Medical School, the University of Texas, and Pittsburgh University. Participants in the Rhetoric Society of America (RSA) Workshop on Medical Rhetoric were an especially exigent and helpful audience.

As always, the loving support of my family sustains my work. My warm and loving thanks are to my brilliant husband, Hugh Grady, and to my two radiant daughters, Laura Rose and Constance. If this book shines, it is because they showed me the way.

Our Bodies, Ourselves
and the Work of Writing

Introduction: Writing *Our Bodies*

IN MAY 1969, the Female Liberation Conference at Emmanuel College in Cambridge, Massachusetts, drew large numbers of politically active and enthusiastic women; scores attended one workshop in particular entitled "Women and Their Bodies." There, they exchanged stories of distress, pain, poor care, and confusion. They decided to explore their own bodily experiences under the twin signs of consciousness-raising and self-help, two reflexive terms that signal the difficulty of the project they were about to undertake. The group met regularly for searching, frank discussions of their own health crises and life passages, and they read papers they had written on health topics. After the inchoate group finished a series of summer and fall meetings and its members revised the papers they had written, they began to share their information in a class called Women and Their Bodies offered at MIT during the winter of 1969–70. Later in 1970, the papers, which had established the outline of the course, were published by the collective as *Women and Their Bodies*.[1] In 1971, the New England Free Press issued the book, slightly revised and with reordered chapters, as *Our Bodies, Our Selves*.[2] The book went into mainstream publication in 1973 as *Our Bodies, Ourselves*, and it has been revised and reissued continually for the past thirty-six years. The Boston Women's Health Book Collective has seen its text through eight major editions in all, with a number of minor revisions.[3] By 2008, the book had been translated and adapted into twenty-nine languages and generated related projects such as *Ourselves and Our Children* (1978), *Ourselves Growing Older: Women Aging with Knowledge and Power* (1987), *Our Bodies, Ourselves: Menopause*

(2007), *Our Bodies, Ourselves: Pregnancy and Birth* (2008), and *Nuestras Cuerpas, Nuestras Vidas* (Seven Stories, 2000). In its various editions, the book has sold more than four million copies.[4]

Our Bodies, Ourselves was not just a routine women's health manual with a feminist twist. Nothing like it was available when the book was first published in 1970. Of course, women had always read and written health books: guides to pregnancy and childbirth, marriage manuals, and texts on nutrition and exercise have been common since the nineteenth century, often written by women physicians and health reformers and addressed to women as family healthcare providers. But in the 1960s and early 1970s, books written by women about women's health did not exist. At that time, a woman searching for recent health texts might find Sherwin Kaufman's *The Ageless Woman: Menopause, Hormones, and the Quest for Youth*, a long advertisement for hormone replacement therapy. Or, if she had an interest in feminism, Simone de Beauvoir's introduction might draw her to *The Sexually Responsive Woman* by Phyllis and Eberhard Kronhausen. There were traditional baby books on infant care and newer books on natural childbirth and birth control, but the popular mass-market label Good Housekeeping Books would not publish its *Good Housekeeping Woman's Medical Guide* until 1974. In 1970, an inquiring woman would have had to consult the generic *The Handy Home Medical Adviser, and Concise Medical Encyclopedia* by Morris Fishbein.[5] *Our Bodies, Ourselves* was distinctive in offering comprehensive, woman-positive information about healthcare, produced by women, in a cheap and accessible format. It reached an audience of women hungry for this information.

One may look at this story in many ways. For members of the collective, it is the "good story" of success against the odds. For feminists, it is a story of survival: an institution formed by the social movements of the 1960s has become a well-articulated, deeply embedded institution. For Donna Haraway, it is a story of feminism as an imperial project, claiming the body as an undiscovered territory.[6] For Kathy Davis, author of *The Making of* Our Bodies, Ourselves: *How Feminism Travels Across Borders*, the book's dissemination demonstrates the rise of global feminism.[7]

These are all good, perceptive stories, fruitful and faithful to the historical record. They are not the story I will be telling. My book reads the history of *Our Bodies, Ourselves* as a story about writers and writing. Indeed, since the women who produced *Our Bodies, Ourselves*, by and large, do not think of themselves as writers—many of them do not think of the book as a piece of writing—this is not the story that the collective would tell about themselves.[8] But they *were* writers. They found new ways to organize and understand the work of writing: they saw the text they produced as a link connecting them to an embodied reader. Struggling to represent their own bodies and those of their readers, they worked out ways of both addressing issues of identity politics and expressing their belief in the universality of the female body. As the book developed, they worked to present more sophisticated and comprehensive medical information and to maintain a critical distance from conventional medicine. These projects responded to a political impulse that developed and modulated as the group's experience grew. *Our Bodies, Ourselves* was a rhetorical experiment, an attempt to construct a new space that opened to public discourse issues that had been consigned to individual privacy. This is not just a story of triumph over adversity, but of continual reinvention, of roads taken and missed, of experiments that were occasionally brilliantly successful. It is a human story, a writerly story.

I examine how this work of writing was done from the first *Women and Their Bodies* in 1970 through the 1984 revision, *The New Our Bodies, Ourselves*, when the book took the form it would maintain until the most recent edition in 2005. (I will refer to all these editions by the most commonly used title, *Our Bodies, Ourselves*.) During this period, the book moved beyond its first audience in the women's movement, became rooted in a nascent women's health movement, and reached out to both mass audiences and diffuse communities of medical advocacy. The important work of the Boston Women's Health Book Collective is worth studying on its own terms. But *Our Bodies, Ourselves* is also a textual crossroads where questions central to writing, gender, and science meet: What does it mean to take on or to refuse the identity of "writer"? Can there be a distinctive feminist account of the biology of women? Can a "lay" audience appropriate and critique the expert knowledge of physicians? These questions prompted my study of the Boston Women's Health Book Collective: my perspective is shaped by my discipline, rhetoric, and specifically by public sphere theory.

As a rhetorician, I am as interested in how texts work as in what they say: I do not see the text as a transparent window into social reality, or primarily as a formal structure; rather, I see it as a work of language that organizes social agency. I see *Our Bodies, Ourselves* as enacting a sustained relationship among writers and readers. Writers selected from the resources available to them to work that subtle change in the minds of readers that we call persuasion; they were open to reciprocal acts of persuasion from readers. Public sphere theorists, beginning with Jürgen Habermas, have shown that the definition of a public issue, who can speak to it, and what counts as an argument for or against it are among the most consequential of all acts of persuasion.[9] They have also identified a paradox that shaped the collective's entrance into the public: the circulation of texts—a central activity that forms the public sphere—connects a wide and abstract audience, "the public," and also activates concrete, socially located readers, "our public."[10]

Our Bodies, Ourselves was written to accommodate women who had taken the collective's health course: the project began as an extension of face-to-face talk. The first editions, quickly and crudely printed on newsprint, spoke to "our public." But "the public" soon arrived, demanding more copies of the book than the first publisher, the New England Free Press, could produce. Negotiating this change was not easy. Simon and Schuster offered the collective an attractive contract, ceding to them control over the book and its marketing and providing for low-cost distribution to clinics and women's groups. Since the collective's central goal was to get *Our Bodies, Ourselves* out "more quickly to more women in more places," moving to Simon and Schuster seemed like a good choice, promising a move beyond "our public" to "the public."[11]

The group approached this decision with great trepidation; in collective meetings, members reported anxious dreams about giving birth.[12] The decision to move to a mainstream house signaled that the collective would not entrust their future to the movements of the 1960s or to the institutions of publicity these movements had sponsored, although they made their decision in ways these movements might have approved. Both Random House and Simon and Schuster had offered contracts; when collective member Norma Swenson wrote to reject Random House's offer, she cited among other issues the press' ownership by RCA, "a war contractor."[13] Still, the New England Free Press was not happy, and it appended a letter (without the collective's permission) to late printings of the 1971 *Our Bodies, Our Selves*:

We at the Free Press feel strongly that "Our Bodies, Our Selves" should continue to be distributed through the Movement where it will help build a socialist women's consciousness. Women are now getting the book from political people and organizations they trust. This makes the book part of a personal process of political education. Selling the book through capitalist distributors in bookstores or even supermarkets will only impede that process.[14]

Of course, nothing would have pleased the collective more than supermarket sales, and they struggled for years to issue the book as a mass-market paperback. Infuriating as it was for the press to expect the collective to sacrifice their own work to the development of the distribution capacities of the press, it was true that the movement in general, and the Free Press in particular, could only have constructed the public space it needed through the cultural and political work of the writers it sponsored.

The move to Simon and Schuster had other consequences for the collective. It prompted them to formalize the loose, participatory writing practices that had produced the 1970 and 1971 editions. Entering a formal contract meant that the group had to incorporate as a nonprofit, so that the group of women who had been working on the book, now organized as a tight group of twelve, officially became the Board of Directors of the Boston Women's Health Book Collective (BWHBC). Boundaries solidified: the collective defined itself as a stable group of twelve founding members and maintained that structure throughout the period described in this book. The early editions, *Women and Their Bodies* (1970) and *Our Bodies, Our Selves* (1971), were written by members of the collective and their close contacts, and women attending the collective's health classes might be invited to help in revision, or their comments might be included in the text. Later, the BWHBC evolved a routine for composing and editing, and then circulating drafts among themselves, to second readers, outside experts, and focus groups. Relations of power and hierarchy operated through these networks and so did relationships of dialogue and mutual support.

Beginning in 1970, the collective organized itself as a networked writer—what I call "a distributed writer"—sharing knowledge and skills. Although many movement publications were collectively written, the complex webs of collaboration that the Boston Women's Health Book Collective evolved were distinctive in their variety and extent; these will be discussed in Chapter 2. The collective included members from different generations, ethnic backgrounds, and levels of experience: some had been with the group since an initial workshop on Women and Their Bodies at the Emmanuel Conference in May 1969; others had joined during the subsequent study group, or at the large MIT classes. Group membership had been fluid from 1970 until 1973: veteran Lucy Candib, one of the writers of the "Capitalism and Medicine" chapter, left in 1971 when she could no longer juggle the demands of medical school with collective membership.[15] Others joined in: Paula Doress-Worters, newly settled in the area and struggling with the demands of a new baby, nevertheless drove into Cambridge weekly through the winter of 1970 because group meetings had become vitally important to her.[16] For the first edition of the book, writers took on chapters because the topics interested them, did research, wrote drafts intended for use in a health course, read the drafts to a shifting group, and incorporated the groups' additions, commentary, and criticisms. Publication of the first newsprint editions brought new members to the group: Judith Norsigian, a health activist, came because she thought the book needed a chapter on nutrition; Norma Swenson, past president of the American Association for Childbirth Education, thought that the chapter on childbirth could be much improved.[17] As I will show in Chapter 1, the members of the emerging collective connected the group to the local women's movement, to the New Left, and to established organizations of health education and emerging practices of the critical social sciences.

The background of collective members also reflects an important development earlier in the 1960s—the entrance of women into higher education. All the collective's members had some experience with higher education when they began their work with the group, and many later earned advanced degrees.[18] Some members of the collective went to women's colleges, including those associated with elite universities (Radcliffe at Harvard, Pembroke at Brown); others went to large state universities (Michigan), or to private schools (Suffolk University). They participated in the opening of higher education to large numbers of women during the 1960s, when, after declines in the 1950s, both the numbers and percentages of women matriculated for undergraduate degrees increased. In 1960, only 38 percent of college-aged women were full-time students; by 1970, 49 percent were in college. During the same period, the college-age men's enrollment increased by only 1 percent, to 55 percent.[19] Young women had few models for working in education: after grade school, they would have encountered few women teachers, and they would have seen almost no women school principals or college professors. But they entered undergraduate education with enthusiasm. Male-only schools became coeducational: women's dormitories were built at MIT; Barnard students were no longer excluded from Columbia's courses; Princeton admitted women in 1970. Older women returned to school, encouraged by Betty Friedan's *The Feminine Mystique* (1964) and supported by programs like the Minnesota Plan for Continuing Education for Women.

Our Bodies, Ourselves was, at the beginning, very much a book from Boston. In Boston, the separation between local counterpublics of the likeminded and a broader national public was relatively thin. Many of the writers were connected, directly or indirectly, to the universities of the city, which offered access to national networks. The publications of the Boston Left were distributed nationally, and the city was a regular stop on the circuits of speakers and other movement travelers. Boston fostered a busy alternative press and an active women's movement. By the mid-1970s, the collective and the book it had produced were seen as models by the Boston women's movement. A document unrelated to *Our Bodies, Ourselves*, an informal history of the Somerville Women's Health Project written by Judy Herman in 1975, described the collective as "a thriving, on-going group, which supported its members emotionally and financially. Sales of *Our Bodies Our Selves* approached the one million mark, a second edition was in progress, and royalties from the collective went to support other feminist health groups, including ours."[20]

Earlier, in 1969, the collective came together as the Boston women's movement was defining itself: the ecology of that movement was rich.

Cell 16, a radical feminist organization equally committed to dialectical materialism and karate, had moved to Boston from New York, publishing its journal *No More Fun and Games*.[21] The group that would become Bread and Roses, a successful, if short-lived, feminist organization, was forming.[22] These groups came together at the May 1969 Female Liberation Conference at Emmanuel College, when the workshop Women and Their Bodies was held. Other workshops included sessions on feminist strategy, black women in society, women and the law, witchcraft, and self-defense. Reports in the movement press suggested that the conference was inchoate, emotional, and very energetic.[23]

The Boston Women's Health Book Collective emerged in a relatively collaborative political climate: the Boston women's movement was not as deeply divided between "politicos" and "feminists" as it was in other cities.[24] Radical feminists and socialist feminists worked on common projects; cultural work and political organizing were seldom opposed to each other; feminists who experimented in personal life and relationships were also deeply engaged in the antiwar movement and in organizing the legal defense of Black Panther Party members.[25] Although it was not their primary affiliation, many members of the Boston Women's Health Book Collective maintained membership in Bread and Roses, and their writers and collaborators also circulated there.[26] Through the early 1970s, the collective maintained an active connection with the women's movement in Boston; their relationship with the national women's health movement developed later and was sustained longer. The collective regularly offered a women's health course in the Cambridge Women's Center, housed in a building taken over from Harvard in 1971. Lesbian Liberation and, for a time, the Combahee River Collective also had offices in the center.[27] When *Our Bodies, Ourselves* became a best-seller in 1973, and the collective was briefly flush with money, they funded local women's health groups, including the Cambridge Women's Clinic. The collective was, for the Boston women's movement, a sign of what was possible for a group that defined its projects well.

During the 1970s and 1980s, the collective's project became more complicated. Their critique of medicine broadened: the issue was no longer the problematic relationship between a male doctor and a female

Figure I.1. Members of the Boston Women's Health Book Collective, 1973.
Standing: Jane Pincus, Vilunya Diskin, Joan Ditzion, Esther Rome, Paula Doress-
Worters, Wendy Sanford. Sitting: Norma Swenson, Pamela Berger, Ruth Bell
Alexander, Nancy Miriam Hawley, Judith Norsigian. Photo: Phyllis Ewen.

patient, but the entire medical system. The collective, like other groups
in the women's movement, confronted issues of identity politics. Becoming more aware of differences of class, race, sexual orientation, ability/
disability, and age, the collective sought to incorporate those differences
into the text. While insisting on "a uniquely OBOS feminist perspective,"
the collective sought to patch in the discourses of medical practitioners,
alternative caregivers, and individuals and organizations whose experiences and views were quite different from their own.[28]

For the collective, these questions began with their location in specific writing communities: many of them were moving from the world
of higher education into the emerging New Left and the women's movement. My book also begins with those relationships. The first chapter, "A Rage for Inscription," considers social movements and higher
education as "literacy sponsors," institutions that promote the literacy
practices of the individuals they encounter.[29] Higher education fostered

practices of research and presentation: college women were encouraged to think about how their education could be put to use, a challenging question when many professions, including medicine, were still unfriendly to women. The writing of the collective was also shaped by the New Left and the women's movement. I analyze the discursive practices of those movements, discussing forms of publication, genres, and styles in the underground press and publications of the emerging women's movement, focusing on how they developed in Boston.

The second chapter, "A Different Kind of Writer," considers what authorship meant to the members of the Boston Women's Health Book Collective and how they negotiated its demands. How did the work of writing change as the book developed? What was required to move from a text that combined the personal experiences of the writers and their friends with the fruits of library research to one that was authoritative and comprehensive? The collective sometimes referred to their authorial voice as "OBOS style." That voice constructed an idealized writer who brings an impossible range of experience and knowledge to bear on the task of writing. She speaks intimately to her readers, but she also invokes the voices of diverse experiences. She is both singular and plural, both lay and expert. Although such a writer might have seemed like a strange figure to traditional literary history, recent scholarship in both literature and rhetoric understands authorship more collectively, placing writers in relationship to collaborators, editors, and readers.[30] Members of the Boston Women's Health Book Collective have always valued their distinctive writing practices, naming them "collective authorship." "Collective," a term used in the early 1970s by many women's groups, including Boston's Bread and Roses, denoted a small group bound by personal ties that undertook political projects. (The increasing importance of the work of writing can be traced in the evolution of the rest of the name from "Boston Women's Health Collective" to "Boston Women's Health Course Collective," to "Boston Women's Health Book Collective.") Since "collective authorship" is an unstable and sometimes disputed term, and since it suggests relationships worked out face-to-face in a close group of collaborators, I describe the collective's mode of work as "distributed authorship." For them, the work of writing was shared among dispersed networks of experts, lay readers, and editors that gathered information,

organized activity, and carried on the political work of the group. Distributed authorship brought the knowledge of experts and advocacy groups
to the text; it helped the collective construct a relationship between personal experience of the body and disciplinary medical knowledge.

Distributed authorship was also a way of becoming more diverse and
inclusive. The collective based its politics on the universality of women's
embodiment: since all women inhabited female bodies—in a sense, *are*
female bodies—a woman's understanding of her own embodiment would
support her political commitment to all other women. But identity politics insisted that women did not all experience embodiment in the same
way and so questioned the universalism of *Our Bodies, Ourselves*. The
issues raised by lesbians and women of color questioned the collective's
notion of unmediated feminine solidarity; forming relationships with
organizations of lesbians and women of color enabled them to frame
these issues as questions of writing.

The third chapter, "A Different Kind of Book," examines the rhetorical structure of *Our Bodies, Ourselves*. This book drew readers in by
breaching its own frame: readers were addressed as "we," encouraged to
identify with personal narratives, and invited to use the book as a prop
for exploration of their own bodies. The text was organized as a set
of nested narratives that could present women's varied experiences as
multiple exfoliating possibilities or juxtapose them to create openings
for critical intervention and suggest ways of reversing or transforming
accepted practices. These techniques were in aid of initiating a public
conversation about women's bodies and their fortunes, a conversation
that became more difficult during the 1980s. As a conservative political
backlash intensified, the text became more closed: *Our Bodies, Ourselves*,
which had entered the world steeped in hope, became a melancholy text.
The fortunes of the sexuality chapter in various editions of *Our Bodies,
Ourselves* illustrate these changes.

Our Bodies, Ourselves has always represented the female body; it has
always aimed to provide reliable medical information. The last two
chapters of Our Bodies, Ourselves *and the Work of Writing* focus on
these projects, tracing the themes and strategies that shaped the text's
image of the active, problematic, connected, and autonomous female
body, and on the uneven and uncertain attempt to correct medicine, to

appropriate it, and to transform it. As a counterpart to the open and experimental address of the text, its description of the body explores the possibilities of reafference: the sensation of touching, viewing, or otherwise manipulating one's own body. Self-exploration was most exigent and consequential in the discussion of sexual anatomy, particularly the clitoris. In successive editions, the collective reconstructed its own experience of reafference, moving from the disgust and alienation of earlier editions to a sense of agency and autonomy, particularly in the discussion of pregnancy.

My book identifies three textual strategies characteristic of *Our Bodies, Ourselves*: authorship is distributed; the text structurally breaches its own frame; the body invoked in the text is reafferent, that is, reflexive and self-referential. These strategies are paradoxical because they at once exceed and enforce the boundaries of textuality. Distributed authorship redistributes agency by including potential readers as collaborators, but also it confirms the collective's overall control of the text. Ruptures in the textual frame include the reader, but they also encourage her to textualize her own body, to write it into the narrative. The reader who investigates herself is both an independent researcher and an agent of the text. These strategies all speak to the book's paradoxical movement between "the public" of anonymous, disconnected readers and "our public" of friends and collaborators. The collective engaged readers as collaborators and used collaborators as surrogates for readers.

Both as a set of professional practices and as an industry, the medicine of 1984 was different from that of 1970. Biomedicine had become an evidence-based science that supported highly centralized and profitable corporations, and the collective struggled to respond to this change. They had begun by investigating the individual doctor-patient relationship and criticizing its power relationships; in 1984, they confronted medicine as a corporate practice that posed questions of access to care. The collective therefore moved from work on the politics of medicine to understanding medicine as politics, as the distribution of scarce resources. *Our Bodies, Ourselves* reflects this work, as the disciplinary registers of medicine are criticized, parodied, or incorporated in the text, particularly in the chapter on birth. I analyze these strategies in Chapter 5, "Taking on Medicine."

This book ends with the 1984 edition of *Our Bodies, Ourselves*. By 1984, the structures of distributed authorship had been consolidated, and the book had taken a stable shape. Since the political situation had changed, the book was no longer a movement publication, but rather a response to the Reagan era, to backlash, and to the first manifestations of managed care. From 1970 to 1984, *Our Bodies, Ourselves* developed from a feminist project to an institution, collaborating with and confronting something like our contemporary medical establishment.

As a rhetorician, I am interested in the work that texts do and in the work that writers do in producing them. I have enjoyed two tremendous resources in examining these issues for *Our Bodies, Ourselves*: the collection of Boston Women's Health Book Collective papers at the Schlesinger Library at the Radcliffe Institute, and the generous help of the eleven surviving members of the original collective. The two hundred or so boxes of the collective's papers offer a rich account of how they worked, how they struggled, and how they related to the social movements of the 1960s. The members of the collective generously consented to interviews that were equally rich resources for understanding how the writers thought and what they were trying to do. The analytic tools of rhetorical study, particularly those developed in public sphere theory and in the rhetoric of medicine have helped me to understand this labor of writing.[31] I do not claim membership in the "we" that speaks and reads *Our Bodies, Ourselves*; my book's project is to explain and analyze, rather than to celebrate, that collective work. But I am grateful to them for the care with which they have preserved their history and for their generosity in sharing it.

1   A Rage for Inscription

O

UR BODIES, OURSELVES was written in the midst of rapid social change, and so it was written amid furious activity and protracted conflict. Its networks of writers condensed points of social activity and political controversy; they concentrated rhetorical resources generated by social movements. These movements shaped the writers of the collective; they encouraged an array of mental habits and writing practices that would make *Our Bodies, Ourselves* both novel and inevitable. Members of the collective also learned skills of analysis and research in higher education, which was opening to women. In the field of literacy studies, such institutional contexts for writing are called "literacy sponsors"; Deborah Brandt has defined them as "agents, local or distant, concrete or abstract, who enable, support, teach and model, as well as recruit, regulate, suppress, or withhold, literacy—and gain advantage by it in some way."[1] We are used to thinking of colleges and universities as sponsors of writing, but it may seem odd to think of the New Left and the women's movement in that way: insurgents of the 1960s and 1970s are imagined picking up guitars or picket signs, not typewriters. But both of these movements were deeply committed to writing and publication; together with higher education, they fostered habits of research, writing, and publication that made the composition of *Our Bodies, Ourselves* possible. Although the book was probably one of the most innovative, and certainly the most enduring, of the publication projects of the 1960s, it was not at all unique.

Higher education, the New Left, and the women's movement each offered distinct models of publicity. The New Left and the women's movement sometimes understood themselves as forming and addressing a universal public that included all possible significant individuals—a broad and undifferentiated mass of potential recruits. At other times, both movements saw themselves as constructing limited counterpublics, specialized groups bound together by texts and practices that expressed their opposition to the status quo. Higher education, especially for women, engaged in a great equalizing mission in the 1960s, so students were encouraged to see themselves as agents of profound social change, to put their education to use "in the world." Later, in the 1970s and 1980s, progressives in higher education continued the New Left's practice of critiquing conventional disciplines, including those related to medicine; they saw themselves as addressing communities of likeminded scholars and activists.

The Boston Women's Health Book Collective (BWHBC) organized networks of authorship in all three of these institutions, reorganizing their networks as social movements faltered or collapsed, reaching out to communities of clinical activists and patient advocates. This chapter shows how *Our Bodies, Ourselves* (OBOS) responded to sponsoring formations, considering the various writing practices and genres, forms of publication, and relations to the public sphere of the texts they fostered. Members of the collective had been formed by higher education and were eager to redeem the promise of their formation. The New Left fostered do-it-yourself publication processes; the genre of power-structure research, imported from the civil rights movement, offered a model for *Our Bodies, Ourselves*. The feminist conversational genre of consciousness-raising offered the collective a persuasive model of argument and a discourse register that mixed colloquial language with political analysis. In the particular local circumstances of Boston, the genre of the open letter, popular in the women's movement, offered a model of pointed, engaged, and expressive publication. These sponsors and practices supported, in contradictory and layered ways, the writing of individuals in the collective; here, I discuss the particular practices of Lucy Candib and Nancy Miriam Hawley. Sponsoring institutions also offered the collective a model of publication as a path to constructing a public and transforming public discussion.

Women learned about writing and research in higher education, which was opening to them in the 1960s, especially at the undergraduate level.[2] Higher education had given women writing skills; social movements gave them a reason to write and confidence in the efficacy of writing. The movements with which many members of the collective were associated—the New Left, including the antiwar and student movements, and the women's movement—provided a rich array of inscription practices, many of them collaborative. Social movements incited their participants to write: leaflets, discussion questions, white papers, chapters, books, and more books. They also made it easy to imagine writing as significant for broad audiences, or even as a tool for changing how medicine was practiced.

Women and Higher Education in the 1960s

Undergraduate education, with all its complexities, was an island of relative equality for women during the 1960s, when women entered colleges in large numbers. The classroom, the library, and the laboratory would be open to them, while the boardroom, the operating theater, and the courtroom were not. This anomaly did not go unnoticed by either college women or their professors: the late 1960s were a period of intense reflection on women's education. Both the United Nations and the President's Commission on the Status of Women issued reports on women's education in 1964. Education for women was on the agenda of such groups as the Ohio Statewide Conference on the Changing Status of Women (1963), and the subject of university symposia at such institutions as the University of Wisconsin (1963), the American Council on Education (1963), the Mississippi State College for Women (1960), Southern Methodist University (1967), and the University of Michigan Center for Continuing Education of Women (1968). When the University of Chicago sponsored a conference on liberal arts education to celebrate its seventy-fifth anniversary (1966), the proceedings included a talk on "Education and the Contemporary Woman."[3]

Once they graduated, many college women faced barriers to further professional training or advancement. Both medical schools and law schools maintained restrictive quotas. Many other professions—journalism, architecture, investment, broadcasting, science, and engineering—discouraged or excluded women. Women were less likely to gain admission to graduate school than men. In 1970, women held 37 percent of the professional and technical jobs in the country, down from 45 percent in 1945.[4] Nearly 20 percent of the working women who were college graduates were employed in clerical, sales, service, or factory jobs—as women's skills, levels of education, and breadth of literacy increased, job qualifications in traditionally feminine jobs were simply revised upward, with no corresponding benefit in pay or status.[5]

The contradiction between women's success in higher education and their exclusion from the professions was pressing, especially at women's colleges. There, discussions of higher education for women could be urgent; a case in point was the Study Group on Women's Education at Radcliffe. Dr. Grete Bibring, a psychoanalyst on the Radcliffe faculty, led the group, which met from January 10 to May 2, 1966.[6] Later that year she would write a report for Radcliffe Dean Mary Bunting about the "defeatist attitudes of Radcliffe students and their lack of opportunities."[7] Fifteen women participated in the study group at one time or another. Among them was Lucy Candib, who was already preparing for medical school: she would work with the Boston Women's Health Book Collective on the first two editions of *Our Bodies, Ourselves* in 1970 and 1971. Other study group members included future attorneys, writers, and other professionals; the poet Rachel Hadas attended regularly, as did Marion Kilson, an anthropologist who would direct the Bunting Institute at Radcliffe from 1977 to 1980, and Margaret Kemeney, who is currently professor of surgery at the Mt. Sinai School of Medicine. But in 1966, such accomplishments were far in the future; the women in the study group were generally worried and uncertain. Bibring opened the group by conceding, "Obviously, we all have subjective doubts which make this process of education productive of problems. We seem to worry about the security of our education for us in the future . . . with the addition of other elements which life will bring (i.e. a family)."[8] The group met biweekly and made a careful record of their discussions about the purpose of education, their speculations about femininity, and their many expressions of insecurity. One member of the group reported that "once she left the college community she was alienated from society. She finds herself always on the defensive, being questioned on all sides."[9] The study group grappled with the paradox of women's higher education in the 1960s: they were demonstrating, daily, their capacity for serious intellectual work, but it was not at all clear where they could do that work once they graduated.

As Rachel Hadas put it during one group meeting, "How can we use our education if we don't keep on with it after our B.A.?"[10] Since there was no obvious venue in which their skills could be used, women put their hard-won analytic capacities to work analyzing their own situation. They valued education: "Elizabeth said [education] produced greatness of heart." But they wondered how to use it: "Dr Bibring then asked why we were such angry young women."[11]

By the late 1960s, these questions had both broadened and attenuated for many of its members: student movements raised questions about higher education in general, rather than women's participation in it. However, many women, including members of the collective, believed that education caused broad social change. All members of the collective remembered writing in college. Some members of the collective valued their classes in writing: Norma Swenson remembers fondly her workshop in writing poetry.[12] Other writers, disengaged as they might have been from academic work, felt that they had learned something fundamentally useful. They had, for example, a new perspective on how stories change: "I knew from being a history major: History changes as different people write it."[13] As a group, the collective were dauntingly literate. Wendy Coppedge Sanford, editor of most of the eight editions of *Our Bodies, Ourselves*, won the 1967 LeBaron Russell Briggs Prize for the best honors essay in English by a Harvard University senior; her *Theater as Metaphor in Hamlet* was published by Harvard University Press.[14] They were at home in language. Planning an exhibit for a women's health fair, the collective considered showing pictures of "many, many cervices," deploying the Greek plural with colloquial ease.[15] As the group moved into research for the book, its process became a hybrid of consciousness-raising and a graduate seminar: women researched papers in the Countway Library at Harvard Medical, wrote up what they found, and read these papers to the group; members responded with stories of their own experiences. Responsive to the sponsorship of the women's movement, they continued to use the forms and conventions of higher education.

Writing and the New Left

If higher education posed problems for women, the New Left and the emergent counterculture seemed to offer solutions. Many members of the collective were New Leftists, working in the civil rights, antiwar, and draft-resistance movements, although others came to the group with little political experience. Founders Paula Doress-Worters, Vilunya Diskin, Joan Ditzion, Nancy Miriam Hawley, Jane Pincus, and Pamela Berger had worked in civil rights, antiwar, and draft-resistance movements before the Emmanuel Conference. Norma Swenson and Judith Norsigian came to the group because of specific health interests in childbirth and nutrition, respectively, but they also had broad political interests and experience with other issues.[16] What would work on the New Left have taught these collective members about writing? What forms of publication would they have seen? What models of producing, publishing, and disseminating writing did that movement sponsor?

The New Left survives in popular imagination as a stew of activities, barely distinguished from the counterculture, politically undefined and averse to disciplines such as writing and research.[17] But the Left was deeply invested in reading and writing, producing alternative or underground papers, magazines, journals, position papers, broadsides, and leaflets.[18] Producing these texts required both formal ingenuity and research skills, but they could be published casually and cheaply to reach broad readerships. Underground newspapers, for example, flourished. These weekly or biweekly tabloids sprung up in cities, towns, high schools, and army bases. The Underground Press Syndicate grew from twenty-five papers in 1966 to one hundred in 1968; by 1971, there were hundreds of papers.[19] These papers combined investigative reporting, foreign news, political analysis, and cultural criticism. They were not necessarily friendly to women; in 1970, women took over the New York *Rat* to protest a pornography issue. But in the undergrounds, by hook or by crook, women learned to write quickly, to edit each other's work, to raise money, to do layout and pasteup, and to manage distribution.

Papers formed a national public for the Left. Linked by the Underground Press Syndicate and Liberation News Service, they freely reprinted articles produced in other cities. Since Lenin's *What Is to Be Done?* (1902), a newspaper had been the mark of a serious Left organization, but the underground press of the 1960s was not interested in that kind of coherence. (The quite different political newspapers of the 1970s, such as *The Guardian* and *The Call*, sometimes approximated it.) Underground papers might publish for a few issues, collapse, and re-form, but this ephemeral structure demonstrated that publication was within anyone's reach. The more established undergrounds assembled a staff, often working in a participatory, consensus-based structure. Papers that survived developed a core of a dozen or so people who sustained the paradoxes of leaderlessness, learning to write quickly, to edit, and to make decisions about the length and placement of articles. Writers of alternative papers generally described themselves as a collective, meaning that the group distrusted hierarchy and valued a fluid exchange of roles. The term was adapted by the Boston Women's Health Book Collective, who described their work process as "collective authorship," although the working relations among collective members and with external collaborators were much more textured and sustained than in the alternative press. The new technologies of photo offset printing made it easy and cheap to mock up the paper using typed copy, line drawings, color, press-on borders and headlines, hand-drawn typefaces, and photographs.[20] The printed word, here, was not the property of experts, but available to anyone; the news was no longer sought out, consumed, or rejected, but produced close to home. In her memoir, *With the Weathermen: the Personal Journal of a Revolutionary Woman*, Susan Stern described her ambivalent relation to her group's ancient offset press:

It had several parts missing, among them the feeder, and one of the "sucking" mechanisms, so you had to push one of the feeder rollers into the ink manually, then run to the other end, and lift out the newly printed sheet. In time we all learned how to run the press, how to load it, ink it, fix it, where to buy supplies for it, and how to find used, inexpensive parts for it. The press was our lifeline.[21]

The writing that ran through these lifelines varied widely. Underground papers were quite capable of publishing a vapid manifesto like "Sgt. Pepper's Political Club and Band," by Walter Bowart and Allen Katzman, which recommended that readers communicate with each other by staring at televisions tuned to empty channels.[22] Some papers offered little more than a steady diet of record and concert reviews. But from the beginning, many undergrounds featured solid reporting and a good deal of investigative journalism. The first volume of the Austin

Rag included a two-part series exposing conditions at the Austin State Hospital. The author, George Vizard, later murdered in suspicious circumstances, reported on his years of working at the hospital: "One of the major problems is money. I have seen many wards without adequate clothing or blankets for the patients. Many of the older 'back wards' have inadequate lighting and heating. The hospital is understaffed, and the pay scale is ridiculously low. An Attendant at ASH [Austin State Hospital] has a take home pay of about $150 a month; a Nurse Technician (two years of college through Blinn Junior College) takes home $200 a month."[23] The *Old Mole* published a similar exposé, "'Man Tends, God Mends,'" in February 1969. Written by five workers at the Mt. Auburn Hospital in Cambridge, the article includes a sidebar recounting a Saturday night in the Mount Auburn emergency room written by Lucy Candib, soon to write for *Our Bodies, Ourselves*.[24]

Underground media reported on political events. Newspapers, magazines like *Seven Days* or *Liberation*, casual publications like the leaflets of the Haight-Ashbury Communications Company, and the films distributed by Newsreel and its Boston and California branches covered demonstrations, conferences, and important speeches. Like the more mainstream reportage of the New Journalism, these stories were not conventional objective accounts: the reporter was part of the action and responded to events emotionally and intellectually. The Boston *Avatar*, not a particularly political paper, carried an account of the November 1967 demonstrations at the Oakland Induction Center.[25] V. T. Ronay's story resonates with the shock of the violent police response, with his own ambivalence about his role as reporter, with his lingering auditory hallucinations of "thousands of people cheering, cheering burning [draft] cards and arrests."[26] It does not tell us what happened at Oakland, but how it looked and felt:

The first and most striking shock in the events was the disparity of size between the police and the demonstrators, mainly kids. I had never noticed how small and skinny students and non-students are. Once the police line stood against the students it was impossible to see the people. . . . The average members of the community, whether male or female, do not exercise nor are they addicted to a notion of the necessity of violence. . . . The people had only their skulls and their screams.[27]

Stories such as these sustained a sense of a national movement, particularly after the fragmentation of Students for a Democratic Society (SDS) in the summer of 1969. Paradoxically, the New Left aversion to bureaucratic structures insured that written texts would be a critical mode of connection among dispersed groups; the underground papers were nodes around which organization, activity, and communication condensed. There were limits to these connections. After 1968, when the Black Panther Party sought alliances with the largely white New Left, exchanges with *The Black Panther* were common, but alternative papers were more or less oblivious to the existence of the traditional African American press. As far as the record shows, they were resolutely monolingual. Within these serious limits, underground papers demonstrated that writing, even casual writing, could establish communication among widely separated groups and encourage the co-coordinated actions and projects. Reprints from Denver's *Big Mama* or Houston's *Space City News* invoked, for readers in New York or Boston, the sense of widely dispersed readers and writers, hungry for information and analysis. Underground papers connected related projects: GI coffeehouses and free clinics exchanged papers and reprinted each other's news.

The style of New Left and alternative press writing was, to put it kindly, uneven. At its best, New Left writing was colloquial, faithful to the tempos and wandering focus of conversation, as in Christopher Tillan's cooking column for the Boston *Old Mole*: "There's probably a large cabbage . . . mouldering in the icebox. The solution to this is butter. If you don't buy it, find some way to get it. If your economic analysis runs in this direction, lift it. (I knew one guy in Berkeley who liked his cabbage this way, so he lifted his one stick of butter, got caught, searched, arrested, handcuffed and jailed, they dropped the butter charge when they found 2 grams of hash in the other pocket.)"[28]

New Left writing was frank about sexuality; underground papers generally relished transgression. The San Francisco *Oracle*, for example, published this open letter of appreciation to Allen Ginsburg from Liza Williams: "You hate war, and speak out. I think you have a tongue like some great bronze bell from the municipality of insight. (And personally I don't care whom you fuck, being delighted that you fuck with pleasure and can convey the delight of fucking, the news about loving, breathing, sweating, tasting, the humanness of contact.)"[29] The explicit, conversational quality of writing from the New Left and the underground press has been widely recognized, but the underground/New Left style included other registers. A wealth of detail established both credibility and presence, as in this account of the San Francisco Human Be-in with its paratactic nouns and adjectives: "Fans, feathers, plumes, and tusks; bells, drums, chimes, and incense; pennants, banners, flags, and talismans; beaded charms, oranges and carrots; balloons, flowers, animal robes and bamboo; flutes and baskets; folded hands, closed eyes, bright brow and smile; prayer cloth and shaman stick. Nearly everyone with something in their hands, except many children darting at the festival through the human forest."[30]

Underground papers offered national coverage, local information, entertainment, and advice on day-to-day life. In the week of April 11, 1969, any of the future members of the Boston Women's Health Book Collective who spent fifteen cents for the Cambridge alternative paper, *Old Mole: A Radical Biweekly*, would have found a range of articles. The cover graphic showed a Rand "Bomb Damage Effect Computer"—a chilling image, given that the bombing of Cambodia had begun. The paper ran articles about the war and the movement against it, including anti-ROTC campaigns and building occupations at Harvard and Boston University, and included short items: "Zaps," a column by a teacher in a prison school who had been reprimanded for wearing a beard and teaching Marx; reports on national repression against the Black Panther Party and on a strike at a local department store; book reviews; quotations from Melvin Laird, then secretary of defense; an article on Boston's property tax policy. The centerfold offered information about substitute teaching, a popular form of white-collar casual labor. The paper also carried a two-page article on abortion by Gene Bishop, later a resource person for *Our Bodies, Ourselves*. Abortion was still illegal, but in "To Control Our Own Bodies," Bishop offered practical advice on obtaining one, quoting from two personal narratives.[31] Bishop's article told readers how to prepare for an abortion, pay for it, and recover afterward; she did not give any description of the actual procedure, offering only vague reassurance that the procedure was short and not too painful. In these months before *Women and Their Bodies*, certain norms of reticence applied, even in the undergrounds.

Bishop wrote regularly for *The Old Mole*, generally on women's issues. In the next edition of the paper, a special supplement reporting on the Harvard student strike, her article, "Women and the Strike," exemplifies the transition from an academic rhetoric that recalled the Radcliffe Study Group on Women and Education to the conversational style emerging in the women's movement:

Despite the myth that Radcliffe girls are smarter, take copious notes, and do nothing but study, many girls never speak up at class, or at meetings. Harvard is male-centered; it is sometimes difficult for women to take themselves seriously. Besides, girls are brought up to feel that they should not assert their brains and their ideas in front of men, and even Radcliffe girls feel that constraint.

Especially at SDS meetings, girls are reluctant to articulate their ideas, and assume responsibility for political activities. None of this is surprising, for everything in the nature of Radcliffe makes women subordinate. When [Radcliffe Dean] Mrs. Bunting defends building dormitories which girls don't want, she says—we must make Radcliffe better, more attractive, so Harvard will want us. So Radcliffe sits and waits, like every other girl, waiting to be courted.[32]

In May 1969, Bishop was not the only writer who alternated "girls" with "women." Both those words appeared in many underground papers until the end of the year. But things were about to change. Printed below Bishop's article was the announcement of the Emmanuel Female Liberation Conference, the birthplace of the Boston Women's Health Book Collective.

The New Left developed a number of characteristic genres, armatures that organized ways of thinking and acting. Power-structure research reports, in particular, offered activists with skills in research and analysis a chance to use them in the service of the movement. The writers of *Our Bodies, Ourselves* adapted this framework; eventually, they would torque and transform the genre. The first editions of *Our Bodies, Ourselves* recalled the newsprint pamphlets in which power-structure research was often published. Like power-structure research, the first projects of the Boston Women's Health Book Collective were based on collective authorship and presented readers with pages of dense information, some

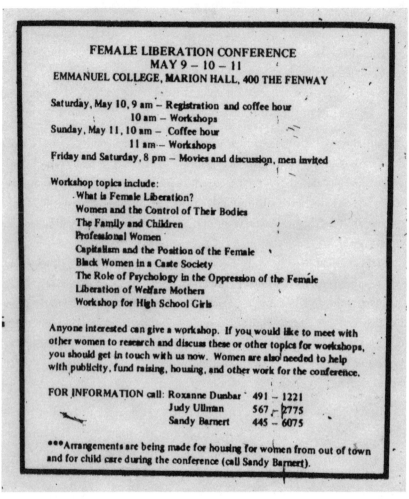

FEMALE LIBERATION CONFERENCE
MAY 9 – 10 – 11
EMMANUEL COLLEGE, MARION HALL, 400 THE FENWAY

Saturday, May 10, 9 am – Registration and coffee hour
            10 am – Workshops
Sunday, May 11, 10 am – Coffee hour
            11 am – Workshops
Friday and Saturday, 8 pm – Movies and discussion, men invited

Workshop topics include:
   What is Female Liberation?
   Women and the Control of Their Bodies
   The Family and Children
   Professional Women
   Capitalism and the Position of the Female
   Black Women in a Caste Society
   The Role of Psychology in the Oppression of the Female
   Liberation of Welfare Mothers
   Workshop for High School Girls

Anyone interested can give a workshop. If you would like to meet with
other women to research and discuss these or other topics for workshops,
you should get in touch with us now. Women are also needed to help
with publicity, fund raising, housing, and other work for the conference.

FOR INFORMATION call: Roxanne Dunbar   491 – 1221
                      Judy Ullman   567 – 2775
                      Sandy Barnert   445 – 6075

•••Arrangements are being made for housing for women from out of town
and for child care during the conference (call Sandy Barnert).

Figure 1.1. Advertisement for the Emmanuel Female Liberation
Conference, May 1969. *The Old Mole* 12 (April 25–May 9, 1969): 5.

of it transgressive. The writers of *Who Rules Columbia?* or *How Harvard Rules* printed memos "liberated" from the president's files; members of the collective snuck into the Harvard medical library.

Both the term "power-structure research" and the first publications in that genre originated in the civil rights movement, and they entered the New Left repertoire through the Economic Research and Action Project (ERAP), an SDS experiment in community organizing.[33] From the beginning, power-structure research combined an academic trust in the transformative power of specialized knowledge with a participatory democratic impetus to egalitarian, collaborative writing processes. The report would show readers that power in their community was held by the rich and powerful who controlled ostensibly democratic processes; readers would be convinced by this presentation to demand political change. Many power-structure projects used social scientists as researchers, but also trained local activists to find the relationships among politicians, members of corporate boards, and foundation experts. The knowledge constructed by power-structure research reports was held to be most effective when it was developed by ordinary people reflecting on common experiences, asking each other who the big men were in their town.[34] The power-structure research report was a connecting node in the networks of movement literacy, a place where skills, knowledge, and experience could be distributed.

Power-structure research established connections between the New Left and student movements. Fred Goff, one of the founders of the North American Conference on Latin America, recalls the writing of *Who Rules Columbia?*: "During the occupation of Columbia University in 1968, we virtually closed down for a few days. NACLA people spent most of their time up there talking to people in the buildings and trying to figure out a more immediate way we could use our research ability. Out of that came the pamphlet, *Who Rules Columbia?* That pamphlet sold a thousand copies the first day."[35] Drawing its title from William Domhoff's *Who Rules America?* and its structure from a publication by the Student Nonviolent Coordinating Committee (SNCC), "The Mississippi Power Structure," *Who Rules Columbia?* quickly found imitators.[36] Sixteen book-length studies with similar titles were published between 1967 and 1975.[37] *Who Rules Columbia?* is a thirty-five–page pamphlet, set in unjustified typescript, illustrated with tables and line diagrams. Like the first such report, "The Mississippi Power Structure," *Who Rules Columbia?* sought to demystify the everyday experience of its readers: students who thought that the business of Columbia was education learned that the school was actually a real estate mogul with interests in the defense industry. Power-structure research reports reconfigured local public spheres: information that had formerly been privileged or private began to circulate to new readers, provoking new questions.

A year later, in Cambridge, the Africa Research Group and *Old Mole* produced a similar pamphlet, *How Harvard Rules*.[38] Written in support of the student strike, the eighty-eight–page pamphlet was produced in eight days, "under great time constraints as well as political and emotional pressures."[39] *How Harvard Rules* included analyses of the Harvard Board of Governors and of the university's relationship to the foreign policy, defense, and intelligence establishments. It ended with short critiques of various disciplines as they were taught in the university. The book impressed and puzzled its initial readers. The *Harvard Crimson* remarked, "What is most fascinating about the book, magazine, or whatever is the range of its analysis." The *Crimson* writers were taken with the foldout, carefully calligraphed chart that connected important Harvard personages to government agencies and corporations. They were struck by the critique of the Fine Arts department: "The art historian at Harvard for the most part is working for and with the ruling class—for those that have time to acquire their particular 'culture.'" Although they found the writing wooden, the *Crimson* writers conceded that "it all holds together."[40]

As campus activism waned during the 1970s, radical scholars turned to the institutions and practices of their own discipline as a site for political work. This emerging academic Left was a resource for movement institutions in the 1970s and 1980s, and it became part of the network of distributed authorship developed by the Boston Women's Health Book Collective. Groups such as Science for the People and the Health Policy Advisory Council (Health-PAC) organized power-structure research projects and published their reports.[41] Health-PAC was particularly important for the collective, since their monthly bulletins often covered issues of interest to women. Here again, power-structure reports condensed the experience of disparate groups and learned ways of working together and sharing information; the reports encouraged similar collaborations among readers. The collective used materials from both groups in their health classes and recommended their publications to readers in the 1973 and 1976 editions of *Our Bodies, Ourselves*.

Power-structure research reports cultivated a distinctive style. The sense of "holding together" mentioned by the writers of the *Harvard Crimson* may have been formed by the high level of detail in *How Harvard*

Rules. Just as articles in underground newspapers insisted on every billy club and police helmet, every flute and shaman stick, power-structure research reports included every corporate tie, interlocking directorate, and government contract that researchers could find. The power-structure chart in *How Harvard Rules* is a thicket of connections and overlapping ties, organized in such categories as "International Corporations and the Imperialists." In this context, even the entry for John Crocker, "former rector: Groton School, Episcopal Minister," seems menacing.[42] Academic conventions were juxtaposed with New Left vernacular. The first page of *How Harvard Rules* argues, a little defensively, that the pamphlet includes information worth publishing by academic standards: "If a premium is placed on originality the main thrust of this booklet regarding who rules Harvard and how Harvard rules is not strikingly original. It does, however, contain a number of rather interesting disclosures."[43] But the last words of the text, the explanation of the inserted power-structure chart, refuse the norms of academic subtlety while invoking those of participation and equality:

By now some eyes will be blinking in disbelief. Can this be true, they will ask. It appears so overdone! It smacks of a crude conspiracy theory of power. Not true; for some reason that shouldn't elude us too long, our approach to power relationships is not the one they teach you in school or the one you find explored in the press. . . . If we still haven't told you enough, don't despair. Pick up the *WHO'S WHO, SOCIAL REGISTER and MOODY'S MANUAL*. Then, make your own chart. It will do funny things to your head too.[44]

The writers were disingenuous in their rejection of academic power-structure research: they had clearly learned the lessons taught by C. Wright Mills, Floyd Hunter, and William Domhoff. They had also learned from the civil rights movement to value the participatory research process as much as its critical product.

The written text of *Our Bodies, Ourselves* drew on many of the styles and genres of the New Left and alternative press. From the first edition of *Our Bodies, Ourselves* to the most recent, writers kept to a colloquial tone. Early editions constructed the writers as ordinary women with no special expertise and a desire to educate others: "By the fall, we were ready to share our collective knowledge with other sisters. Excited and

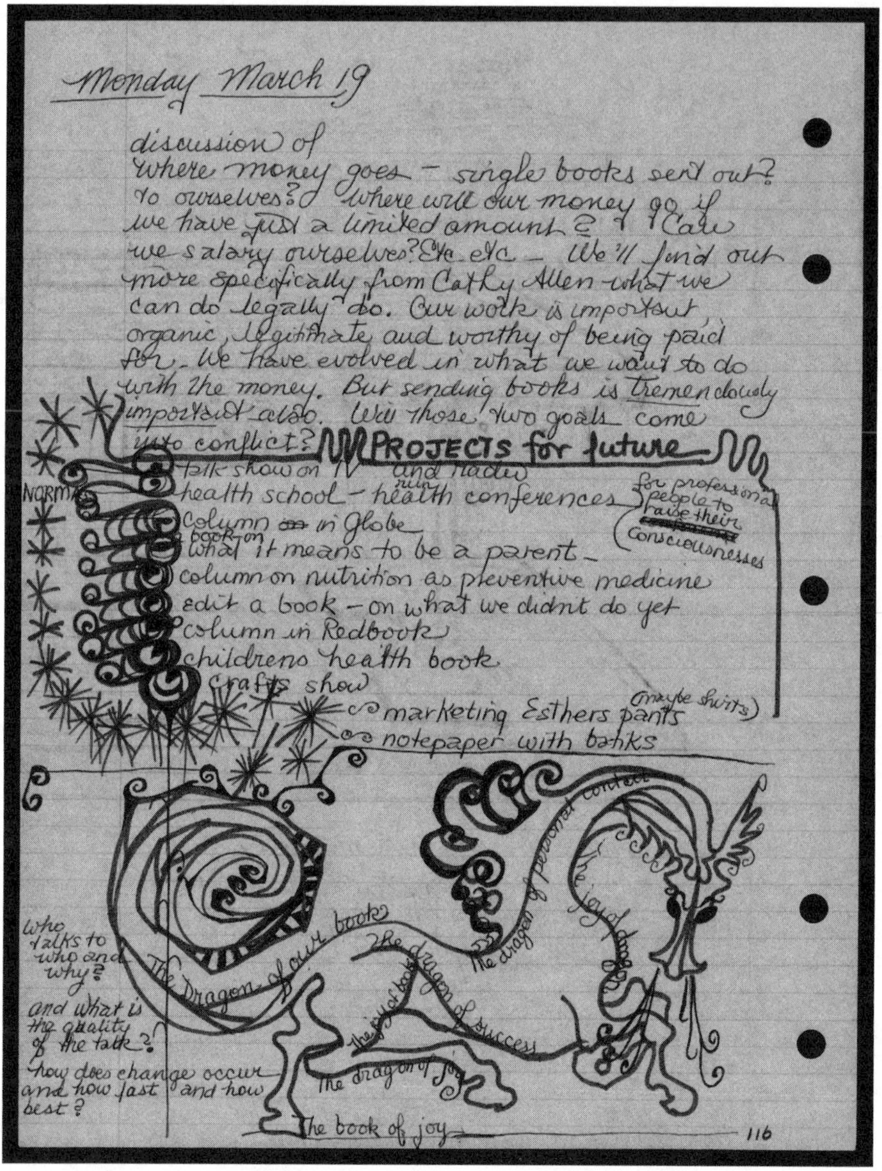

Monday March 19

discussion of
where money goes — single books sent out?
to ourselves? Where will our money go if
we have just a limited amount? & Can
we salary ourselves? Etc. etc — We'll find out
more specifically from Cathy Allen what we
can do legally do. Our work is important,
organic, legitimate and worthy of being paid
for. We have evolved in what we want to do
with the money. But sending books is tremendously
important also. Will those two goals come
into conflict?

PROJECTS for future

talk show on TV and radio
NORM health school — health conferences for professional people to raise their consciousnesses
column in Globe
book on
what it means to be a parent —
column on nutrition as preventive medicine
edit a book — on what we didn't do yet
column in Redbook
childrens health book
crafts show
marketing Esthers pants (maybe shirts)
notepaper with batiks

who talks to who and why?
and what is the quality of the talk?
how does change occur and how fast and how best?

The Dragon of our books
The dragon of personal context
The dragon of success
The dragon of joy
The book of joy

116

Figure 1.2. "The dragon of our joy," Boston Women's Health Book Collective
Minutes, November 1971. Boston Women's Health Book Collective;
Schlesinger Library, Radcliffe Institute, Harvard University.

nervous (we were *just* women; what authority did we have in matters of medicine and health?) we offered a course to sisters in women's liberation."[45] The language of the text was frank: the chapter on sexuality did not speak of "fucking," (although you can find that word in the chapter on relationships), but it did talk, in some detail, about sex, masturbation, virginity, and orgasms. Members of the collective had more than one feeling about their project: they feared both failure and success.

In the early editions of *Our Bodies, Ourselves*, no detail of anatomy or physiology was too small to include. Like the writers of power-structure research, the collective moved from the proud assertion that they were ordinary women who had just done a bit of research to a hypercorrect parody of disciplinary writing. If doctors used technical language to mystify women, the writers of the collective would go them one better, as in this paragraph from the 1970 edition: "A follicle . . . is a hollow ball of several layers of cells. In the case of a Graafian or mature follicle, there is an egg cell in the center. The ovary contains thousands of follicles, but only about 300 will become mature. The others are termed atretic (their development is abortive); yet they perform the essential function of secreting constant low levels of estrogen."[46] While the word "abortive" was never casual in any feminist text of 1970, the atretic follicle was here a decorative element, assuring readers that these writers have learned their anatomy, gone beyond the diagrams in high school biology, and could be trusted to guide the reader in her investigations of her own body.

The Boston Women's Health Book Collective hoped women would use the book as a tool to provoke changes in the healthcare system: the text is intended to be exigent and consequential: "The purpose of this paper [the anatomy chapter] is then to help us learn more about our own anatomy and physiology, to begin to conquer the ignorance that has crippled us in the past when we have felt we don't know what's happening to us. The information is a weapon without which we cannot begin the collective struggle for control over our own bodies and lives."[47] They saw the book as an incitement to "collective struggle," an organized, public, political project of transforming the healthcare system that would necessarily bring to the public sphere issues and questions that had been private, restricted to the rare conversation between a woman and her doctor. *Our Bodies, Ourselves* would frame nutrition, body image, sexual experience, and childbirth as political questions, like abortion and birth control, open to public debate and organized activity. While *Our Bodies, Ourselves* carefully deployed technical language, the writers also shared the commitment of the New Left and underground press to amateur production and ordinary speech. The book had the feeling of conversation, if an unlikely conversation. No one has ever spoken like this, careening from detailed technical information to the expansive assertion of a political manifesto to the directness of colloquial body talk.

The Women's Movement

While the genres and styles of New Left writing influenced the Boston Women's Health Book Collective, *Our Bodies, Ourselves* was created in the crucible of second-wave feminism and helped to shape the discursive style of that movement.[48] The writing practices of second-wave feminism have been authoritatively analyzed by Kathryn Flannery, in her *Feminist Literacies, 1968–75.*[49] Flannery gives an account of the 560 feminist periodicals published during the late 1960s and early 1970s, and of the political polemics that circulated from hand to hand in feminist collectives and political groups, prompting women to cut their hair, leave their jobs, or divorce their husbands. These texts are as vital as they are ephemeral: they were the expression of a decentralized movement that encouraged its participants to read, to think for themselves, and to write. Early feminist efforts at nonhierarchical publishing left writers exhausted and frustrated, and the quality of work produced was uneven. But taken together, these publications were a remarkable experiment in popular literacy. Feminist newspapers encouraged a participatory relation with their readers, actively solicited new writers, and maintained supportive relations with their contributors.

Writing in feminist papers was much less closely tied to immediate exigencies than the writing of the New Left. Some newspapers, like Denver's *Big Mamma Rag* or the Washington, DC, *off our backs*, covered women's actions and conventions. Others, like *Furies*, were political and cultural journals in tabloid form. Ginny Berson, member of the *Furies* collective, observed, "Although we called ourselves a 'newspaper,' our interest in news was relatively insignificant."[50] Poetry and fiction were integral to second-wave feminist texts, included in most women's newspapers, and widely circulated in self-published chapbooks. Feminist performance practices, from the street theater of "zap actions," to concerts, dances, and full-fledged theater companies, supported second-wave feminists in the impossible task they had set themselves: creating an alternate culture, with all the institutions and practices that project implies.

The central speech practice of the early women's movement was consciousness-raising, and the forms of language characteristic of consciousness-raising shaped early editions of *Our Bodies, Ourselves.* A private practice of disclosure and reflection adapted from the civil rights movement, consciousness-raising could be deeply transformative and was a common entry point into feminism.[51] Forty years after the fact, collective member Ruth Bell Alexander characterized the Boston Women's Health Book Collective as "essentially a consciousness-raising group."[52] According to collective member Paula Doress-Worters, the "Women and Their Bodies" workshop at the 1969 Emmanuel Conference—their point of origin—began with brief presentations by Nancy Miriam Hawley and Nancy Shaw. Then women began to talk directly about their medical experiences:

We got really excited because a lot of us were dealing with these issues in our lives. And, you know, a lot of us had begun to be in consciousness-raising groups, and we were just fascinated with this whole ideas of exploring our own lives and figuring out what was going on, what was wrong. So, there were a lot of us who were in the midst of trying to deal with birth control and abortion and all those reproductive rights issues. And there were another whole group of us who were having babies, or had just had babies, or were about to have babies, were about to have a second baby, whatever. So, that was a very relevant issue. And then as we went around the room it just seemed like everybody in the room had a story about some way that the medical profession was not responsive to what we wanted to know about our bodies, that we didn't even always know what questions we should be asking. And by the end of that workshop—that's an hour and a half, a couple of hours, whatever it was—most of us were convinced that we had to continue working on this issue, talking together. And we set a meeting.[53]

The collective's women's health classes were, in effect, consciousness-raising groups punctuated by short presentations of medical information.

Jane Pincus described the collective's first class, a large session held at MIT: "Fifty women. Tremendous feeling of sexuality, freedom, and excitement. A lot of women for the first time talked about themselves, their experiences, how they felt. . . . People just had a sense that we could learn about ourselves, that what we learned would give us a lot of control, a lot of power."[54]

The central trope of consciousness-raising was synecdoche, the figure in which a part or detail invokes a whole. In consciousness-raising, high heels invoked the confinement of women; a pink romper signified enforced gender roles: what a woman had understood as private experience was shown to be emblematic of wider issues of gender politics. These tropes of understanding released excitement; as another guide to consciousness-raising said, "CONSCIOUSNESS—RAISING is not a confessional but intimate secrets may be spoken of when they are relevant. It is very consciousness-raising to discover that others' guilty secrets are the same as one's own."[55] For the collective, excitement traveled from the private space of consciousness-raising to the more open forum of women's health classes: class participants asked for written information, and the papers written in response to those requests, lightly edited, became *Women and Their Bodies: A Course* (1970). These figures supported and textualized the collective's commitment to the universalism of women's embodiment: women found, in consciousness-raising, that they shared similar experiences of pregnancy, abortion, and birth, and they considered these common experiences both a political and emotional bond.

Since they had experienced consciousness-raising as transformative, and had seen it transform others, the collective organized *Our Bodies, Ourselves* to replicate that experience. Women's narratives were included in the text. Sometimes, these stories would have been collected in a health class: when a woman told a memorable story, she would be asked to write it down, and it would be incorporated into the book.[56] Sometimes, the collective would solicit narratives by posing questions to readers or to audiences at a talk, a practice that the group has consistently maintained. (For the most recent 2005 edition, the author of the chapter on identity and lesbian, queer, and transgendered people asked for anecdotes on various listservs; a year after the call, she was still receiving responses.[57]) Writers wove together narratives that demonstrated the range and variety of women's experiences, working against the notion of a single normative model of female embodiment and suggesting possibilities for new relationships, health practices, and ways of thinking of medical authority.

The collective also drew on written feminist texts, including a Boston feminist adaptation of the power-structure research report. *How Harvard Rules Women* was produced in 1970 by women in the New University Conference, an organization of progressive academics.[58] *How Harvard Rules Women* refers explicitly to *How Harvard Rules* in both its title and its text—the *How Harvard Rules* power-structure chart was actually tucked into the back cover of the copy I consulted at Temple University's Contemporary Culture Collection. But it is quite different in organization and tone. For the women of the New University Conference, Harvard was as much about the exploitation of women workers and the marginalization of graduate student wives as it was about the production of elites and the conduct of military research. Sometimes, the language of the text, locked into traditional contradictions of higher education for women, recalls that of the Radcliffe Study Group: "Ultimately the feeling of temporariness induced by the knowledge that you will undoubtedly live where your man wants to live, that your work will of course be interrupted by children, etc., means that women often have great difficulty applying themselves to long-term tasks or occupations."[59] At other times, we hear the cadences of consciousness-raising: confidential, frank talk about what everyone knew and nobody had said in public:

The relation of Harvard to its women is similar to that of the missionary to his heathen. And your feelings, if you're a woman who has made it to America's loftiest and oldest bastion of intellect and the ruling class, are often similar to those of the heathen imported for cultural development to imperialist shores—a mixture of gratitude, awe, doubt that you're worth the honor, and sometimes, dimly or blazingly, resentment that you're considered inferior. Those sober-suited gentlemen who, with scholarly purpose and carefully averted eyes, sidestep you in the shadowy corridors of the Widener stacks, those men younger and older who, as you enter the Widener reading room inspect your legs as you pass to your set; or who, in Holyoke offices, inspect your legs as you pass to your desk; all of the masculine Worthies on the conglomerate Harvard faculties, with their mild manners, their green

bookbags, their after-dinner-sherry gentility and their government affilia-
tions, overwhelm you with the sense that your womanhood is never neutral,
but always provocative—of intellectual opprobrium, of patronage humorous
or curt, of sexual appraisal, of sexual advance.[60]

How Harvard Rules Women, like *How Harvard Rules*, included discussions of Harvard professional schools and of the curriculum in psychology, the social sciences, and literature. In this version of power-structure
research, however, the emphasis was not on the exposure of elites but on
the capillary relations of power. The research procedures of the psychology department connected to the difficulty of obtaining contraceptives
from the student health center.

There is a strong family resemblance between *How Harvard Rules
Women* and *Women and Their Bodies*, issued later in 1970: photo offset
production, unjustified right margins; rivers of text punctuated by photographs, drawings, and diagrams; a nicely calligraphed table of contents.
The covers of both books featured a single photograph and a hand-drawn
title; from beginning to end, both books had a do-it-yourself feel. And
the books have similar purposes: to make transparent a system that had
been alienated and mystified. Both collective authors used their well-
developed academic skills to undertake an amateur production. Both texts
combined research and discussion of public issues with individual experiences. And both reoriented the conventions of power-structure research
to the analysis of everyday life. The fact that Radcliffe women changed
into their jeans when they came back to their dorms, the discomfort of a
hasty pelvic exam, the lack of day care on the Harvard campus, the rise
in syphilis infections, and the boredom of secretarial work—all were
presented in these two books as disparate demonstrations of the power
and reach of patriarchy. Like the writers of *How Harvard Rules Women*,
the writers of *Our Bodies, Ourselves* worked quickly, under pressure, and
relied on unconventional distribution to disseminate their text widely.
They deployed detail in the text to establish their authority and show
that they had things to say, using the genre of power-structure research
as a nodal point or staging area from which both readers and writers
moved from ignorance to knowledge. Writers presented the everyday
circumstances of their lives in new ways; readers learned names for experiences and ideas they had only vaguely registered.

Figure 1.3. *Women and Their Bodies,* 1970, cover. Boston Women's Health Book Collective. Author's collection.

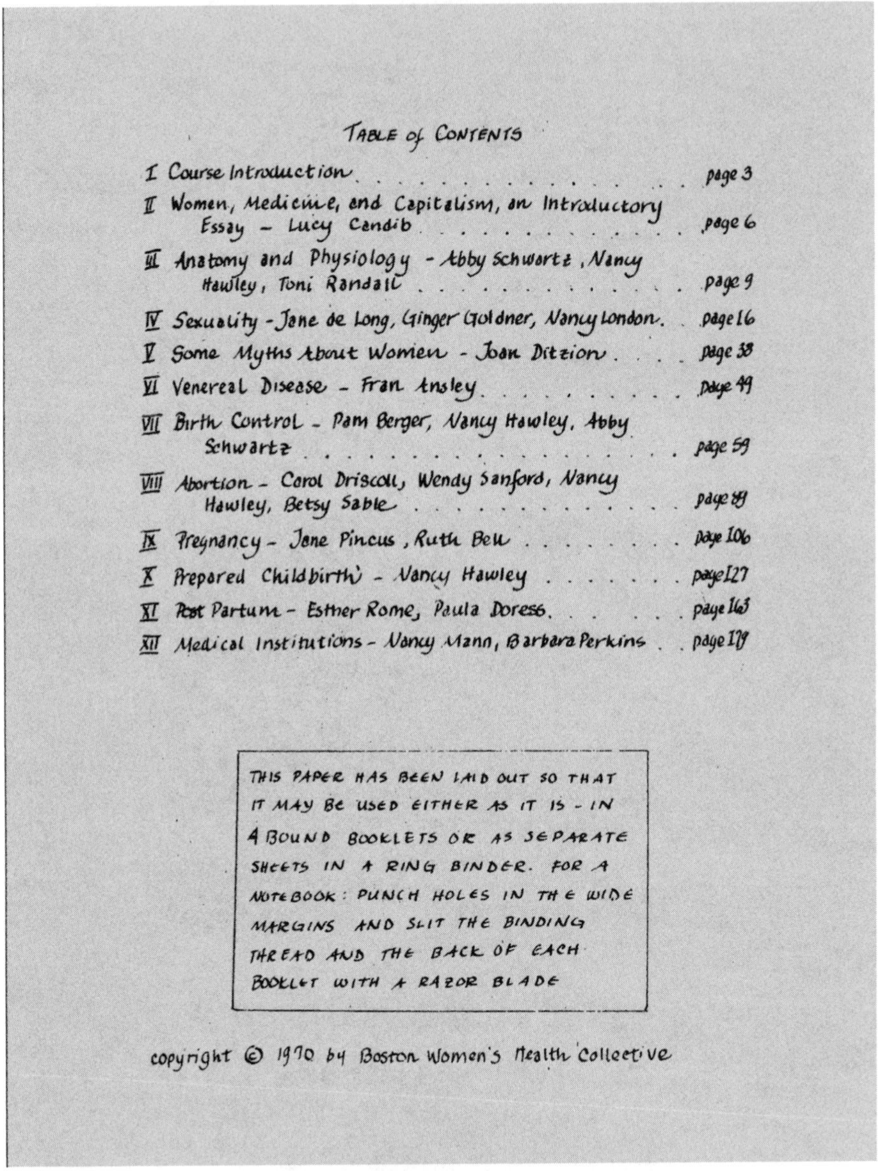

TABLE of CONTENTS

THIS PAPER HAS BEEN LAID OUT SO THAT
IT MAY BE USED EITHER AS IT IS - IN
A BOUND BOOKLETS OR AS SEPARATE
SHEETS IN A RING BINDER. FOR A
NOTEBOOK: PUNCH HOLES IN THE WIDE
MARGINS AND SLIT THE BINDING
THREAD AND THE BACK OF EACH
BOOKLET WITH A RAZOR BLADE

Figure 1.4. *Women and Their Bodies*, 1970, table of contents. Boston Women's Health Book Collective. Author's collection.

Figure 1.5. *How Harvard Rules Women*, 1970, cover. © New University
Conference; image from Temple University Contemporary Culture Collection.

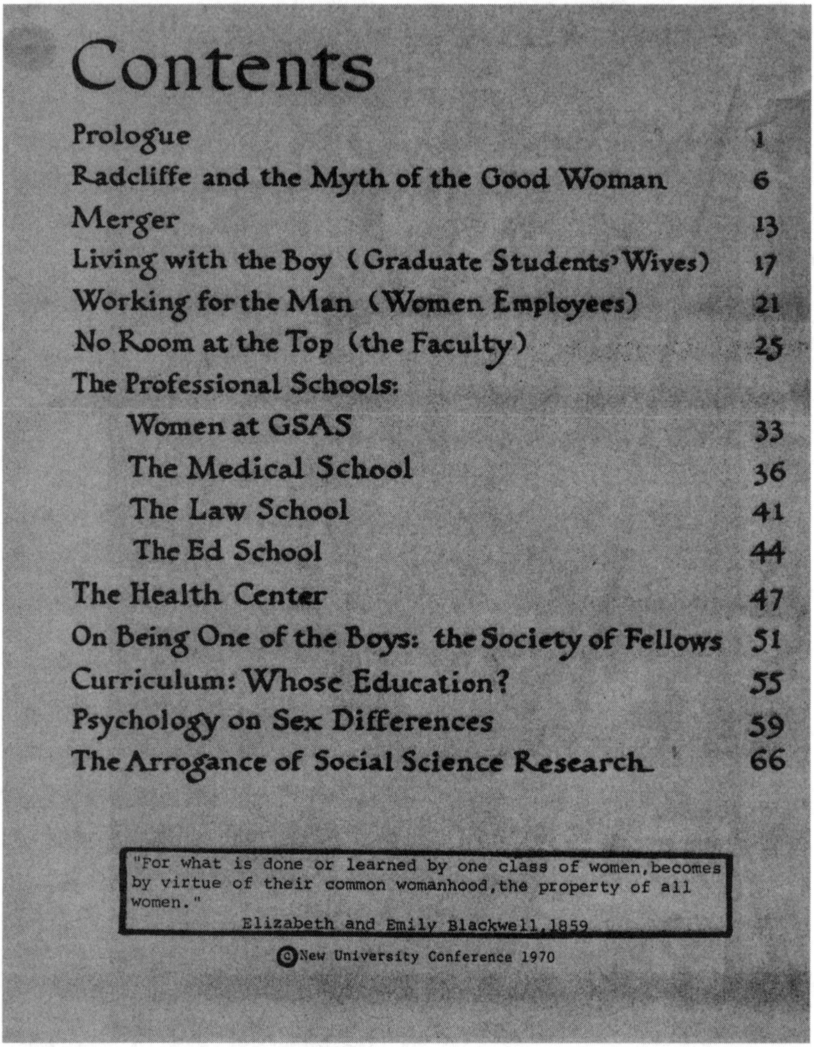

Contents

Prologue 1
Radcliffe and the Myth of the Good Woman 6
Merger 13
Living with the Boy (Graduate Students' Wives) 17
Working for the Man (Women Employees) 21
No Room at the Top (the Faculty) 25
The Professional Schools:
Women at GSAS 33
The Medical School 36
The Law School 41
The Ed School 44
The Health Center 47
On Being One of the Boys: the Society of Fellows 51
Curriculum: Whose Education? 55
Psychology on Sex Differences 59
The Arrogance of Social Science Research 66

"For what is done or learned by one class of women, becomes by virtue of their common womanhood, the property of all women."
Elizabeth and Emily Blackwell, 1859

©New University Conference 1970

Figure 1.6. *How Harvard Rules Women*, 1970, table of contents. © New University Conference; image from Temple University Contemporary Culture Collection.

The Collective and the Boston Movement, 1969

The writers of *Our Bodies, Ourselves* drew on writing practices, such as the manifesto and the open letter, which were popular in Bread and Roses, Boston's feminist umbrella organization. Open letters were typed, often with handwritten headlines, and photocopied or duplicated with mimeograph stencils. Letters ranging from a single page to seventeen carefully documented pages circulated through personal networks, collectives, or "mass meetings" of the organization. They might record passing reflections, observations on a common problem, or thoughts on the organization's direction.[61] For example, Nancy Shaw's letter, "Working on Women," dated April 28, 1969 (two weeks before the Emmanuel Conference), begins with the common experience of dreading a gynecological exam. The letter muses about the causes of this fear, remarking that "few of us know anything about our genitals or wombs."[62] Shaw, who would work on the 1973 *Our Bodies, Ourselves*, developed a list of demands and proposals and ended with a call to organize patients. She concluded, "Doctors will continue to work on us and not with us as long as we are all docile patients and each is only one. We've just got to get together."[63]

Most open letters followed the same template as Shaw's: an observation, developed in political analysis, led to a proposal for action. Some letters were broad and reflective, like Meredith Tax's "Working Notes on Labour, Leisure, Recuperation, Play and Sex."[64] Others were less formal, but just as heartfelt. An undated letter from Shierry began, "The plenary session wigged me out," and complained of abstract, contentious discussions. The letter proposed that "political meetings should start with free movement dance sessions, so that people realize that they're physical beings in their bodies."[65] Early chapters of *Our Bodies, Ourselves*, such as "Our Changing Sense of Self" and "Sexuality," circulated from hand to hand like the open letters of Bread and Roses.[66] In early editions, chapters of the book often adapted the experience-analysis-demand-proposal template of the open letter.

The paper that Nancy Miriam Hawley wrote for the Emmanuel Conference, "Women and the Control of Their Bodies," was essentially an open letter. This five-page, single-spaced document observed that women have begun to organize around their own needs, advocated that they work on health, and proposed an organization something like the collective.[67] Hawley began, "We women of the New Left have gained our 'Movement Credentials' by picketing, alongside our men, against Woolworth's, Chase Manhattan Bank, United Fruit, the Harvard corporation, and all other corporations that oppress poor and minority groups at home and abroad."[68] She asserted the importance of a liberatory practice of the body: "We need to assert ourselves against those forces that have controlled our bodies and ignored our minds. Since the alienation of women from their bodies has been one of the main aims of male domination, we must take control of our own bodies before we can liberate our minds and be our own people." Hawley listed the ways in which women's bodies are "manipulated"—health and beauty; ignorance of anatomy and physiology; sex; birth control and abortion; and childbirth.[69] "Women and the Control of Their Bodies" ends by proposing a project of disseminating information to women about health and sexuality, the germ of *Our Bodies, Ourselves.*

In a later paper, Hawley defended the practice of the collective to Bread and Roses, arguing that women's health courses were more profoundly liberating than the routine of writing leaflets and calling meetings.[70] Hawley and her coauthor Myra Levenson were responding to a proposal that Bread and Roses solve its perennial problem of political direction and focus by organizing around healthcare issues in Cambridge; their paper also responded to discussions about the collective's work in Bread and Roses. Hawley and Levenson criticized the health-organizing proposal for "defining politics as primarily making demands upon institutions, and turning to 'organizing' other women instead of moving and taking risks ourselves." The women's health courses were proposed as an alternate model of organizing: "We think that the model of the health course that is currently being taught and rethought by women is an important women's action. . . . They [the health group] feel that our awareness of our experience as women relating to our bodies ties us to other women."[71] Reflecting on the divisions between their group and organizations of African American and white working-class women, Hawley and Levenson urged a more personal, pluralistic, and coalition-based style of organizing. "None of us," they observed, "got turned on to the women's movement by a leaflet."[72]

Both "Women and Their Bodies" and the Hawley-Levenson letter illustrate the collective's sponsorship by and accountability to the local women's movement. That movement offered them the genres of consciousness-raising and the polemic letter; the collective was almost immediately required to give an account of their practice to a wider movement community as a matter of political strategy. The women's movement offered models for speaking and writing and venues in which to learn that work, but also pressed the emergent collective to articulate an understanding of women's embodiment and its political consequences. (Members of the collective might dispute this account, since they rightly see their work as coeval with, and intimately connected to, the nascent women's movement. But during its first years, the collective articulated a political presence for two audiences: "the public" of ordinary readers and "our public," the emerging women's movement.) The text of *Our Bodies, Ourselves* sometimes reads like a warm bath of affirmation, but the early editions were shaped by conversations that could be critical and challenging as well as supportive.

The collective shared an interest in alternate forms of publication with the rest of the Boston women's movement. Feminist health groups were particularly interested in graphic texts. A pamphlet titled "Women and Health," produced by the Women's Health Ring, combined health information, political analysis, anatomical diagrams, and home remedies. The double-sized handout opens to a graphic of women's faces, a declaration that "We are getting ANGRY and we are joining TOGETHER," and the words of "Our faces belong to our bodies," a song that was important to the collective. On the reverse are referrals to community clinics, pregnancy counseling services, and the Medical Committee for Human Rights. The centerfold offers information about cancer and pap smears, yeast infections, and breast exams. Illustrated with a drawing of the sexual organs and pictures of women with raised fists, it warns against colored toilet paper, feminine hygiene sprays, and individual solutions: "Good hygiene and good intentions will not cure our crumbling health system." The style of the drawings was distinct from that of the underground comics, where bodies were often grotesque and exaggerated; this poster was designed to combine modern clarity and homemade rough edges.[73] Although the open letter, addressed to

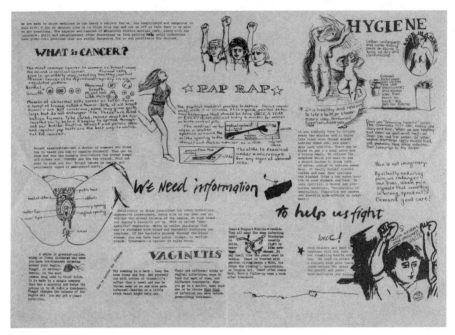

Figure 1.7. Women's Health Ring wall poster, c. 1970. Schlesinger Library, Radcliffe Institute, Harvard University.

Figure 1.8. Sticker used in a Valentine's Day "zap action" by Bread and Roses, c. 1970–72. Schlesinger Library, Radcliffe Institute, Harvard University; reprinted with permission of Fran Ansley.

"our public," resembled traditional essay forms, Bread and Roses also produced texts for "the public," inventive alternatives to the print-dense leaflet. The "Zap" collective of Bread and Roses printed stickers for one-time events: leafleting women on Valentine's Day, inviting them to "join women's liberation," and decorating store windows with stickers reading, "It's not your heart he's after."[74]

These practices of writing and reading offered the emerging collective a heady dose of sponsorship and a rich, responsive, public space. The women's movement and the New Left offered models of consequential writing; these practices animated the rhetorical resources offered by higher education and to the emerging networks of health activists and patient advocates.

From Movement to Advocate:
Sponsorship in the 1970s and 1980s

In general, the late 1970s and early 1980s saw the development of new sponsors and new networks for the writing of the collective. They collaborated with women of color and cultivated networks of health activists, antirape groups, organizations of midwives, and other advocacy groups. For example, the collective developed a working relationship with the Massachusetts Coalition for Occupational Safety and Health (Mass COSH), an alliance of union locals, workers, health activists, and lawyers. They published *Our Jobs, Our Health* with Mass COSH in 1983, and Mass COSH coauthored "Environmental and Occupational Health" in the 1984 edition of *Our Bodies, Ourselves.*[75] Although the 1973 contract with Simon and Schuster did not sever ties between the collective and the movements of the 1960s, their decision to leave the New England Free Press was coherent with the project of looking outside the New Left and second-wave feminist movements for both sponsorship and public space. "Our public" was disintegrating; the collective worked to reconstruct it.

Our Bodies, Ourselves continued to be an important book for many members of the women's movement and the organizations that developed from the New Left. The Denver women's paper *Big Mama Rag*, for example, praised "groups of women putting together such fine materials as *Our Bodies, Our Selves.*"[76] But other feminist periodicals put distance between themselves and the collective. *Off our backs*, which functioned as a national clearing house of feminist opinion, reviewed the 1973 *Our Bodies, Ourselves* critically. Reviewer Chris Hobbs was clearly alienated from this "slicker, expanded edition."[77] She appreciated the information in the new book, but felt that the move to a mainstream publisher had weakened other women's publishing projects and produced a tamer, less provocative, text.

In the mid-1970s, some members of the collective left Boston: Jane Pincus moved to a farm in Vermont; Ruth Bell Alexander, to California; both maintained active ties to the group. Those who remained in Boston focused on writing the book, developing the group's growing international connections, establishing a Women's Health Information Center, and on their own developing careers and young families. The Boston women's movement was no longer their primary context. When I spoke to a writer for *Sojourner*, the Boston feminist paper, about the collective's relation to Boston movements in the mid-1980s, she observed, "I think of individuals being very engaged in a broad range of issues. And their personal connections were so strong. . . . But I don't see them as being particularly closely connected to other sorts of things that were happening in Boston. I don't think they were removed, but they really created themselves as a separate organization they maintained."[78]

The conventional views of how the social movements of the 1960s ended alternate between apocalyptic collapse (we knew it was all over at Altamont, or the Flint Conference, or the Days of Rage) and mysterious slow attrition. The decline of the social movements looked different in the Left press. In 1973, Kirkpatrick Sale published an optimistic article that reported large numbers of demonstrators in 1972 in "The New Left: What's Left," but the very title of his article suggests an inventory of remnants.[79] A longer, more realistic view of the receding tide of activism was written by Elinor Langer in *Working Papers for a New Society*. Collective member Jane Pincus remembered this essay, "Notes for Next Time: A Memoir of the 1960s" as prescient.[80] Langer begins with the bald assertion, "These days I take it for granted that The Movement is dead."[81] She coolly assesses the situation of the Left, including the women's movement, in 1973: "We 'failed' as a revolutionary generation. Everything we thought was wrong is still wrong, and more besides, and we are without the institutions, influence, or understanding to help change it."[82] Langer's long essay includes both a moving account of her own experiences and astute analysis: she is particularly telling in her critique of such movement pieties as false consciousness and repressive tolerance. Sometimes, the essay becomes impenetrable: "Many of our errors come from that curse by an undefeatable law whose meanings are concealed in a Rosetta Stone we cannot yet read."[83] Langer criticizes precisely the movement practices that the collective successfully avoided: sectarian infighting, jargon-ridden writing, guilty self-examination. Her recommendation for the future anticipates the collective's program of work: "to spread out and imbed ourselves with all our demands and visions, incomplete as these may be, in every institution in the country: in schools, colleges, unions, hospitals, churches, community organizations, political parties, radio stations, newspapers, libraries."[84] Whether Langer had directly influenced Pincus and other members of the collective, their project of constructing an alternate public sphere to support feminist health practices coheres with her recommendation of a long march through the institutions.

In modulating their relations of sponsorship, publicity, and distributed authorship toward a diverse network of health activists and away from movement organizations, the collective both gained and lost. Their political formation in the women's movement had prompted them to zealously seek connections with ordinary women, and mainstream publication enabled them to do that; the stream of letters from grateful or curious readers assured them that they were reaching more women than they had ever hoped. The direct conversational engagement of the early editions gave way to a thinner relationship to readers, but the collective found ways of compensating for this distance. More fundamentally, the mid-1970s saw a contraction of the public spaces occupied by the New Left and the women's movement and an attenuation of their power of sponsorship: they could no longer offer access to an expanding public, or even reliable reactions to early drafts of chapters. Collective members desperately needed specialized, constantly updated medical information; they could no longer survive with the skeleton staff and the shoestring budget of a movement organization. If they wanted to continue to play a public role, they had to find a new public. If they wanted to continue to operate in the economy of sponsorship, they had to become sponsors themselves.

Two Writers and Their Sponsors

Members came to the Boston Women's Health Book Collective at different ages, with different experiences, from different parts of the country. Two writers—Lucy Candib and Nancy Miriam Hawley—demonstrate how relationships among multiple literacy sponsors affected practices of writing for individual writers. Although Candib and Hawley illustrate the sponsorship of higher education for women, the New Left, and the women's movement, they each developed as writers in complicated ways; both of them spoke to multiple publics, in a range of voices and media. I have chosen these two writers because the archival record of their work in the late 1960s and early 1970s is rich; other members of the collective, less active in the New Left or less comfortable with spontaneous writing, might have had quite different profiles.

Lucy Candib's collaboration with the collective was brief: she worked on the first edition, *Women and Their Bodies: A Course*, writing the opening chapter on capitalism and medicine. That chapter was moved to the end of the book in the 1971 edition for reasons that no one now can recall. Candib was a student in Harvard Medical School, having finished her undergraduate work at Radcliffe—we have already met her as a member of Bibring's study group. By the time the collective incorporated in 1973, Candib was a hospital intern, and her consuming schedule left no time for the accelerating pace of the collective's work. She left the collective, although she reviewed draft chapters from time to time, and she continues to be in touch with some of its members.

Although Candib's undergraduate years at Radcliffe, 1964–68, saw changes in the relation between women and higher education, this issue was not central to Candib's own interests at the time: she joined the Radcliffe study group because she was "very moved by and attracted to Bibring as a powerful woman figure."[85] By 1968, questions about the purposes of higher education for anyone were being raised by students and faculty everywhere, and Radcliffe was involved in the student strike: one of Candib's closest friends was Gene Bishop, who wrote on women's

issues for the *Old Mole*. Candib was active in the strike: her papers, archived in the Schlesinger Library, include carefully preserved oversize
newsprint copies of strike posters (see the illustration in Chapter 4).
That spring, Candib also wrote her undergraduate thesis, a history of
neighborhood health clinics; revised during her first year as a medical
student, it was published in the *New England Journal of Medicine*.[86]

At Harvard Medical School, Candib found very few women medical
students, and she shared few common interests with them. She worked
with the Harvard Student Health Organization, a group of leftist medical students and their allies. The summer after her first year of medical
school, she "tripped over a mimeograph machine," bought it, and so the
organization began to produce a newsletter, *The Red Nucleus*. *The Red
Nucleus* was published both simply and irregularly: Candib's archived
collection, which is not necessarily complete, includes a dozen editions
published during a period of two years. The newsletters range from
two to eight pages, mimeographed in the distinctive purple ink of that
low-budget, labor-intensive form, with a hand-drawn headline and the
motto, "The Red Nucleus, lying deep within the established white matter, relaying vital information outside the traditional pathway."[87]

The Red Nucleus discussed the war in Vietnam and the "doctor's draft,"
covered the American Medical Association convention, and explained
why medical school lectures were so bad. The newsletter reported on
the medical school's role in university expansion and its effect on Boston neighborhoods, a particular interest of Candib's. In one issue, the
writers reflected on their first year in medical school. The essay juxtaposed traditional complaints about "God knows how many bleary-eyed
mornings in amphitheater C" to analysis of medical education as a social formation:

Something subtler has been going on all year long. Stated simply, we have
been trained for a career in middle-class medicine, for a life of endeavor on
the exciting frontiers of super-scientific medicine, and in the upper echelons
of an academic medical establishment that is almost totally indifferent to the
vast inadequacies of healthcare planning and delivery in this nation. What
have we heard about infant malnutrition in Mississippi or South Carolina,
about unsanitary health conditions in the South End or in Roxbury? How
many lectures have we had by doctors mainly involved in clinical practice, in

public health, or in community health organization? And how much emphasis has been placed on careers outside of research and academic medicine? The answers to these questions are nothing, none, and damn little.[88]

This critique—medicine served few patients, and many of them badly—motivated Lucy Candib's long career, devoted to the theory and practice of feminist family medicine. But it was from the collective, and from Bread and Roses, that Candib learned feminism. She was a member of a personal group of Bread and Roses that included Gene Bishop, who would write the chapter on rape in the 1973 *Our Bodies, Ourselves*, Nancy Miriam Hawley, a member of the emerging Boston Women's Health Book Collective, and Winifred Breines, who would later write an important article on race and feminism that analyzed Bread and Roses.[89] Candib began organizing women health workers, and wrote a position paper on health for Bread and Roses.[90] All these experiences shaped Candib's writing in "Women, Medicine, and Capitalism."[91]

"Women, Medicine, and Capitalism" opened with a quotation from Marcuse: "Health is a state defined by an elite," and it developed the argument that the capitalist organization of U.S. medicine does not work for women.[92] Candib developed this general point through discussions of the ideology of control and submission as it was enforced through medical uniforms, rituals of education, and "pseudoscientific jargon."[93] She connected medical mystification to women patients' reluctance to bother their doctors, and to the objectification of the patient as "the vehicle which brings the disease to the interventionist," an object to be kept "horizontal, passive" and hospitalized.[94] Women, alienated from their bodies and their genitals, convinced that they lack something important, are especially targets of objectification. The first readers of *Women and Their Bodies* might have been puzzled by this chapter or exhilarated by it. Candib herself is now of two minds about the "Women, Medicine, and Capitalism" chapter. Conceding that she has "this sort of theoretical approach," she reads the chapter as moving from the abstraction of capitalist medicine to the details of everyday care for women. It was important to her at the time to open the chapter with Marcuse, "because I think you need to sort of say where the stuff comes from," but she thinks that if she were writing the chapter today, she would begin with concrete examples and move to abstractions. Candib connects her earlier deductive approach to her education: "Certainly getting educated where I got educated, being abstract was valuable and was rewarded."[95] Candib adapted the norms of writing developed in higher education to her work with *Our Bodies, Ourselves.* She cited sources, however informally, developed arguments, and defined terms. Even as she critiqued the mystifying power of medical language, she deployed other terms of art. Candib had made a conscious choice to continue her medical education at a time when many activists were leaving campus; she saw herself bringing the ideas of the Left and the women's movement into medicine.[96] Her work as a writer would develop with her professional identity in family medicine, but at this very early stage of her life, she wrote from the crossroads where the emerging institutions of radical medicine met the inchoate women's health movement. At this juncture, she responded to the sponsorship of both higher education and the women's movement; her text shuttled between those two very different languages. Today, she feels that she "did write something that had life in it."[97]

For Nancy Miriam Hawley, academic preparation seemed like a distraction from the work she had to do on the Left. At the University of Michigan, Hawley joined Students for a Democratic Society and consigned academic work to the intervals of her political activity: "I was in college as a political activist, and I took courses because that's what you do. It's like I wound up majoring in history because I had more courses in history."[98] When she came to Boston, Hawley met the women who would become members of Bread and Roses; with them, she helped organize the Emmanuel Conference, where she gave the workshop on Women and Their Bodies. Although most members of the collective trace their origins to that workshop, in Hawley's memory it is not a particularly central event: she dates the beginning of the collective from the meetings on health issues that the group sponsored later that summer in their homes. Nonetheless, the five-page paper that Hawley wrote for the Emmanuel workshop sketched the outlines of the project that *Our Bodies, Ourselves* was to become. Hawley asserted the universality of women's embodiment, and that conviction led her to argue for a book project: "I thought that early on when we were doing papers and the courses it just wasn't enough. We couldn't get it out to

enough women, and the message was so central, that we all have bodies, they don't look the same, but they function the same and we had
similar needs too. The knowledge provided power to me; it will provide power to you."[99] At one collective meeting in 1973, she predicted
that the book the group was preparing would sell more than a million
copies. Everyone had a good laugh.

Although Hawley was deeply committed to the production of a book,
she did not see herself as a writer: "I never thought about myself as a
writer and whether I could write well or not write well."[100] Like many
other members of the collective, she saw writing as a communicative,
organizing activity modeled on conversation. For her, writing *Our Bodies,
Ourselves* was such a direct record of experience that it scarcely counted
as writing, but rather as "just a vehicle to share your experience."[101] Hawley worked closely with the collective for the first New England Free
Press editions, continued to collaborate on the 1973 and 1976 Simon
and Schuster editions, and was central to the controversy over whether
to include a chapter on psychotherapy in the 1984 edition.

Members of the collective must have argued in their years of working together, but the dispute about whether to have a chapter on psychotherapy is the only one that they specifically remember, and the only one
directly reflected in their records. Hawley, who had trained as a therapist
and had established her practice, wanted the book to support women
who were seeking therapy; Norma Swenson felt that therapy medicalized women's lives and disagreed with its focus on individual problems.
In the end, the collective agreed to include a chapter on psychotherapy
cowritten by Hawley and Wendy Coppedge Sanford, with "help from
Judy Norsigian and Norma Swenson."[102]

Argument is, as Habermas has observed, an extremely costly activity, and examples of explicit disagreements being argued to coherent
resolutions are rare.[103] The psychotherapy chapter, published in four
compact pages, is no exception to this rule. The chapter was structured
as an envelope: it opened and concluded by talking about the benefits
of therapy, and it discussed the dangers and problems of therapy in the
middle. So, the chapter suggested in its first sentences that when "we
feel depressed, anxious, or hopeless . . . we may . . . carefully choose a
trained psychotherapist who will offer . . . objectivity, skill and attentive-

ness."[104] A personal narrative followed: a woman described her therapy as useful, indeed transformative. Then, the chapter began again: "Women must approach psychotherapy with caution."[105] Therapists stereotyped women, focused too much on individuals, and exercised too much power. While every sentence is qualified, these paragraphs contained some of the strongest criticism of health caregivers anywhere in the book. For example: "Some [therapists] have molested and raped us in the name of 'therapy.' Most widely, they have used myths about woman's supposedly passive, masochistic nature to keep us 'in our place.'"[106] The final pages of the chapter suggested that some schools of therapy might be better than others, described common therapeutic approaches, and gave practical advice about choosing a therapist. Again, a personal narrative presented therapy as a benign, fruitful process: "Working with the help of therapists . . . I felt stronger as a person after each session and clearer about my life."[107] Ultimately, the chapter offered readers two contradictory accounts of psychotherapy.

In this text, Hawley's developing commitment to an emerging practice of feminist psychotherapy was at odds with the critique of medicalization adopted by the collective to structure the 1984 edition. That conflict was intractable. The introduction to *Our Bodies, Ourselves* characterized the psychotherapy chapter as a "compromise that we could live with," but there was little common ground between positive experiences with therapy and principled rejection of it. Members of the collective were familiar with psychotherapy, and some had found it useful. They did not see talking to a therapist as medical abuse in the same way that an unneeded caesarian or the hasty prescription of birth control pills might be. At the same time, critiques of psychiatry by writers like Thomas Szaz were at the height of their influence, and it would have been inconsistent to encourage women to resist seeking medical advice at every juncture of their lives and also to recommend psychotherapy as a way of handling emotional problems. As a writer, Hawley was faced with the difficult task of brokering between two intellectual frameworks: one in which therapy is a liberatory practice, and one in which it was oppressive to women. The sponsorship of her emerging professional identity was at odds with one of the health advocacy sponsors in the collective's developing circle of contacts.

In subsequent editions of *Our Bodies, Ourselves,* Hawley's writing focused on issues of therapy and emotional health. Her identity as a founder of the Boston Women's Health Book Collective is part of her public presence, mentioned on the Web site for her consulting partnership and on publicity for a book that she is currently coauthoring. After having urged the group to produce *Our Bodies, Ourselves* and offering them the models of literacy sponsorship common in the New Left, Hawley focused and concentrated her collaboration with the collective, which became a sponsor for her own work in psychotherapy and, more recently, in business.

The experiences of Candib and Hawley demonstrate how collective members moved in and out of close collaboration with the group, and how they situated themselves in varied relationships to the movements and historical developments of the 1960s and 1970s. For these writers, literacy sponsors were not stamping machines: they appropriated the practices of higher education, the New Left, and the women's movement in varying combinations, with evolving emphases, and with quite individual inflections. But while, in their personal histories, both writers moved from one milieu to the next—from the New Left to the women's movement or the feminist practice of radical medicine—relations of sponsorship are not easily discarded. Both writers drew on practices of abstraction and documentation that their education had cultivated. For Candib, in particular, questions about the role of expert knowledge remained at the center of her intellectual work. For both Hawley and Candib, writerly authority was based on control of detail and immediacy: they had absorbed the New Left ethos of the engaged reporter or the power-structure researcher. Hawley was especially committed to the collective process of writing, expressed in the metaphor of conversation—an ideal drawn from the civil rights movement, and central to early New Left practices. Both writers, with quite different inflections, juxtaposed personal narrative with political analysis, deploying the central trope of feminist consciousness-raising.

These writers also exemplify two different models of engagement with the collective. Candib participated in the loose, freewheeling composition of the first two editions; the boundaries of the collective were porous, and no one reviewed the text for continuity. The collective was not particularly worried by the abstraction of Candib's chapter, which was stylistically at odds with the personal tone of much of the rest of the book. Once the chapter was done, it was out of Candib's hands: she neither knew nor cared why it moved from the beginning of the book in 1970 to the end in 1971. Hawley's relationship to the collective reflects the higher stakes of participation from the mid-1970s to the 1980s, when the central members of the group formalized their status, first as "members" and later as "founders." Like other collective members, Hawley sometimes engaged deeply with the work of writing, and sometimes she took a more marginal role, depending on her life circumstances. In 1973, Hawley is listed as an author of the chapters on anatomy and physiology, sexuality, and relationships, and as a consultant on the chapters on abortion and childbirth. In 1976, she is an author of the chapters on sexuality and relationships, and one of many consultants for the chapter on considering parenthood. In 1984, Hawley, working with Wendy Sanford, served as project coordinator, keeping in mind "all the people, tasks, and stages of this project," but she limited her own writing to the chapters on psychotherapy and alternative medicine.[108] The collective encouraged its members to move from chapter to chapter, to develop and relinquish areas of special interest, to try out various roles in the process of drawing the book together. After 1973, the boundaries between the collective and its collaborators were clear, but inside the collective, roles were flexible, evolving from one edition to the next.

Our Bodies, Ourselves and Public Discourse

Our Bodies, Ourselves was a grand public telling of secrets. The collective raided medical libraries to collect the secrets of physicians and told them shamelessly: they demonstrated how doctors dismissed women's problems and maintained their ignorance of women's bodies. The collective's own talk about menstruation, masturbation, abortion, and orgasm was fashioned into a new story of female bodily experience, revised and reshaped through all the editions of *Our Bodies, Ourselves.* The collective insisted that these narratives were not just private matters, that they were not to be confined to either the consulting room or the kitchen table. They opened the public sphere to new issues and new agents. Public discourse, of course, has always been concerned with gendered embodiment. The citizen, as Jürgen Habermas concedes, was assumed to be male (and we might add, white and able-bodied).[109] All the messy details of particular bodies, their limits and their leaking temporality, were the seamy side of this fabric, supporting the composed image of rational critical discourse but generally ignored. *Our Bodies, Ourselves* reversed the fabric. Women's experience of the body was consequential: it spoke to how women could live and move in the world, to their access to resources, including medical resources, and to the life story they could expect to shape for themselves.

The women's health movement developed a counterpublic sphere in which a new discourse of the body, modeled on *Our Bodies, Ourselves*, had both currency and consequence. While the development of alternate forms of women's healthcare probably was prompted by the movement of healthcare into a competitive market economy in the 1970s as well as by the work of the women's health movement, those alternative forms also prompted women, their doctors, and the public agencies responsible for deploying medical resources to learn a new way of talking about women's health.[110] A new incarnation of "our public" had arrived.

Our Bodies, Ourselves, then, incited any number of face-to-face meetings, public projects, and other political activities: the social project that it represented was dense, and it included both personal transformation and public agitation.[111] Whether we understand the public in broad, Habermasian terms, as the discursive domain of all subjects, or in the terms developed by Mary Ryan and Geoff Ely, as one of many discursive domains cross-hatched with multiple publics, counterpublics, and alternative publics, publics are created by discourse.[112] As Michael Warner observes, "The way *the* public functions in the public sphere (as the people) is only possible because it is really *a* public of discourse. The peculiar character of *a* public is that it is a space of discourse organized by discourse. It is self-creating and self-organized; and herein lies its power, as well as its elusive strangeness."[113]

Before 1973, *Our Bodies, Ourselves* sold 450,000 copies, organizing spaces of the women's movement such as consciousness-raising groups and women's health classes. After 1973, millions of copies circulated, invoking readers directly and thereby creating an imaginary but powerful public of women who shared each other's secrets, stole secrets from their doctors, and were prepared to tell these stories in an even broader public space.

Historians of the public sphere have identified secrecy and its violations as central issues in the development of public culture. Norbert Elias identified the "civilizing process" of removing to a zone of privacy such bodily functions such as spitting, urinating, or having sex; he saw this removal as a critical step in the construction of a modern subject, and *Our Bodies, Ourselves* attempted to fold back that veil of privacy.[114] For the collective, secrecy supported professional power: rather than making an inventory of their bodily experience to be confided to a personal physician, the women of the Boston Women's Health Book Collective wrote about these experiences in colloquial language, sometimes de-medicalizing them and sometimes claiming for their own the lexicon of conventional medicine. They understood bodily experiences as universal, available to all women, and open to everyone for discussion, research, and reflection. The domain of female sexuality and reproduction, the very basis of women's exclusion from public life, was for the collective a site of rational critical discourse. (A down and dirty rational critical discourse, to be sure.) But like Habermas's public citizen, the writer of *Our Bodies, Ourselves* searched for arguments and proposals that would work for all women, whatever other identities they shared. Armed with an anatomical chart, these daughters of the Enlightenment fashioned a new public and constructed a new universalism.

The collective mobilized the paradox identified by Michael Warner: public discourse is at once personal and impersonal; it is addressed to any woman who opened the book looking for information on, say, cervical dysplasia, and also to the stranger, the abstracted and universalized "woman" she was the moment before she opened the book. The writers of *Our Bodies, Ourselves* deployed personal narrative to heighten this sense of a community of intimate strangers. Identity politics directed them to widen their networks of authorship and increase the range of experiences represented in the text, so that readers encountered the universality of women's embodiment as a series of differentiated, vivid examples. Writers of personal narratives spoke directly, with distinct individual voices— highly edited individual voices, to be sure—but they were never identified as particular, named people. Even members of the collective appeared in

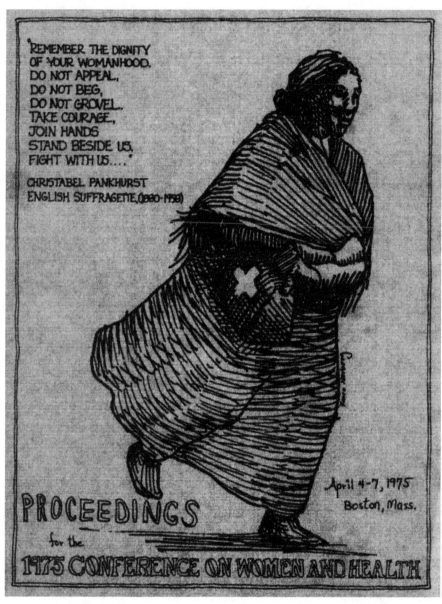

Figure 1.9. *Proceedings* of the 1975 Conference on Women and Health, cosponsored by the Boston Women's Health Book Collective. Drawing: Karen Norberg; Boston Women's Health Book Collective.

the book as loci of experience rather than as discrete individuals ("We have found . . ." "Some of us have tried . . ."). No member of the collective speaks as an individual in any edition of *Our Bodies, Ourselves*, and until recently, no member of the collective was identified in any photograph, not even in the iconic group picture of the collective published at the beginning of most editions. Even now, as members of the collective comment on draft passages of this book, they refuse credit for individual contributions, objecting that "everybody did that." The writers' relative anonymity enacted the universalism of discourse they were constructing. Although many of them refer to their relation to readers as a "conversation," it had become something different and something more.[115]

The collective was not alone in the project of entering, constructing, and transforming the public, or in suffering the vicissitudes of that project as the social movements of the 1960s ebbed. The transformation of public life those movements had sought quickly became both impossible and mystified. Harold Mah has shown how the public sphere can become, rather than a place of disagreement and negotiation, a "single, unified being, a mass subject."[116] This mass subject fuses persons into "a unitary, collective subject, no longer 'a public sphere' but now 'a public.'"[117] (Not, I should note, the universal category of "the public" that I have been discussing.) While public discourse is all about conflict, the mass subject is univocal: it does not dispute, but proclaims. The New Left and second-wave feminism constructed such a phantasmic subject and then invoked it as a unitary agent, variously named "women," "the Movement," or even more elusively, "the people." Beginning in 1969, in emulation of the Black Panther Party, the New Left worked to brand itself as representative of "the people": the park taken over by Berkeley radicals was "People's Park;" the counterdemonstrations planned for the U.S. bicentennial in 1976 were the "People's Bicentennial." These phantasmic agents had lives of their own: the "people" could learn, decide, or act through their agents, specific political organizations that invested themselves with representative power.

Phantasms could also become objects of identification for individuals whose exhausting and dangerous activity now required legitimation. No gesture is more common in accounts of the 1960s (or more exasperating to contemporary scholars) than the veteran's claim to a magnified historical agency, a power of representation that came unsought and left unexplained. These reflections by Todd Gitlin on the demise of SDS are a case in point:

All my thinking had been predicated on the intelligence of the movement itself as the embryo—like the classical Marxian proletariat—of a new society taking shape in the shell of the old. Now the premise decomposed. Therefore, the more predestined the Weathermen and the SDS crackup seemed, the more depressed I felt. "Can't separate things," I wrote Chris Hobson: "Grief over SDS & all that; sense of displacement from 'the movement'—which seems to require quotation marks now; . . . discovering that I had believed in the movement *itself*."[118]

Like writers of the *Harvard Crimson*, who did not know what to call *How Harvard Rules*, Gitlin had no name for the thing he has seen for the first time: the movement as a phantasmic identity, understood at the moment of its fragmentation.

Historians of the French Revolution have studied the relationships among subjects, the nation, and the public with attention, and their observations are relevant to the experience of the 1960s and 1970s. Keith Baker traces the process whereby "the nation was constituted symbolically as the ontological Subject, its unity and identity the very ground of individual and collective existence."[119] Those who lost contact with that symbolic, indeed magical, nation (or "people") tried to restore it through efforts of the will. A frustrated Jacobin or antiwar activist might hope that greater, more reckless, efforts would realign them with this lost Subject—efforts that might be expressed as ideological or political violence. Like Gitlin, casting about for an identity but unmoored from the symbolic subject of the movement, New Leftists became anxious when the momentum of radical activity subsided. For writers on the New Left or in second-wave feminist movements who did not summon themselves to exercises of radical will—and the women of the Boston Women's Health Book Collective were certainly among them—the alternative was melancholy. The collective's internal papers and the introductions to *Our Bodies, Ourselves* written after 1976 express a sense of having been carried, almost involuntarily, into an exhilarating identificatory relation with history, and then left adrift. Continuous political crisis, tolerable only because one was invested with a magnified historical agency, gave way to an airless sense of isolation, loss, and belatedness. An identity that once seemed coherent and integral had decayed into something fragmented and partial:

It is more difficult to be a feminist these days than it was in the optimistic climate of the early seventies. . . . Sometimes the great differences between us—race, class, ethnicity, sexual preference, values and strategies, turn us against one another. . . . Acknowledging the past and present hurts, the inner fears of difference and the external realities which separate us can enable us to learn to hear each and every woman's voice clearly, to nurture each and every woman's life.[120]

From the dream of social transformation, it was difficult to awaken to a modest project of organizing and maintaining a counterpublic, particularly when even this modest project proved to be killingly difficult. The women of the Boston Women's Health Book Collective were able to make such a transition, to institutionalize their political and intellectual energies in a form that could transform and conserve them. The collective took up the promise of the public—free access to the discourse by any stranger willing to attend, or in Robin Morgan's terms, any woman who "picked up the book out of anger, or defiance, or on a dare, or from genuine curiosity, or cynical amusement."[121] They would serve the needs of this reader and offer her both rationality and representation, both an accessible critical analysis of scientific medicine and a new way of thinking about her own body. If possible, they would draw her into their networks of correspondence, direct her to the institutions of the women's health movement, and integrate her into the fragile feminist counterpublic of the 1980s. Or they might entrust their future to this reader's conversations with her sister or her neighbor, with their promise of replicating the transformation they had experienced in their long talk with each other.

2　　A Different Kind of Writer

THE WRITER OF OUR BODIES, OURSELVES has had a long and successful career. Industrious and well published, her powers of research and investigation honed in thirty-five years of work, this writer assists at homebirths and cancer surgeries, chiropractic sessions and self-defense classes. Invoked in first-person plural, as "we" or "us," she is consistently feminist, sensitive to the differences among women, and determined to include a range of diverse voices. Woven into the text she writes are the words of individual women narrating their own health and reproductive histories.

Such a writer is anomalous for traditional literary studies, focused on the individual author. She recalls Foucault's dictum that the author function as a concept "does not develop spontaneously as the attribution of a discourse to an individual. It is rather, the result of a complex operation which constructs a certain rational being that we call 'author.'"[1] But unlike Foucault's author-function, this writer does not give the impression of an individual person's voice. It is impossible to call this writer "they," but it is inaccurate to call her "she." The writer is not an individual, but a group, the "we" who sorts out an impossible range of medical information and an equally impressive range of personal experiences. The voice is personal; the writer is not a person. It called for complicated subject positioning from the writers, as in this quote from Norma Swenson: "We learned to speak in that voice, even though it maybe was mine, but probably not."[2] This is a voice that could be realized only as text, not in health courses, public meetings, or any other conversational venue. A growing line of literary scholarship addresses such paradoxical forms of authorship, framing authorship as intrinsically collaborative, always imbricated in networks of readers, editors, correspondents, and other texts.[3]

Members of the Boston Women's Health Book Collective called their writing practices "collective authorship." "Collective," a term used in the early 1970s by many women's groups, including Boston's Bread and Roses, denoted a small group, bound by personal ties, that undertook political projects. The evolution of the group's name demonstrates the increasing importance to them of the work of writing: they began as the Boston Women's Health Collective, became the Boston Women's Health Course Collective, and ended as the Boston Women's Health Book Collective. But while all members of the group valued collective authorship, they meant very different things by it. For some, collective authorship described the group's decision-making process, the intensive meetings sorting out various proposals for the overall organization of the book and the direction of its chapters. For some, collective authorship meant intensive line editing of each manuscript by members of the collective. For some, collective authorship meant that parts of the project would be delegated to trusted individuals whose work would be accepted as authoritative. For all the members of the group, being in a collective implied bonds of friendship and mutual support: collective minutes are punctuated with accounts of sleeping toddlers and menus for potluck suppers. All collective members describe the book as being spoken by a voice different from that of any individual writer, but personal and distinct, and they valued that voice more than they valued their own. These contradictory formulations raise questions about where authority and agency were located in the writing process of the group, about how knowledge and expertise were constructed, and about how the writing of a book intervenes in and reconfigures a public sphere. Authorship is a conceptual nodal point that organizes issues of authority, knowledge, and publicity; the collective's distributed practices of writing gave them time and space to work these problems out. They learned how to produce a book, then they learned how to produce a comprehensive book, which eventually became a book that responded to the identity politics of the late 1970s.

Distributed Authorship

Our Bodies, Ourselves is an instance of distributed authorship: writing is done by multiple authors, often removed from one another in space and time. The efficacy of the text is understood as a relation with a deep network of readers and writers, but control of the text is dynamically invested in a central group. Early editions of the book were compiled from a range of documents, including the papers produced by collective members, contemporary pamphlets and essays, and medical textbooks. The book was released into feminist and alternative press communities that encouraged active response. From the beginning, *Our Bodies, Ourselves* was understood as a collaborative production. Later, the Simon and Schuster contract encouraged a regularization of collective structures. The collective settled on its membership, established business procedures, and began to keep careful records; in 1976, for a brief period, the collective dutifully had their minutes notarized each week.[4] After 1973, the boundaries of the collective became less porous, but its network of outside resources expanded. By 1984, eleven of the book's twenty-six chapters had a first author who was not a member of the collective, including two chapters ("Violence Against Women" and "Occupational Health") assembled by progressive groups. The logic of distributed authorship would accelerate in subsequent editions. Relations with collaborators were regularized with written agreements; print resources were organized in a library; collaboration became structured.

For collective members, the experience of writing for the group was both taxing and exhilarating. They felt free to write what they wanted, to speak openly, to consult both the authorities they knew and their own experience. The responses of their readers were gratifying: their writing had never been taken this seriously. So intense was this work that, for some members of the collective, it seemed like a direct imprinting of personal experience, and not writing at all: "When something comes out of your lived experience it's not seen as an activity like writing. It's just words and paper, just a vehicle to share your experience."[5] The text itself vanished at the very moment when it was realized. Collective members took up new chapters and topics in their work on different editions; few of them can recall offhand just which chapters they had written for which editions, but all remember moving from one topic to another as their interests evolved.

Distributed authorship created the sense of a public sphere in which issues of health, medicine, and feminine embodiment could be discussed and debated, enabling the writers to redefine these issues as matters of feminist politics. Abortion and birth control had become political issues in the late 1960s, but when the collective began its work, they were seldom understood as matters of women's rights: they were framed as issues of sexual freedom, or individual liberty, or overpopulation and poverty. Other questions—women's sexuality, socialization, and knowledge of their own bodies—were relegated to conversations between individual women and their barely informed doctors, and not regarded as political questions at all. Part of the collective's work was constructing a public space in which these issues could become consequential for women: their conversations with each other and with their collaborators were a prototype of that space.

The collective developed plural networks of expertise, including sympathetic medical practitioners, groups of medical consumers, and alternative healthcare sources, and it used them as sources of information, or as writers, reviewers, and editors. Many members of these networks wrote for the book; many others were interviewed—one of the collective's main strategies for gathering information. Some attended small group meetings with writers, or answered particular questions. The collective sponsored the construction of long chains of readers, reviewers, and correspondents who monitored the development of the text. For them, distributed authorship implied oversight of the project, preferably by several members. The identity of the oversight group, and balances of power within it, were shifting and dynamic, but each edition of the text after 1971 was pulled together by a relatively small group of women who worked on tone, continuity, and overall coherence. This chapter examines how practices of distributed authorship evolved in early editions of *Our Bodies, Ourselves* from 1970 through 1984, with a brief excursus into the 1990s, when issues of identity politics became salient. As the book developed, strategies of distributed authorship organized the collective's response to differences in race, ethnicity, and sexual orientation, shoring up a collective voice, a "we" of authorship, in the face of serious political differences in the women's movement.

The term "distributed authorship" was developed in studies of copyright and intellectual property and adopted in avant-garde art circles in 1983.[6] More recently, Sarah Robbins used "distributed authorship" to refer to the complex networks of editing and publishing characteristic of the antebellum public sphere in the United States.[7] Robbins shows how American women discounted their books as casual domestic productions, so that authorship was shared by the woman writer and those who saw to the book's publication: her study recalls similar disavowals of authorship by the Boston Women's Health Book Collective, whose members sometimes protested that they never meant to write a book, or at least not one that would be so popular.[8] The concept of distributed authorship, developed to sort out the changing contours of authors' legal and property rights, can direct our attention to ways in which multiple authors are integrated into the production of the text over extended processes of production.

For the writers of *Our Bodies, Ourselves*, the choice of plural rather than individual authorship was rooted in the practices of two of the group's sponsors, the New Left and second-wave feminism. Although the New Left cooperated with the mass media in generating stars, many organizations inherited a collaborative, democratic style from the civil rights movement; the Port Huron Statement calls for "a democracy of individual participation."[9] And the women's movement was emphatic in its distrust of movement celebrities.[10] But members of the collective had also been formed by a third literacy sponsor, higher education, which valued expertise and associated it with individual authorship. The collective rejected the individualism of authorship, but continued to value expertise. Distributed authorship allowed them to broker this contradiction: a collective member developed a base of knowledge in an area and shared that knowledge with the collective through reports, collections of articles, and interview transcripts. Such sanctioned knowledge would be reevaluated from the perspective of many individual experiences— those of the writer herself, of other collective members, of participants in health classes, of women who wrote letters to the collective. Accounts of individual experience were considered authoritative; the revision process constructed a virtual consciousness-raising group, revising standard expertise. As the networks of the group developed, the balance between expertise and experience shifted: the collective asked experts to draft chapters, but revised these drafts to include narratives of direct experience. In both cases, distributed authorship opened medical expertise to feminist reevaluation. Although individual authorship was always acknowledged in chapter headings and tables of contents, the dynamics of writing became more participatory.

Just as members of the collective refused solo speaking engagements, traveling in pairs to train new speakers and support veterans, they refused to take on the identity of authors. The 1970 introduction ends by soliciting "all your ideas, comments, suggestions, criticism," proclaiming "Power to our sisters!!" and acknowledging nineteen women by name, as well as "all the other women who took the course and read the papers."[11] Almost every chapter of the first edition has more than one author; the credit lines grew longer in subsequent editions, as more collaborators and editors were acknowledged. If the text was not really written, but simply transcribed a direct record of lived experience, its writers would potentially include all those who shared the experience of living in a woman's body.

Authorship seemed too dangerous for any one woman to hold. All my interviews with members of the original collective ended with the question, "How have you changed as a writer during your years with *Our Bodies, Ourselves*?" Almost all responded by refusing the term "writer": these women saw themselves as researchers, or editors, or organizers. They did not refuse authorship as a matter of principle: almost everyone named one or another collective member as a "real writer." Almost everyone was surprised to hear that the woman they named didn't consider herself a writer, either. By any objective measure, these women were writers: they had been engaged in a publication project for nearly forty years, and many of them had individually published books. When I probed further, collective members identified being a writer with modernist icons of authorship: "having worlds inside your head, like Faulkner," or effortlessly producing beautiful prose, or working for years in solitude.[12] This kind of aesthetic production was clearly alien to members of the collective. None of them would have been happy with the isolation implied in this model of authorship, although they could imagine it as an identity for others. Books had been transformative for them: Nancy Miriam Hawley became a feminist because Kathie Sarachild, a member of the radical feminist Redstockings, had handed her a copy of Simone de Beauvoir's *Second Sex*.[13] Although the collective aspired to that kind of writerly power, they each separately refused the identity of "writer" in favor of some other role that engaged them in an ongoing conversation that they valued. Distributed authorship was a way of producing a book without becoming a writer.

Speaking as "We"

Distributed authorship operated in three dimensions: it was realized in the text as a speaking voice; it operated to maintain the collective's control over the published book; and it operated through complex networks of authorship. In 1971, the collective stopped referring to women as "they" and adopted a systematic, all-embracing "we" that marked the relationships of distributed authorship in the text. (Conventional health books, written by physicians, established a clear demarcation between the instructing "I" and the docile, reading "you;" New Left journalism and the early documents of the women's movement were sometimes written by a "we," but often by an individual "I.") This "we" was a universalized Woman, and the collective was her voice. Thirteen years later, when Paula Doress-Worters and Diana Laskin Siegal instructed the writers of *Ourselves, Growing Older* on the use of "we," the word had come to mean a plural female author rather than a universal female body. At a writers' meeting on October 21, 1984, Doress-Worters and Siegal explained:

Generally author's voice is "we" or "we women," rather than the more distant "they." Individual authors should use "we" rather than "I," because all chapters will have multiple authorship after readers' comments and editing. . . . Do not use "we" when it would appear presumptuous; i.e., the majority of writers on this project are white, therefore we can hardly say "we Black women." However, we are midlife *and* older women; therefore don't use "we" for one group and "they" for the other group based on your age.[14]

Distributed authorship created a strangely concrete abstraction: the voice of the book was the voice of the women writing it *as a group*. Voicings were remarkably complex, parsing the speaker to represent women in general, groups of women, groups of women who were not active in writing, or intersections of groups of women. The only voice that distributed authorship did not support was that of an individual woman writer: there was no authorized use of the pronoun "I" outside of inset personal narratives. By 1984, this exclusion had become normalized: in a book with so many writers, "I" made no sense. "We," therefore, carries the process of writing into the text itself, marking the book as the work of many women, any women, maybe you. "We" included disabled women; in meetings with Boston Self-Help, members of the collective learned that the group disliked being referred to as "they," which they considered "too distancing," and wanted all readers to think of being able-bodied as a temporary state.[15]

Members of the collective were proud of the move from "they" to "we," but critics of the book challenged their right to that collective voicing. Paula Doress-Worters and Vilunya Diskin described that process:

We didn't want to create distance that said "you out there." We said, "Wait a minute, it's not their bodies out there; it's our bodies." And later we really had to think about when we were saying "we." So it got much more complicated as our group got more diverse and complex. When we started out with "we," it was a very inclusive solidarity sisterhood thing. And in the intervening years many groups, as they differentiated themselves said, "Don't 'we' baby me!"[16]

The initial universalized "we" and the later concrete "we" were layered into the text of *Our Bodies, Ourselves*. The pronoun "we" sometimes expressed the collective's understanding of female embodiment as universal: all women shared similar experiences, so they could be invoked in the plural pronoun. Sometimes "we" represented the specific collective writer of the text, encompassing a broad range of individual voicings, but not necessarily including the full range of every woman's experiences. The collective saw female embodiment as universal, and universal female embodiment as the ground enabling collective authorship. But they also recognized that their own specific practices were situated, local, and partial.

The "we" of *Our Bodies, Ourselves*, circulating among the collective, their collaborators, and their readers, also expressed a political project.

The collective wanted its conversation to become both general and consequential. They thought that women who learned basic health information from other women would understand themselves, their relation to other women, and their capacities in new ways. New insights would be expressed as projects, programs, new ways of relating to healthcare providers, new ways of talking about the body: these practices would ultimately transform American medicine. Today, members of the collective see their hopes as naïve, but they still consider conversation to be a transformative practice. The very first editions of *Our Bodies, Ourselves* are animated by the energy of telling and discovering secrets: the secrets of embodiment as women experienced it, but had not spoken of it; the secrets of the medical lexicon and medical training. To bring these discourses into a public sphere was to transform public discourse, to put in train a political story. To describe some medical indignity—and in 1970, when it was illegal to prescribe birth control to unmarried women in Massachusetts, or to perform abortions almost anywhere, indignities were thick on the ground— was an act of thrilling resistance. Well into the 1970s, these actions were deeply and immediately satisfying: the women's health movement grew steadily in both numbers and influence; clinics and information centers were organized; the global connections that would become so important to the collective in the twenty-first century were initiated.

In a quite different register, theorists of the public sphere have made a similar point. Jürgen Habermas's influential *Structural Transformation of the Public Sphere* argues the importance of conversations among private individuals in the eighteenth century for the development of the politics and culture of the enlightenment.[17] Conversations initially focused on the characters and situations of novels, creating a space for discourse outside official or ecclesiastic channels. This public sphere, which eventually sponsored newspapers, journals, and letters, established a discursive terrain that was theoretically open to all comers, and where the force of argument, rather than a speaker's office or rank, could be persuasive. The distributed writer of *Our Bodies, Ourselves* opened new public spaces to new participants. What had been a private matter between a woman and her doctor was redefined as a political issue. The causes and cures of health and disease became matters for deliberation in the emerging feminist counterpublic.

Central Control

The Boston Women's Health Book Collective wanted control over their texts, and so the collective negotiated distributed authorship to maintain their editorial authority. The contract with Simon and Schuster vigilantly protected the collective's right to final approval of the text. They gleefully tussled with "Red Pencil," the collective's nickname for the Simon and Schuster copy editor who tried to sanitize their language, and the collective usually won.[18] Other conflicts were more difficult. Original plans for the 1976 edition included a chapter on drugs; although members of the collective worked long and hard on the chapter, they were never able to produce a version they wanted to publish.

In 1984, the collective decided that they wanted a more coherent book, one that argued against the medicalization of women's lives, and that they would assert consistent central control over its content. Carrying out this policy was not simple. The collective had asked an activist in reproductive technologies to produce a draft chapter; her work seemed "antimale" in its characterization of reproductive technologies as imposed by men on women. This radical feminist framework was at odds with the projected critique of medicalization. Representatives of the collective negotiated with the author, who explained that, while not all men are "into new reproductive technologies, men are still oppressing women." Collective members countered that readers would reject the chapter's wholesale condemnation of men; they argued that the writer should "*want* to convince people*," and that this work of persuasion was worth some small changes.[19] The writer decided that writing "researchers and doctors" in place of "men" was not such a small change: "What you define as 'anti-male bias,'" she wrote to the collective, "I see as clarity."[20] She was paid for her work, but her draft was rejected.

The collective understood themselves as voicing the reactions of potential readers. Having given talks and classes, talked to readers about previous editions, and read readers' letters, they had a sense of what kind of language worked. Their own copy had been edited, and they expected the distributed writers to engage in the same process. Judith Norsigian described the arc from reader to collective member to writer: "I, at that point, had had enough experience knowing that the particular language that was being used was problematic because I had already seen people

not understand it. So, I had already been convinced by other people saying, you know, 'You've got to use this language instead because more
people will understand it.'" She made the same argument to invited writers, asking for changes in language to make the text "just a bit more accessible. And some will say, 'Fine.' Another group will say, 'No, I want
my original words.'" After a few of these conversations, the collective
stipulated that writers did not have "the final editorial consult."[21]

More painful decisions involved members of the collective. In 1984,
a collective member living in California undertook revision of the birth
control chapter. The rest of the collective felt that her draft reflected a
"cafeteria-style" approach to birth control rather than the outright advocacy of barrier methods that they had planned. They also felt that,
rather than reflecting the more inclusive tone that they were searching
for, this draft was "racist and patronizing." The draft was rejected, and
Susan Bell was asked to write the chapter. The correspondence about this
issue is frank and emotional: nobody was happy about the decision, or the
way it was reached. The dynamics of distributed authorship, in this case,
favored a central political vision over a long-standing collaboration.[22]

Networks of Authorship

The networks of authorship constructed by the collective began as
complicated friendship networks within second-wave feminism. Early chapters of *Our Bodies, Ourselves* chapters circulated in the Boston
women's movement. The collective itself was the first network: as each
edition was revised, the group—still an informal collection of interested women—met to consider new emphases, suggest new sources of
information, and plan changes to the text. While minutes of the Boston
Women's Health Book Collective Board of Directors, the name under
which the collective became an nonprofit corporation, periodically lament
that they no longer have time to "really talk" to each other, the group did
periodically settle in for a prolonged stocktaking. In response to group
prompts, members wrote long self-evaluations, or reports on their own
healthcare practices, or reactions to proposed drafts. For members of the
collective, collaboration mitigated the anxiety of writing: the text was no
longer a display of oneself, but a convivial project. As one member put
it, "I like writing collectively. I love the way different eyes on the same

subject, even when you're all coming from the same place, you tend to do a much better product. And one of the things that's good about not being an identified writer is that you don't have a big investment about your own words, that things not be changed."[23]

Beginning with the first Women and Their Bodies class at MIT in the winter of 1970, the women who took health courses were resources for the book. Their comments were gathered, compiled, and discussed. The collective continued to teach in formal and informal settings for decades. "Women and Their Bodies" was offered periodically at the Cambridge Women's Center, which was also the home of Lesbian Liberation, the writers of "In Amerika They Call Us Dykes" (1973). Community groups and clinics requested the course or used the collective's materials to mount it themselves. Members of the collective stopped giving health classes during the rush to produce the 1973 and 1976 Simon and Schuster editions, but they continued to consult with women on health issues and to teach in academic institutions or community schools. Esther Rome, for example, offered a course on "Wandering Through the Food Maze" at the Cambridge Adult Education Center in 1981; the notes for this course are the framework for her revision of the nutrition chapter; questions and comments from students are part of the submerged dialogue that shapes the chapter. After the chapter was drafted, Rome recruited three of her former students to read it as "lay women" and give her suggestions for revision.[24] In 1981, as the group was preparing to write the 1984 edition, they invited women to participate in issue groups at their Women's Health Information Center, offering sessions for women over age forty (led by Norma Swenson) and on feminist women and relationships with men (led by Paula Doress-Worters). These groups collected experiences, identified emerging problems, and tested ideas.[25]

Members of the collective traveled and spoke. The group fielded twenty-seven speaking engagements in the first five months of 1979: some were general talks such as "Women and Health," given to both the Taunton Women's Alliance and the Boston State College Psychology Club; others were specific presentations on such topics as Depo-Provera (to an FDA Consumer Meeting) or on the regionalization of maternity and newborn care to the International Childbirth Education Association Eastern Regional Conference.[26] These talks could lead to collaborations, extending the networks of the collective deeper into the ranks of activists and caregivers. Paula Doress-Worters relates such an encounter in a memo on revision of the sexuality chapter for the 1984 edition: "E. H. [Eleanor Hamilton] is a woman in her 70's, a leading sex educator, whom Wendy and I met at the sex educators conference in Vermont. Would like to interview her on this [pleasure anxiety]. She believes we are taught to interpret good feelings as bad and bad feelings as good. This reinforces the sex negativity of the culture."[27] In the end, neither Eleanor Hamilton nor the idea of "pleasure anxiety" appeared in *The New Our Bodies, Ourselves*; like many other discussions, interviews and group meetings, this conversation informed the writing rather than emerging directly in the text.

The collective also sponsored institutions and events that sustained its network of contacts. Beginning in 1980, the group funded and helped to staff a Women's Health Information Center (WHIC) in Watertown, Massachusetts. The WHIC maintained a library, actively monitored women's health issues, and responded to inquiries from advocacy groups and individuals. From 1975 to 1995, the collective periodically distributed Women's Health Information Packets (WHIP) to U.S. health activists and a growing list of international contacts. Packets included reprints, clippings, flyers, clinical materials, patient handouts, and letters. Like the punk zines that were circulating as envelopes of drawings and stories to round-robin mailing lists, the WHIP project was a proto-Web site, offering women's health activists a cheap, convenient way to keep in touch and share information. In 1975, the collective cosponsored the first national Conference on Women and Health, with twenty-five hundred women participating. They were also active in the Rising Sun Feminist Health Alliance, a loose organization of women's clinics and health centers that sponsored periodic weekend retreats from 1978 to 1987. Rising Sun retreats featured karate classes, clinical demonstrations, and intense discussions of common problems. Managing these activities prompted the collective to expand: Pamela Morgan began working for the group in 1979 as coordinator; Sally Whelan joined in 1980 as documentalist.

Almost from the beginning, the collective's conversations included letters from readers.[28] These letters could lead directly to revision. For

example, in 1976, readers objected that the book's discussion of conization, a procedure in which abnormal cells are removed from the cervix,
was threatening and vague; it was rewritten in 1984 to offer a much more
detailed account of the procedure and its possible complications. More
significant than this specific change was the realignment of reader and
text. The writers could not resolve all ambiguities: in 1984, one sentence
read, "a cone biopsy involves some risk of future infertility because it
may weaken the cervix," which, although more specific than the general reference to complications in 1976, is scarcely definitive.[29] But now
the reader knows what the writer knows. The letter writers had effectively policed the collective; the text is repositioned so that uncertainty
is shared rather than transmitted.

Correspondence and meetings with readers told the writers of *Our
Bodies, Ourselves* what information readers wanted, and they always wanted
more. Information was gathered from sympathetic experts, including
health professionals and activists. Some such early efforts were painful
improvisations. In 1975, searching for information on rape, a collective
member called James Selkin, director of the Violence Research Unit of
the Denver Department of Health and Hospitals, to ask why men raped
women.[30] They had never met Selkin and had no further contact with
him after his polite and puzzled reply. By 1984, however, the collective
would compile the "Violence Against Women" chapter from materials
produced by experienced advocates in the Boston Area Rape Crisis Center and the Alliance Against Sexual Coercion.

Members of the collective had a long-standing interest in public
health and began attending the annual meetings of the American Public
Health Association in 1975.[31] Some of the collective's close collaborators
were academics working in the new field of critical studies of science and
medicine. An important node of this network developed around Irving
Kenneth Zola (1935–94), professor of sociology at Brandeis University.
Zola was a leading scholar in disability studies, founder of both the *Disability Studies Quarterly* (1982) and Brandeis's program in medical sociology.[32] In the late 1970s, collective member Norma Swenson matriculated
in the Brandeis program; Zola's critique of the medicalization of social
problems cohered with her growing understanding of the systemic,
social nature of medical problems. A 1981 memo to writers who were

revising *Our Bodies*, probably written by Swenson, includes this advice: "I think Nancy [Hawley] and Pam [Berger] should interview Irv Zola, ask his advice, have a mini-tutorial with him about concepts of health and illness, belief systems, etc. After interviewing [for the projected chapter on alternative health] is done, perhaps before. He's an invaluable resource."[33] In 1981, Judith Norsigian and Irving Zola married, and the ties among Zola, his colleagues, and the collective deepened. The 1984 edition repeatedly discusses "medicalization," a key concept in Zola's work, and the "Special Acknowledgments" page thanks him for "reading and carefully criticizing all our most problematic chapters . . . [his] advice never failed to be right on the mark." Zola, who publicly acknowledged his own intellectual debt to the collective, helped to connect them to the resources and institutions of social studies of medicine.[34]

Susan Bell, a student of Zola's, developed a sustained collaboration with the collective.[35] Bell did the revisions of the birth control chapter in the 1984 and 1992 editions of *Our Bodies, Ourselves*; she described her 1984 rewrite as a competent and technically comprehensive revision of the original chapter.[36] By the time she began work on the 1992 edition, Bell had been convinced by new scholarship in feminist body studies, particularly Emily Martin's *The Woman in the Body*, which argued that conventional medicine saw pregnancy as the goal of every menstrual cycle. Bell decided that her own writing for *Our Bodies, Ourselves* had fallen into that trap. So, instead of describing a disintegrating uterine lining, as she had in 1984, Bell told a different story about the same hormones: "Approximately *days 26 to 27 to 28*. If pregnancy is prevented success-fully, *corpus luteum's* manufacture of *estrogen* and *progesterone* slows down to a very low level. This drop creates an 'appropriate environment for reducing the excess layers of tissue lining your uterus.'"[37] Bell rejected as sexist both the technology of birth control and the language used to describe it. Her own translation of the specialized language of science would mediate between the biology of birth control practices and the worlds of the book's many readers, women who might not have insur-ance, or who might live in their parents' homes. Bell used the concep-tual framework of situated knowledge, developed by Donna Haraway, to support her work, bringing the early texts of postmodern feminism to the collective's attention.[38]

Although higher education was one of the sponsors of the collective's writing, they did not want the book to seem academic. Connections with scholars, however, opened broad avenues of research to the group. In the 1981 revision memo, writers are urged to "familiarize yourselves with dominant (usually male) thinkers and feminist critics' critiques in both popular and academic/scientific/intellectual realms. Be prepared to identify the issues and prepare readers to cope with them—in society, in government policy, in readers' self-evaluation as women. Special critical attention goes to medicine and medical ideology in every area, so as to build an effective critique. This means reading books as well as articles."[39] Notes on particular chapters make such suggestions as "Foucault (*History of Sexuality*) for challenges to the notion that we live in a sex-repressive age," and "everything Ellen Willis has written."[40]

Thirty-five years later, Jane Pincus could readily name four women who collaborated with her on the 1971 childbirth chapter; all of them now healthcare advocates.[41] The 1981 memo to writers on revision suggested consultation, variously, "with feminists who are teaching fertility awareness courses," "Baltimore RESOLVE women," and organizations such as Science for the People and the Reproductive Rights National Network.[42] These collaborators could become coauthors, taking on responsibility for drafting chapters, or interviews with them might inform writers' treatment of a topic. They might serve as readers and critics of draft chapters; those who did substantial work on a chapter were listed as coauthors and were paid. The collective valued their networks as guarantees of the vitality of the text: they wanted to maintain close contact with women "on the front lines" of healthcare struggles because of the stories they had to tell. In an April 1979 collective meeting, for example, Norma Swenson reported on a visit to the Cambridge Women's Health Center. The minutes record her comments: "I learned a lot at the community health center; it has a steam that we don't have. Things are going well. They have a strong desire to communicate. We should try to run a seminar workshop series of meetings in addition to speaking there."[43] The clinic, like other feminist health groups, was seen as a site for learning and collaboration, not only because of their clinical expertise but because of their "steam"—their political energy.

Jane Pincus: Distributing Writing

Jane Pincus's history as a writer for the Boston Women's Health Book Collective illustrates the movement of distributed authorship from the immediate circle of the collective to distributed networks of experts. Distributed authorship began with the work of individual members of the collective, women whose capacities as writers were developed as they wrote. Jane Pincus wrote the pregnancy chapter in the first newsprint edition, continued to work on issues of pregnancy and childbirth in all editions up to 2004, did overall editing on the 1984 edition, and, with Wendy Sanford, wrote and edited for all editions through 2004.[44]

Born in 1937, Pincus grew up in Westchester in a middle-class family. She went to a public high school and graduated from Pembroke, the women's college of Brown University, in 1959. She was interested in French literature—her undergraduate thesis had been on Andre Malraux, the socialist novelist and art critic—and she also did graduate work in art at Columbia University. She moved to Cambridge, Massachusetts, with her husband, Ed Pincus. There, she taught high school French and had two children. A civil rights advocate since childhood, she worked on fair housing issues and draft counseling before finding her way to the emerging feminist movement. After the Emmanuel Conference, she began working with the Doctor's Group, the nascent collective, and a personal group loosely connected with Bread and Roses.

Pincus drew on a wide range of textual practices for her work on *Our Bodies, Ourselves.* She had been keeping personal journals for years and drew on these records of her own pregnancy and childbirth. Within the collective, Pincus circulated frank, detailed accounts of her personal life, of medical events, and of the problems she faced. In her hands, even routine documents became festive. The group rotated the work of keeping minutes of their meetings and of writing letters. Pincus's minutes were ornamented with drawings, especially if the meeting was boring. She decorated the margins of difficult letters with designs and borders. Pincus was frank in narrating her own experience, and she developed these accounts in conversations with other members of the group: "I just wrote. . . . I don't even think I looked anything up. I remember writing down some things about pregnancy. It was easy because you just sort of wrote down what you knew, which wasn't much. And then you would bring that down and talk to people and then add questions that you'd look up the answers to if you couldn't answer it there."[45]

Pincus was looking for answers to her own questions. During her second pregnancy, she had read the medical record of her first childbirth, then an unusual act, and found that "a lot of dangerous things were happening to me that I didn't know anything about."[46] Her reaction was alienated astonishment: "My record, I didn't recognize my record, I said 'that's not *my* record.'"[47] For Pincus, writing *Our Bodies, Ourselves* corrected the unrecognizable medical language that described her body and her baby at risk and beyond her control. This writing juxtaposed medical discourse with that of the personal journal and the intimate conversation "so what you got was a whole range of personal and medical events, physiological events that were mixed together."[48]

While she worked on the very first editions, Pincus was also experimenting with film. Her husband, Ed Pincus, founded the new MIT film department, and he was beginning work on *Diaries (1971–76)*, a record of his life and of their open marriage. Jane Pincus started a course in cinema photography, made some short films, and collaborated with three other women on a film about abortion, still illegal in 1970. When women learned about the project, they sent the filmmakers audio tapes describing their experiences with illegal or overseas abortions. These accounts were intercut with extended interviews; the composite story of a back-alley abortion, ending with the patient's scream, and a political analysis of birth control, including a critique of contraceptive drug testing on Puerto Rican women. The film ended with a "spoken song":

Our bodies are ours to control.
My mind defines the rage inside of me.
Every woman who says she is my sister
Will stand and fight with me.[49]

The initial politics of *Our Bodies, Ourselves* are concentrated in these lines: feminine autonomy as a relationship to the body; the body as an external object and a source of identity; rationality as a means of organizing affection; universal womanhood; the movement from solidarity to opposition. The structure of the film—integrating multiple personal accounts, a narrative constructed from various sources, and political analysis—anticipates the structures of *Our Bodies, Ourselves.*

This film, and Pincus's work on pregnancy and childbirth, illustrates the first phase of the collective's distributed authorship. For Pincus, writing *Our Bodies, Ourselves* began as a way of coming to terms with personal experience, particularly the experience of pregnancy and childbirth: "One of the ways that we understood experience was to write about it."[50] But while Pincus mined her own journals for examples, she also talked with other women in her personal group, with mothers of the children in her playgroup, with members of the collective, and with women who took the health course. The impulse to write was sparked by her rejection of her own medical record, an alienated and threatening account; writing was a way of taking back bodily experience and countering a medical discourse seen as pervasive and threatening. Pincus speaks of the "incomparable 'high' of collective discovery and connection with other women, both in the BWHBC and elsewhere," as "the invisible fuel that inspired us and that was literally in the air!"[51] At the same time, the limits of the medical resources available to the collective in the 1970s forced Pincus to lean heavily on what information she had. Nearly forty years after the fact, she recalled: "There was a book by Anthony somebody called *The Body*, which I actually copied right into the first newsprint of *Our Bodies, Ourselves*, which talked about how the fetus grew from week to week."[52] *The Body*, by Anthony Smith, whose other books are about travel and adventure, had indeed been published in 1968, and in the first edition of *Our Bodies, Ourselves* the appendix to the pregnancy chapter draws freely on Smith's account, although the text characteristically adds technical language to Smith's graceful popularization.[53] In the early 1970s, distributed authorship mediated the collective's relationship with each other and with other activists in the women's movement.

From 1975 through 1980, Jane Pincus lived in Vermont and concentrated on her own artwork. Removed from daily interactions with the collective, she handled the distribution of free copies of the book to women's groups and clinics, and she traveled frequently to Boston for group meetings. In the 1984 edition, *The New Our Bodies, Ourselves*, she worked with Norma Swenson to expand the section on pregnancy and childbirth to more than a hundred pages, organized around the contrast between conventional medicine's "climate of doubt" and the "climate of confidence" that *Our Bodies, Ourselves* advocated. Swenson and Pincus took notes on medical textbooks, read articles in the medical press, and held scores of interviews. The networks of distributed authorship grew to include medical experts and health activists. Pincus and Swenson worked up a text in conversations and review sessions, trading and correcting drafts. Jane Pincus and Wendy Coppedge Sanford were also overall "editors and midwives" of the 1984 edition.[54] They reviewed chapters for clarity and focus; they meticulously copyedited every line of text. Jane Pincus, like most members of the collective, does not consider herself a writer, but she admits to being an editor: "I love to make sentences active and strong."[55] Pincus continued to work with the collective for subsequent editions, especially on the childbirth and pregnancy chapters. Because of disagreements about content and authorship, she withdrew her draft of the pregnancy chapter from the 2004 edition, although her name is still on the childbirth chapter.

As the network of distributed authors grew, all members of the collective became more skilled and critical in their use of medical information. In later editions, Pincus's conversations with informants deepened, and her use of both medical and personal authorities sharpened. She still returned to her own diaries for accounts of pregnancy, and she relied on a reference work—Ethel Sloane's progressive text, *Biology of Women*—but these texts are integrated with others, interrogated, and continually juxtaposed with personal narratives more extended and varied than those in earlier editions. Pincus attended a childbirth-preparation class taught by midwife Becky Sarah; consulted with medical sociologist Susan Bell; translated *La Genèse de l'homme écologique: l'instinct retrouvé*, a manuscript by Michael Odent, a French doctor, whose book she would later co-translate.[56] She heard papers on medical topics at the University of Vermont, interviewed dozens of women about their experiences in pregnancy and childbirth, and testified at Vermont hearings on reproductive rights.[57] The text crystallizes relationships among health activists, members of feminist communities, and supportive health professionals. It expresses a focused perspective, the advocacy of a "climate of confidence" that Swenson and Pincus had developed in their own conversations and in political discussions with the collective.

Pincus's development as a writer reflected the development of the collective's networks. Some of these networks were casual and temporary—the MIT film department had no formal relation to the collective, but it subsidized Pincus's early experiments with film, offering her new models of collaboration and outreach. Other relationships, like Pincus's long-standing collaborations with collective member Norma Swenson, her work with midwife Becky Sarah, or with sociologist Robbie Pfeufer Kahn, were to shape the texts she wrote through many editions.[58] Pincus connected the collective with the emerging networks of lay midwifery and home-birth activism; she also shaped the distinctive style of the text, ruthlessly pruning out movement jargon while carefully maintaining the markers of individual style in personal narratives. Her work as a writer, like her early experiment with film, focused on collecting, selecting, and arranging narrative and analysis assembled from dispersed networks of correspondents and potential readers. Her understanding of her own embodiment and of her own experiences with medicine was intricately bound up with her research and writing on conventional medicine and its alternatives. For Pincus, the distribution of authorship was not a matter of convenience; it expressed her understanding of knowledge as situated in practice and plural. It sharpened her commitment to individual voicings of the text, and it supported a writing practice that was inclusive rather than polemic.

The Politics of Distributed Authorship

As Pincus's story illustrates, second-wave feminism had encouraged the collective to see authorship as plural and had undercut the authority of the solitary writer. In the mid-1970s and 1980s, the politics of the women's movement became more complex: African American feminist organizations emerged; political differences sharpened with the development of cultural feminist and lesbian separatist politics; the growth of feminist institutions raised serious practical and political questions. Distributed authorship was a strategy for responding to these challenges, particularly to the claims of identity politics, which focused on specific identities such as race, gender, and sexual orientation as a basis for political resistance and group solidarity. Identity politics fostered the development of collective consciousness and a program that claimed rights and status based on group membership. Women of color were important theorists of identity politics in the 1980s; cultural feminists asserted a worldview based on values associated with femininity; lesbians demanded distinct institutions and political priorities.

For the Boston Women's Health Book Collective, issues of identity emerged first in a project of translation, itself a venerable form of distributed authorship. Kathy Davis's *The Making of Our Bodies, Ourselves: How Feminist Knowledge Travels Across Borders* is a magisterial account of the translations and adaptations of *Our Bodies, Ourselves*, detailing the movement of the text from the European translations of the 1970s to the Asian, African, and Middle Eastern adaptations of the 1980s and 1990s.[59] Relationships with translators raised issues about what kind of public sphere the collective wanted to construct and how discrete groups would participate in that work. The collective wanted their book to reach women who did not read English, but any translation project would require collaboration outside their immediate networks. Necessarily, central elements of distributed authorship were worked out in these early efforts at translation, particularly translation into Spanish.

The collective had first attempted a Spanish translation in 1974, negotiating funding of $3,000 for it in their contract with Simon and Schuster. The collective paid a small group to begin this work, but the Spanish text that emerged seemed dogmatic and failed to present choices to readers. This unsuccessful attempt to distribute authorship prompted the collective to define, for the first time, the elements of their style and tone—features of the book that they wanted preserve in translation. The list they formulated, essentially a style sheet for the book, reads:

a) no rhetoric

b) using *we*

c) giving choices

d) non-directive—never saying *this is the way*

e) respecting that the person reading it can make the choice herself[60]

"No rhetoric," on this list, should be understood as "no heavy-handed movement rhetoric," since *Our Bodies, Ourselves* is a rhetorically sophisticated text, and its writers were proud of their ability to present radical ideas in colloquial language. The collective eventually refused to publish a translation that diverged from both the politics and spirit of their book; experiences like this one consolidated a key practice of distributed authorship, the maintenance of central authority by the collective. Davis has shown that, in their relationships with global translators and adaptors of the book, the collective has held this authority very loosely, deferring to the experience of women in the countries where the translation was to be published. But in the United States, in 1976, their decision was peremptory: this translation would not do, and the book was straightforwardly translated in a version produced in 1976 by Raquel Scherr Salgado and Leonora Taboada and distributed informally among health activists.

In the early 1980s, Elizabeth MacMahon Herrera, a Columbian immigrant woman originally drawn to the group by the need for a more thoroughgoing adaptation to the needs of Latinas in the United States, was working with Amigas Latinas en Acción pro-Salud (ALAS). ALAS developed a broad practice in health issues important to Latinas and worked from 1980 to 1992 on adapting *Our Bodies, Ourselves* to new media suited to the needs of the Latino community: they were not translating the text, but transforming it. (ALAS was, in fact, quite critical of the existing Spanish translation of the book.) Elizabeth MacMahon Herrera worked as a member of the collective, also serving as liaison to ALAS. ALAS's materials, especially their films, circulated to the collective's Latin American contacts.[61] ALAS's work influenced the writers of the full adaptation, *Nuestros Cuerpos, Nuestras Vidas* (2000), composed in what editor Ester Shapiro called "a transformational 'trialogo'" between the writers of U.S. *Our Bodies, Ourselves*, Latin American and Caribbean health activists, and Latinas living in the United States.[62] She credits Rosie Muñoz Lopez, a member of the editorial group, with translating the book's "we" to meet the conceptual needs of the Latina editors:

Muñoz Lopez noted that *OBOS* itself incorporated the voices of a shifting "we" which was textually interpreted in context as sometimes referring to all U.S. women, and other times to specific women. Through the participation of Latinas in the organization the U.S. Latina perspective had been expanded beginning with the 1984 edition. Why not use a similar strategy in the Spanish cultural adaptation, letting the "we" who speaks be defined in context while further expanding the sections dealing with U.S. Latinas?[63]

The translators saw ALAS, with its ongoing work on health issues, as an essential support for producing an animated, engaged translation. They sought out similar groups of Latin American activists to write particular chapters. Distributed authorship sponsored cascading relationships of delegation and collaboration: the Boston Women's Health Book Collective and ALAS; ALAS and the writers of *Nuestros Cuerpos, Nuestras Vidas*; writers of *Nuestros Cuerpos, Nuestras Vidas* and the Latina health activists who helped develop the book.[64]

Many of the changes made to adapt *Nuestros Cuerpos, Nuestras Vidas* to the needs of its readers restored the structure and feeling of *Our Bodies, Ourselves'* early editions. In *Nuestros Cuerpos, Nuestras Vidas*, as in the very first editions of *Our Bodies, Ourselves*, political analysis come first, before the chapters of medical information. The text is seen, not as a comprehensive resource, but as "an expression of [a] movement."[65] Of course, the book was not framed as homage to Anglo American second-wave feminism: writers were wrestling with the question of how their work on *Nuestros Cuerpos, Nuestras Vidas* would build a Latina health movement. As Shapiro put it, their vision of using the book as a tool for transnational organizing "remains a work in progress."[66] The collective continually negotiated a tension between broadening the boundaries of "the public" and sharing control of "their public."

While the Spanish translation posed complex problems, those raised by lesbian and African American activists went to the heart of the collective's local practice. The politics of *Our Bodies, Ourselves* were based on the idea that all women shared a common experience of embodiment, and so writers understood the practice of writing about medicine as rooted directly in their own experience and their own political identities. The work of translating the text foregrounded the ways in which the body is shaped by the words that describe it, and common experiences are mediated by distinct languages. These issues emerged as specific questions of textual organization, word choice, and book design; nothing in the experience of the collective's sponsors was comparable to the complexity or political stakes of the problems translation posed for them. As the collective worked to find adequate translations, they began direct collaboration with groups who felt that *Our Bodies, Ourselves* did not express their own experiences of feminine embodiment.

Lesbian Identity Politics

When African American or lesbian women reflected on their quite concretely embodied experiences, they did not come to a sense of universal solidarity with other women, but to a sense of their difference, and very often to an angry recognition that their difference had not been recognized by white heterosexual feminists. Lesbian organizations posed these issues forcibly in the 1970s. The collective was eager to respond and planned a chapter on "Lesbianism" in 1971; a draft version of the chapter, known as the "Gay Paper," circulated in the collective in 1972.[67] Since all the members of the collective were at the time heterosexual, they asked a group of women meeting at the Cambridge Women's Center (known at the center as Lesbian Liberation) to write the chapter, agreeing to their demand for final control over the chapter.[68] The draft Lesbian Liberation produced was exuberant and raw; it was included in the 1973 edition with minimal editing. One writer's use of lowercase "i" for the first-person pronoun was regularized; some of the purple passages in personal narratives were cut, but the overall tenor and direction of "In Amerika They Call Us Dykes" is unchanged from the original draft by Lesbian Liberation. While this text was anything but a nuanced political statement, the collective understood that their book had to include material by lesbian writers without tampering or censorship. Scores of lesbians accepted Lesbian Liberation's call for letters, and many wrote that "In Amerika They Call Us Dykes" had been the first sympathetic writing about lesbianism they had ever encountered.[69] The lesbian chapter framed issues of sexual expression as political questions; the health problems of lesbians were presented as issues of equal access to care. The question that lesbian readers had posed to the collective—why are you writing a women's health book focused on heterosexual reproduction?—was broadened, and prompted the airing of a new set of secrets.

By 1974, when the collective was preparing a more carefully shaped book, they moved toward a resolution of issues of authorship and collaboration. Lesbian Liberation, honoring its own collective authorship process, refused to make changes unless all their members agreed, but few of them were still interested in working on the text. It was unlikely in any case that Lesbian Liberation would write the text the collective wanted, and the BWHBC was certain that they wanted to assert editorial control of the chapter; minutes of the collective reflect a desire for something "softer" and "more mature."[70] Wendy Sanford wrote a letter to "the women who worked on the lesbian chapter of *Our Bodies, Ourselves*" (December 15, 1974) summarizing conversations about balancing the chapter; she conceded that both groups were weary of the difficult negotiations around revision. Since the collective's lawyer had found no agreement ceding editorial control to the original writers of the chapter, Sanford proposed to bring in new writers to collaborate with the collective, or with the former writers, individually or as a group. This strategy seems to have been effective, since a subsequent letter "to all who worked on the lesbian chapter revisions," reported on publication dates, book prices, and other practical matters and invited everyone to a "women's party for people who have worked on revisions."[71]

The text of the 1976 chapter supported an accommodation between the identity politics of the Cambridge lesbian feminist community and the collective's desire for an inclusive text. The chapter is, in its outline and in most of its specific content, the same as it had been in 1973, but the principle of the collective's editorial control had been established, and some significant changes had been effected. There were new personal narratives, from an African American lesbian and from older women, and a general critique of homophobia in psychiatry was cut. One of the most striking changes is the rewriting of the chapter's final paragraph, which in 1973 had read:

Look! Women are the source of life! Blood-lined bellies, soft-thighed nourishers of a billion million infants—wild, moon-ridden creatures of such lushness that a thousand wars have not burned us out. . . . When two of us are suddenly made able to see into each other, there is no course, no end for that journey. The earth trembles before our collision as we walk a path this side of loneliness, this side of what can be known through words alone— that side of revolution and madness—and everywhere love.[72]

Some might find this writing lyrical; others, incoherent. But the last paragraph of the 1976 chapter strikes a different note:

As we said initially, this chapter just begins to offer a picture of what our lives as lesbians are like. There is no one way to describe who we are. . . . As women, as gay women, we have started to find the ways that our lives connect. . . . At the same time, we define our struggle. It is one that goes on in many forms, and yet we understand that together we can, and do, make the changes we all (gay and straight) need.[73]

In 1976, the collective published a chapter on lesbianism that did not quite express the "unified feminist vision" of *Our Bodies, Ourselves,* although it was valuable to many readers and connected the BWHBC to the lesbian political community. This experiment in distributed authorship developed the collective's experience and constructed networks that would support a more congenial revision in 1984.

For that edition, Sanford worked with new collaborators, the "Lesbian Revisions Group," to completely revise the chapter. As the collective's networks developed, and some of its members came out as lesbians, the dissonance between "In Amerika" and the rest of *Our Bodies, Ourselves* became more salient. As it stood in 1976, the "lesbian chapter" jarred against the warm tone of the rest of the book. And the chapter raised its own issues of identity, since it was oriented to white, young women. In reworking this chapter over three editions, distributed authorship had enabled the collective to maintain editorial control, to abstain for a time from exercising it, and to develop a more cohesive group of collaborators. The relations of distributed authorship had allowed the collective to manage their disagreements with coauthors while they developed more congenial collaborators.

The collective at first projected a long section of the book on sexuality and relationships, and then decided to discuss lesbianism in a separate chapter, "Loving Women: Lesbian Life and Relationships."[74] "Loving Women" adapts the narrative frame used so often in *Our Bodies, Ourselves;* in this case, we read the story of coming out, to oneself, to friends, to a wider community, of finding a place in the lesbian community and of establishing or deciding not to establish relationships. Personal narratives are frequent, varied, and short; the chapter includes sections on older lesbians, lesbians of color, disabled lesbians, and lesbian mothers, as well as discussions of legal and medical issues. The chapter constructed a collective voice of "we" lesbians, and it also provided a range of positions for various readers: sometimes it addressed lesbian readers; sometimes, women in the process of coming out; sometimes heterosexual readers to whom the authors wished to give "a clearer picture of our lives."[75] The comprehensive organization, supportive tone, and shifting address of the chapter link it to the rest of the book. Through distributed author-ship, the identity politics of lesbianism had been successfully integrated in *Our Bodies, Ourselves.*

African American Identity Politics

The collective's collaboration with African American identity politics was more protracted, difficult, and uneven. Boston was a national center for African American feminists: the Combahee River Collective, a very important Cambridge group, constructed identity politics as a mandate for "focusing upon our own oppression. . . . We believe that the most pro-found and potentially the most radical politics come directly out of our identity, as opposed to working to end somebody else's oppression."[76]

The Boston Women's Health Book Collective began collaborating with African American feminists early in the 1970s. They acknowledged the limits of their own experience of race: "We are white, our ages range from 24 to 40, most of us are from middle-class backgrounds and have had at least some college education, and some of us have professional de-grees."[77] While this self-description flattened the contours of ethnicity, national origin, and class within the collective, it placed and identified them within the nascent identity politics of the early 1970s, especially in Boston, with its relatively small African American population and its reputation for progressive politics.[78]

In the late 1970s, the African American community in Boston suf-fered from a violent white reaction to school bussing. The Combahee River Collective was organized as a response to these events. Combahee's first meetings during the 1970s were held at the Cambridge Women's Center, where they shared space with ongoing Women and Their Bodies courses and the lesbian collective who had written for the 1973 edition.[79] Combahee was an important political force, both nationally and within the Boston movement; they set the terms of the feminist encounters with racial identity politics. Combahee focused on political theory and the formation of activists. They sponsored a series of retreats for African American feminists in the late 1970s, encouraged the publication of a number of important books, and, with Audre Lourde, founded the influential Kitchen Table: Women of Color press. The Combahee River Collective Statement originated the term "identity politics," declaring, "We are actively committed to struggling against racial, sexual, heterosexual, and class oppression and see as our particular task the development of integrated analysis and practice based upon the fact that the major systems of oppression are interlocking. The synthesis of these oppressions create the conditions of our lives."[80]

The Combahee River Collective was not alone in raising these issues; the early 1970s was a very active period for African American feminists, marked by the formation of the National Black Feminist Organization, Third World Women United, and Black Women Organized for Action. Women's health organizations were also formed by Latinas, Asian Americans, and Native Americans, for whom health issues, especially forced sterilization, were organizing priorities. The savagery of racist attacks in Boston and in other cities, the exigency of forming alliances with African American feminists around health issues, and the influence of the Combahee Collective all meant that in the late 1970s and 1980s, the Boston Women's Health Book Collective struggled to come to terms with race, both as a political issue and as a question of daily work. The writers of *Our Bodies, Ourselves* established a working relationship with Barbara Smith, a central figure in Combahee, who is acknowledged for her help in the 1973 and 1976 editions, and they also began constructing networks of collaboration with African American women's organizations.

From the beginning, the Boston Women's Health Book Collective shared with Boston second-wave feminists a commitment to antiracist politics, although like most new Left groups, they understood the 1966 endorsement of Black Power by the Southern Nonviolent Coordinating Committee as a rejection of integrated organizations by the entire African American community. The collective saw their universalized understanding of women's embodiment as antiracist: all women shared the same body, and this common experience of embodiment was the basis for feminist unity and solidarity. Women's bodies offered, for them, an undifferentiated material basis for feminism. At first, these commitments to antiracism and feminist universalism operated on parallel tracks. As Wini Breines put it in her analysis of antiracism and Boston second-wave feminism:

Despite relatively sophisticated understandings of class and race, of difference, white socialist feminists simultaneously conceptualized women as an undifferentiated oppressed group. These contradictory themes persisted alongside one another. . . . Numerous published and unpublished socialist feminist documents refer to women as a group, often comparing women to other oppressed groups such as African Americans, which was deeply offensive to African Americans.[81]

Our Bodies, Ourselves did not compare women in general to African Americans in general, but the book also seldom discussed race until 1984. These contradictory impulses did not support a productive relationship between the collective and African American activist women. Within the framework of identity politics, living in a white female body was incommensurable to living in an African American female body. If white women understandably felt that all women were united by the experiences of pregnancy and childbirth, African American women correctly perceived that their experiences were racially marked by limited access to healthcare and the oppression of sterilization abuse.

The movement of health issues and experiences into a public sphere foregrounded the ways in which the experience of medical care, seldom a positive one for any woman, was shaped by race and class. The fragile relations of publicity, always thin and potentially abstract, did not organize the necessary dialogue about these differences between African American health activists and the collective, and the nascent counterpublic sphere of women's health fragmented under the pressure of antifeminist backlash, as did other institutions of the women's movement.[82] Members of the collective had no better handle on the complex problems posed by multiple identities than the other participants in movement communities; they could only continue to build networks of connection that would bear fruit in the 1990s. Audre Lorde, an African American feminist writer close to the Combahee River Collective, described the pressures that identity politics placed on her as an African American lesbian:

Being women together was not enough. We were different. Being gay-girls together was not enough. We were different. Being Black together was not enough. We were different. Being Black women together was not enough. We were different. Being Black dykes together was not enough. We were different . . . [italics in original]

It was a while before we came to realize that our place was in the very house of difference rather the security of any one particular difference. . . . It was years before we learned to use the strength that daily surviving can bring, years before we could appreciate each other on terms not necessarily our own.[83]

Lourde accurately captures the antimony of early identity politics: devised as a way to make sense of the layered and overdetermined experiences of multiple oppressions, identity politics also developed a fragmentary and self-replicating logic.

Racial identity politics demonstrated that there had always been discord in the house of difference, and that race, class, and sexual orientation affected women's embodiment deeply. One way the collective came to terms with identity politics was to distribute more widely the work of authorship; another was to broaden their orientation to service. The Women's Health Education Center supported collaborations with health activists in African American, Latino, and white working-class communities. Breaking with the practices of the New Left and second-wave feminism, the collective actively recruited women of color as writers and advisors.

In 1981, Norma Swenson met Byllye Avery, an African American woman working on issues of reproductive health and woman-centered birthing in Gainesville, Florida. Both were on the board of the National Women's Health Collective, and Avery had attended the 1975 National Women's Health Conference sponsored by the Boston Women's Health Book Collective.[84] With the encouragement of the NWHC, Avery began to plan for a National Black Women's Health Project, launched in 1983 at a large, very successful conference. After redirecting her work to the needs of African American women, Avery continued to maintain ties with the Boston Women's Health Book Collective.[85] She joined the Collective Board of Directors and continued to collaborate with the group, writing a preface to the 1998 edition praising the book's importance. Avery's remark that "white women had no idea about certain issues affecting Black women," often quoted, aptly expresses the frustration of many African American health activists with the largely white women's health movement; this frustration should be read in the context of the sustained collaboration between the National Black Women's Health Project and the Boston Women's Health Book Collective.[86]

The 1984 edition of *Our Bodies, Ourselves* was reshaped by these collaborations, but the deepest challenges and the most significant accomplishments in the collective's struggle to construct racially inclusive relations of distributed authorship did not occur until the 1990s, when the collective brought significant numbers of women of color into their staff, board, and advisory bodies. In 1998, an internal document summarized that process: the inchoate structure of the organization "made it more difficult to move effectively towards one of the BWHBC's main goals in the 1980s and 1990s, that of becoming a more diverse organization at both the staff and board levels. Serious tensions arose along lines of race, class, and seniority, ironically at the same time as the BWHBC was making important strides in supporting and being part of an international and multi-racial women's health movement."[87] The staff unionized, and African American and Latina staff members filed discrimination complaints against the collective, complaints that were dismissed by the Massachusetts Commission Against Discrimination in April 2004. It took time to resolve the grievances, negotiate a contract, and begin sorting out these problems.

Distributed Writers, Distributed Bodies

For the Boston Women's Health Book Collective, distributed authorship brokered the conflicting claims of identity politics and universal feminine embodiment as dispersed networks of writers corrected the limits of the collective's experience and new personal narratives gave the book a located specificity. It described what happened to all of us, what every woman experienced, by recounting particular moments of bodily experience. Francesca Polletta, in *It Was Like a Fever: Storytelling in Protest and Politics,* shows that narrative is particularly useful to social movements because it holds in suspension contradictory explanations and values, and the collective used narrative to bridge contradictions that resisted logical resolution.[88] They relied especially on personal narratives, the everyday practices of public discourse. Most political agents seldom encounter such prestigious forms as the political oration and the manifesto; these genres emerge at critical moments. For most health activists, the public sphere is shaped by a day-to-day exchange of stories. The Boston Women's Health Book Collective appreciated these exchanges, constructed them from available materials, incorporated them into their text, and institutionalized them as practices of distributed authorship. The text held in suspension the contradictory values of universal feminine embodiment and identity politics. The collective needed the political and rhetorical resources concentrated in those values, and distributed authorship was a strategy for bringing them into alignment.

Beginning in 1984, and more insistently in each subsequent edition, the text of *Our Bodies, Ourselves* described women's experiences as they varied across classes, races, and ethnicities. In early editions, writers had drawn conclusions from their own experiences with perfunctory disclaimers. Consider these selections from the 1970 "Introduction to Pregnancy":

We, as women, grow up in a society that subtly leads us to believe that we will find our ultimate fulfillment by living out our reproductive function and at the same time discourages us from trying to express ourselves in the world of work. . . . Because our opportunities, hence our motivations, are limited we ourselves often begin to believe that in motherhood we will find greater satisfaction than as student, worker, artist, political activist, etc.[89]

The writers went on to report on a conversation among themselves in which they admitted to negative feelings about pregnancy: "We all have them to some extent."[90] They recognized that for some women, maternity presents more material worries: "For some of us and most of our third world sisters very real economic pressures make pregnancy and motherhood a nightmarish rat-race for survival."[91] The writers' initial "we as women" invoked a feminine experience, presented as universal, of being conditioned to seek fulfillment in motherhood. The sliding "we" allowed the writers to universalize their experience without reflection, and to deploy that generalization as a corrective to repression: we *all* feel this way; we just don't talk about it. "We" meant every woman, and also the "group of five" who spoke frankly one afternoon about ambivalence, but not exactly "our third world sisters."

By 1984, the collective had learned some of the lessons of identity politics. The chapter about deciding on parenthood became a broad, diverse narrative. In the chapter on abortion, personal narratives described specific problems women of color face, such as being put under general anesthesia because of stereotypes that "Black and Hispanic women are all screamers."[92] The chapter also discusses insensitive counseling— "just because they give you a white woman to talk to doesn't mean you get counseled."[93] The text criticized opposition to abortion by African American leaders, quoting an unnamed African American women's health activist on the importance of abortion to women of color. What emerges is a much more complex and nuanced story of the politics of abortion, a story that connects abortion to other forms of reproductive freedom, raises issues of access, and suggests that women should be cautious in drawing political conclusions solely from their own experience, or in organizing for reforms that simply meet their own needs. The direct line from bodily education to political program has been knotted; knowing one's own body is not enough.

For this edition, feminist health policy required investigation, consultation, and collaboration; it could not be directly read out of a conversation among friends. The first mission of the book had been defined as the transmission of information, "as much information as could fit between the covers of a book," and reliable information required collaborating experts.[94] Gathering information had developed the collective's capacity for building alliances and made the book useful to a wider range of readers. Precisely these skills increased the distance between the writers—skilled navigators of the networks of health—and readers, who could only draw upon their individual experiences. Evaluating health information had become a specialized practice; political analysis became another service offered to readers. The last words of the introduction to the 1998 edition invoke the universality of women's embodiment as the fragile goal of a long conversation and proposed distributed authorship as a tactic for constructing it:

> We are still evolving ways to form communities that will stand in solidarity with one another. Too often, differences in race, class, ethnicity, financial circumstance, sexual orientation, values, strategies, and degrees of power make it difficult to listen to one another, and these differences divide us. By telling the truth about our lives, women with dissimilar backgrounds and experiences make it more possible for every woman's voice to be heard and for every woman's life to be nurtured. To transform the world into a healthy place we need the energy of *all* women.[95]

In the first editions of *Our Bodies, Ourselves,* personal experience confronted conventional medicine. By 1984, identity politics constructed a mediating step: many different women spoke about their experiences; various communities united around their common understanding and mutual nurturing of "women with dissimilar backgrounds"; this unity created a transformative energy that would confront conventional medicine. Universalism was no longer an assumption of the text, but rather a rhetorical figure, or perhaps a utopian aspiration.

This reorientation of the mission of *Our Bodies, Ourselves* was in no way an error; the book could not survive as a relic of a certain moment in Boston feminist politics. As the movements of the 1960s retreated and collapsed, the book's original enraged militancy would have become an atrophied gesture. The collective kept faith with their transformative project by transforming themselves, constructing a multiracial network of women's health activists. Their movements toward inclusion and service increased their knowledge, developing the project beyond the collective's first impulses. In an early essay, Elizabeth Grosz described the tension that the collective experienced: feminist theory is at once a politics, a "response to the broad political aims and objectives of feminist struggles," and an intellectual project, "a self-conscious reaction . . . to the overwhelming masculinity of privileged and historically dominant knowledges."[96] *Our Bodies, Ourselves* was at once a political text, drawing communities of women together, and an intellectual project, arguing against the masculine assumptions of conventional medicine and asserting feminine embodiment as a norm. Grosz resolved the tension between feminism as a political program and feminism as an intellectual project in the usual way: she invoked Gayatri Spivak's concept of "strategic essentialism," the conscious use of essentialist categories in order to fight the dominant culture. But I do not think the "different kind of writer" described in this chapter was a strategic essentialist. She was a paradoxical essentialist who saw the claims advanced by identity politics as both real and aspirational. Members of the collective are not at all strategic in their belief that women share something concrete and politically consequential based on their female embodiment. These were serious commitments to which they devoted decades of their lives. Their solution to the tension between feminism as politics and as intellectual project was a historicized universalism that they realized as a fluid engagement with identity politics.[97] Strategic essentialism poses ethical problems, since it assumes an agent who knows that the essentialist position being proposed is in some sense an error, but advances it in any case. The collective's historicized universalism, by contrast, was sincere, if logically inconsistent. Their text avows both essentialist and constructivist positions; the writer hopes that both influence the reader, always identified, on some level, as "someone like the writer."[98]

Distributing the work of authorship among many writers of various identities transposed the issues of identity politics and essentialism from the intractable domain of personal motivation to the negotiable territory of the text. It was no longer a question deciding whether or not a specific text was racist, but of producing text that included African American readers. Distributed authorship recognized the density of identities that women bring to their experience of their bodies and provided a space where that identity could be written in private, but read in public. Identities were understood as real without being seen as essential. They were held to be historically formed, partial, multiple, and contradictory, but not for that reason inconsequential. There has been no more consistent critic of identity politics than Judith Butler; she has recognized that "in the face of the prospective silencing or erasure of gender, race, or sexual-minority identities by reactionary political forces, it is important to be able to articulate them and to insist on these identities as sites of valuable cultural contest."[99] Linda Alcoff has also argued for an identity politics as a way of asserting the right to construct identity, rather than merely accept its socially given terms. She argues for "realist" concepts of identity: "Identities refer to objective and casually significant features of the world. . . . They are thus non-arbitrary, and that experience provides both an epistemic and political basis for understanding." Alcoff also insists that "a realistic identity politics, then, is one that recognizes the dynamic, variable, and negotiated character of identity. . . . It recognizes that social categories of identity often helpfully name specific social locations from which individuals engage in, among other things, political judgment."[100]

The collective's negotiations with identity politics were, in Alcoff's terms, realistic—they were consequential and necessary, not artifacts of a social location or ideology. The collective made a political judgment and chose inclusiveness over consistency; they displaced their own experiences from the center of the text and initiated a series of partial, unevenly successful collaborations with women whose experiences and identities were quite different from their own. They put to work the capacities of distributed authorship.

3   A Different Kind of Book

F ROM THE FIRST, the Boston Women's Health Book Collective saw their book as a kind of conversation, an extension, in fact, of their conversations among themselves. Joan Ditzion said, "I feel that the book was always to get people talking. It was a re-source, it was a guide, but it was that interpersonal connection and how it applied to people lives and going from the book to the conversation, to the book. I mean, it's not one or the other."[1] To replicate the uneven pace, the swooping logic, and the rapid shifts of intimate conversation, and somehow to splice into this text blocks of complex medical informa-tion, the collective had to invent new forms for writing about the body. Although they did not see themselves as rhetorical innovators—they thought they were avoiding rhetoric altogether—they developed a way of organizing the book that deployed the traditional rhetorical figure of metalepsis, an opening in the textual frame. Metalepsis structured *Our Bodies, Ourselves* on every level: the physical design of the book, its over-all narrative structure, and the texture of individual sections.

A Homemade Book

The first editions of *Our Bodies, Ourselves* proclaimed that every woman was a potential writer, and that her body was a potential source of both medical knowledge and political enlightenment. Like the other "books, pamphlets, or whatever" produced during the 1960s and 1970s, *Women and Their Bodies* offered readers a new sense of what it meant to write books and of what it meant to live an embodied life, inciting corporeal acts of self-persuasion. It was a porous text, a ground where readers and writers met. The writers entered the text as images or personal narratives, and they also encouraged readers to move into the book. The rhetorical term for these solicitations is "metalepsis," the figure of excess, of breaking frames. Traditionally, metalepsis was a figure in which a writer refers to something by naming an object only remotely related to it. For example, a lead-footed driver is one whose foot is heavy, or leaden, on the accelerator.[2] The figure only makes sense when the reader enters it, completes it, and takes up the reference; it does not sit easily in the field of the text. Narrative theorists, following Gérard Genette, extend metalepsis to include other intrusions of the narrator or the audience into the universe of the story, which "produces an effect of strangeness that is either comical or fantastic."[3] In *Our Bodies, Ourselves*, metalepsis creates a relationship between readers and writers that, for the writers, recalled conversation; it also joins lines of argument and registers of language, enlisting the reader in the construction of knowledge. Since readers generally believe knowledge that they have constructed, the textual objects presented in *Our Bodies, Ourselves* seem to be real things rather than propositions in a text.

Members of the Boston Women's Health Book Collective did not see themselves as writers; the book was for them a vehicle for investigating embodiment in ways that combined scientific research and political reflection. Although they did not know the word, they wanted metalepsis: they expected readers to enter the text, to mess with it. Textually, they incorporated readers' words into the book, composing from layered quotations of letters and conversations. Materially, they encouraged readers to reconfigure the book to suit their needs. The writers of *Our Bodies, Ourselves* imagined the book as part of a conversation that was both intimate—the reader, book in hand, would look into a mirror at her genitals—and consequential—the book would provoke political organization and activity.

The collective undertook its project at a time when publishing and printing were changing, both as technologies and as business practices. They took advantages of these developments to produce a book that they could revise easily, that their readers could rearrange to suit them, and that almost anyone could afford. The 1960s saw changes in print technology that made it easy and relatively cheap for an informal group to publish its work. Specifically, offset lithography became available and cost-effective for small publishers.[4] Hot-type composition, a skilled trade, had been replaced by photocomposition using keyboard typesetting machines or photo setters. Many movement publications did not aspire even to cold type, setting their copy on photocopied plates from unjustified typescript. As Lucy Candib's account of *The Red Nucleus* demonstrated, a group that wanted to publish blue mimeo copies required nothing more than a lucky find at a garage sale. *Women and Their Bodies* was among these low-end publications, set directly from typescript; the publishing bill was $1,500: a lot of money for a small group of women to raise by themselves, but not beyond the reach of an active feminist community, or the 250 members of Bread and Roses.[5] The first printing of the book sold for seventy-five cents; later, the price went down to fifty cents.

The first editions of *Our Bodies, Ourselves* were published by the New England Free Press, although their imprint only appeared for the first time on the 1971 *Our Bodies, Our Selves*.[6] They printed the book cheaply on newsprint, binding it, according to the note inside the front cover, "so that it may be used either as it is—in 4 bound booklets or as a separate sheets in a ring binder."[7] Readers who wanted to put the pages in a notebook were instructed to punch holes in the margin, to slit the binding thread and the back of each booklet with a razor blade, and to put the book into a binder. Health classes could take it apart and distribute each of the four booklets separately. The book looked handmade, and in that first edition, readers were encouraged to participate in making it over themselves. From the time she first took it into her hands, the reader of the 1970 or 1971 edition of *Our Bodies, Ourselves* was encouraged to shape her copy to her own needs. She could separate out the divisions, reorder them, loan them to others, interleave her own notes or diagrams into the binder where she kept the book, or write in its generous margins. The writers metaleptically invited the reader to design the book she wanted, to become her own publisher.

The 1970 edition was set from typewritten copy, cut to size and pasted up on layout pages, with space left for photographs and drawings. The text was not left-justified; page numbers were hand-written on each page; chapter titles were typewritten in capitals, centered, and underlined. Captions and picture credits were rare and almost always hand-written. In the second, 1971 edition, the text had been set by machine and justified; some chapters were set in columns. The book, while still printed on pulp and bound in four parts, included such graphic features as variations in type size, captions, printed page numbers, and occasional decorative borders. In both versions, the hand-lettered cover featured a distinctive picture of two women, young and old, holding a sign that says "Women Unite." This image would appear on every cover until 2005. Both editions of the book carry the mark of the makers' hands; they feel a bit like school literary magazines, and a bit like the printed zines that were emerging: publications the reader could have produced herself. The look and feel of the book pulled the reader metaleptically into the text.

Our Bodies, Ourselves was not alone in using this newsprint format to cheaply disseminate information to a wide audience; this was the characteristic format for power-structure research reports, particularly the feminist *How Harvard Rules Women.* Produced within months of each other, both are set from unjustified typescript, and both offer the thrill of a public airing of secrets. The amateur style of these texts supported the writers' desire to establish their own authority against that of received academic and medical institutions. Both publications pushed at the boundaries of the book as an object: both spoke of a convivial process of publication, a kind of long party organized by a craft project rather than the solitary work of academic writing. For the writers of *Our Bodies, Ourselves,* the new offset technologies were tools for distributing authorship, allowing them to delegate the writing of a chapter to a friend or an allied group, to review the manuscript as a group, and to see the text they produced through editing and layout. The final pasteup work was done by the New England Free Press.

Our Bodies, Ourselves was laid out quite conventionally, with text and graphics aligned to the edge of the page. The collective has never used color in the text, and they did not favor the loose, florid style of other movement publications such as the Boston *Women's Liberation Newsletter.* (The *Newsletter* was a monthly mail-out, printed on poster-size paper so that its announcements page, covered with a flurry of type-written blurbs, assorted graphics, and poetry, could be conveniently hung on a wall.) Still, images were central to the book, and the collective exploited the spontaneity photo-offset printing afforded to those who wanted to use them. The 1970 edition included eighty-seven images, not counting a feature that showed photographs of a normal labor and delivery. Many images were instructional graphics—anatomical diagrams, charts showing the stages of labor, a picture of a vacuum aspirator used for early abortions. The rest were general illustrations: they showed women to themselves, as collective member Ruth Bell said, "in a different light."[8] There were many pictures of babies, children, and their mothers. Pregnant women were shown naked, or with a partner, or doing yoga. Many photos were snapshots of the writers of the book, their friends, and their relatives. Most readers would have had a drawer full of similar photos: intimate, straightforward, and unremarkable.

What set the illustrations in *Our Bodies, Ourselves* apart was their treatment of the female body, particularly the naked female body: these were pictures of women at ease with themselves. Typical were the photos in the 1970 edition of two women, nude to the waist, working vigorously in a garden plot, and of a naked pregnant woman, seen from the side, looking outside the frame of the camera. The women in these images were vital, composed, integral—and absorbed in their own world, doing what they are doing. The sexuality chapter included a number of nude photographs, a line drawing of two nude women, and a drawing of a woman lifting her dress to look at her genitals: these are images of sexual actions, but they are not sexual solicitations. Although some of the images are quite lovely, the drawing of a woman lifting her skirt and looking at her genitals is direct, oddly proportioned, and stiff. This very ungainliness gave the drawing metaleptic force: self-exploration did not require a body that was a beautiful object. It was an ordinary activity, just as the drawing was little more a directional sign for the action "looking at yourself." The drawing did not make this action pretty, but showed that it was possible, and for many readers, it was the first image of a woman investigating her own genitals they had seen. For founders Paula Doress-Worters and Vilunya Diskin, many years later, the drawing recalled their initial engagement with the book: "It's somebody looking at themselves, you know. It's taking control. It's saying, Ooo, because the discussions at the time were that men always had the entrée to women's bodies, much more than women

(what modern man wants a clinging vine?) and a sex-kitten at the
same time.

Why is it that women still resist so much advertised liberation? Why
is the advertising still necessary some 50 years after the propaganda
for women to enjoy sex as much as men began? Why do women and men
still think sex is dirty? Maybe they're right. When women feel power-
less and inferior in a relationship it is not surprising to feel
humiliated and unsatisfied in bed. Similarly, a man must feel some
contempt for a woman he believes to be not his equal. (1)

"Frigidity" or inadequacy in bed is not divorced from the social
realities we experience all the time. This male dominated culture
embues us with a sense of second best status, and there's no reason
to expect this sense of inferiority and inadequacy to go away between
the sheets.

SEXUAL FEELINGS

Part of the reason so many people have problems about sex is because
sexual feelings are considered separate or different from other kinds
of feelings we have. Sex has got to do with the body---that alien part
of us residing below the neck that has needs and responses that we don't
understand. But all our feelings reside in the body. Fear usually
makes its presence felt by your heart pounding, your chest feeling
caved in, your stomach turning. Joy is tingly--your head feels a
little light, fingers and toes sort of shimmer, and the rest of you
feels warm and all in one piece. For some people anger feels like a

1. "Sexual Liberation": More of the Same Thing, by Roxanne Dunbar, in
    No More Fun and Games, Issue Three, was the source of many of these
    ideas.

Figure 3.1. Women gardening, *Women and Their Bodies*, 1970,
p. 17. Boston Women's Health Book Collective.

Some women masturbate by moistening their finger (with either saliva or juice from the vagina) and rubbing it around and over the clitoris. The amount of pressure and timing seems to vary among women. Some women masturbate by crossing their legs and exerting steady and rhythmic pressure on the whole genital area. A smaller number learn by developing muscular tension through their bodies, resembling the tensions developed in the motion of intercourse. Some ways of doing this is by climbing up a pole or a rope or even chinning parallel bars. Other techniques for masturbating include using a pillow instead of a hand, a stream of water, and electric vibrators. Some women find their breasts erotically sensitive, and rub them while rubbing the clitoris. It's nice sometimes to make up sexual fantasies while masturbating. Some women like to insert something in the vagina while masturbating (like a finger or vibrator), but few women get more satisfaction out of vaginal penetration than they do from clitoral stimulation.[2]

If you have never masturbated, don't feel you are confined to these techniques. Finding what you like to do is what it's all about.

VIRGINITY

The "cherry" that is to be every man's prize on taking a virgin symbolizes a traditional conception of the male-female role. The woman is to be nurtured, watered, trimmed and cared for like the most delicate of cherry trees, raised in the anticipation of the moment when the fruit will be juicy and ripe. Then it will be "plucked", "ravished", consumed by the man, for whom all this preparation was actually intended. The more delicate the tree, the more satisfying the deflowering.

Few of us would choose to look at ourselves this way. It would be a sign of great alienation to see ourselves not as people, but as sexual objects, as trees with cherries. Yet the concept is so imbued in our culture that few men can entirely avoid it. We make ourselves pretty for men. We take infinite pains with the curl of our eyelashes, with our hair. In many ways, our daily actions reflect the fact that we have accepted and internalized this conception of ourselves as sexual objects.

Virginity – the constant preoccupation of teenage and college women – has its base in our perception of ourselves as objects for the eventual enjoyment or consumption of another. One asks oneself not "What will be best for me–spiritually and physically?", but "What will they (other people in general, but especially one's future husband) think of me?" To use one's body in this way, as a physical pledge of the appropriateness of one's conduct in the eyes of others, is to deny oneself in the most basic way. Certainly there are many valid reasons for not going to bed with a man, but the preservation of one's hymen is not one of them.

Men traditionally have made a big production of the bursting of the hymen. Marriage manuals spend chapters on it. Pornographers go wild over it:

At length by my fierce rending and tearing thrusts the first defences gave way, and I got about half-way in... as I oiled her torn and bleeding cunt with a perfect flood of virgin sperm. Poor Rose had born it most heroically, keeping the bedclothese between her teeth, in order to repress any cry of pain... I now recommenced my eager shoves, my fierce lunges, and I felt myself gaining at every move, till with one tremendous and cunt-rending thrust I buried myself into her up to the hilt. So great was the pain this last shock caused Rose that she could not suppress a sharp shrill scream, but I heeded it not; it was the note of final victory and only added to the delicious piquancy of my enjoyment... I drew her to a yet closer embrace, and planting numberless kisses on her rosy lips and blushing face, which was wet with tears of suffering which the brave little darling could not prevent from starting from her lovely eyes, I drew out the head and slowly thrusting it [sic] in again: my fierce desires goaded me to challenge her to a renewal of the combat. A smile

Figure 3.2. "First tentative look," *Women and Their Bodies*, 1970, p. 14. Boston Women's Health Book Collective.

did, and much more than girls did. And we talked about that a lot, . . . and shared experiences of how difficult it was to look at yourself. . . . And I think that's what that was. It's the first tentative look."⁹

In the 1973 edition, the "Anatomy and Physiology" chapter also included a very simple photograph of a naked woman holding a mirror under her genitals; the image, labeled "Esther's vulva" in the proofs, is unsentimental, unsexualized, and explicit. On one level, the photograph is a transcription of the anatomical drawings that surround it—it shows what these structures look like in the flesh. On another level, the photograph, like the early line-drawing of a woman with a lifted skirt, invites women to look at a woman investigating herself. In this case, it is no longer a "first tentative look," but a graphic and matter-of-fact display, one which the text will invite the reader to imitate. (In interviews, writers who looked at this image warmly remembered the late collective member Esther Rome's ease and openness with her body, a level of comfort that the photograph metaleptically invited readers to share.) These images opened the frame of the text, encouraging readers to model a new relationship with their bodies on them.

Many members of the collective associated writing with hard work, but all of them enjoyed working with pictures. They were willing to answer my puzzling questions about particular words, but they were eager to look at images: it was like flipping through a friend's photo album. Many of the photographs in the early pregnancy chapters are of founders Jane Pincus and Joan Ditzion. Pincus had recently given birth when she began working on the book, and Ditzion became pregnant early in the collective's history. The "Childbirth" chapter is illustrated with pictures of Pincus's cousin giving birth.¹⁰ Looking through the text, Judith Norsigian tenderly pointed out a lovely image of elderly women dancing together as a photograph "of two Armenian women that my uncle took, and he's very proud that we've kept that photo in most of the editions."¹¹ If a writer wanted a particular image, she might go out and take a photograph herself: for the 1973 edition, Norsigian photographed the General Foods Plant in Woburn, Massachusetts, so that the book would include an image of the food industry. The images are a ghostly realization of the collective "we": collective members frequently appeared in photos, but without identification; they were silent witnesses on the pages they had written, surrounded by relatives, friends, and mementoes of their travels.

When the group ended its collaboration with the New England Free Press in 1972, their move to a mainstream publisher prompted them to adopt more conventional procedures. They asked for permission to use the pictures they published and began to screen their copy more carefully for legal liability. By 1974, the group hesitated to display an anatomically correct Raggedy Ann doll at a women's fair. "We are afraid that the Raggedy Ann with pubic hair might be slanderous—we could be sued. Paula will take responsibility for finding out legality of R-A with vulva."[12] Since this comment comes late in a long meeting, and Paula Doress-Worters never reports on the legality of the Raggedy Ann doll, it is entirely possible that it is self-parodic, an expression of the group's giddiness as it negotiated the new languages and conventions of publishing.

Publication by Simon and Schuster offered all the bells and whistles of professional typesetting, and a much broader range of graphic effects. Their sales increased with broadened distribution—from 250,000 copies between December 1970 and March 1973 to 3.5 million copies between April 1973 and 1996.[13] The collective appreciated that *Our Bodies, Ourselves* could now reach women in places where there was no organized women's movement. It was available in remote rural areas; it was on the shelves of school libraries (although not without battles against censorship). Their original contract with Simon and Schuster provided for parallel publication of a mass-market paperback, a cheap, small-format version of *Our Bodies, Ourselves* that could have been sold in drugstores and supermarkets; that publication never proved practicable. Instead, the book itself became longer and more comprehensive; the 1973 *Our Bodies, Ourselves* was almost twice as long as the 1971 New England Free Press edition. Conventional publication meant clearer images, a more readable layout, and graphic support for some of the hallmarks of the collective's style, such as personal stories and anecdotes, which were now indented and set in italics. The new edition was indexed, so that readers could finally find information on a specific topic. There were other improvements large and small: the book became more sturdy and durable; the layout, cleaner and more readable; photographs were more clearly printed.

Telling Stories

The text of *Our Bodies, Ourselves* was organized and embellished to draw readers in. The text they encountered was a series of nested narratives, each of which included the reader and writer in a common endeavor. From 1970 until 1984, *Our Bodies, Ourselves* told two interlocked stories: the story of the female reproductive lifecycle, and the story of the growth of a women's health movement. These narratives were linked by the concept of body education: an individual woman's coming to consciousness of her own embodiment, of her need to understand her body, and of its social location and conditioning. In both of the book's larger stories, the text reaches metaleptically beyond itself, invoking the reader, inscribing the story of her changing body, and enlisting her as an activist for women's health. Within these two overarching narratives, the book included such smaller stories as the story of childbirth or the hormonal cycle, and the micronarratives of a particular woman's abortion or amniocentesis.

In the 1970 and 1971 editions of *Our Bodies, Ourselves*, chapters read a lot like academic papers. Writers called on the familiar genre of the term paper to organize their information, and the emerging genres of consciousness-raising to inflect and interpret it. The structure of the book, rather than the information it presents, was the source of its power. *Our Bodies, Ourselves* made sense of the ordinary vicissitudes of life in a female body. Women did not respond to the text because it gave clear information about what it called "venereal disease," but because it presented sexually transmitted diseases matter-of-factly, as a part of sexual life, and because the chapter's critique of failures in the public health system was provocative, connecting a woman's struggle to find dignified treatment with broader social forces. Readers are invited to see their struggles to obtain information and care as confirmations of their solidarity with other women, rather than as casual humiliations. The reader who turned to the book, and therefore to other women, for health information has metaleptically affiliated herself to the women's health movement that *Our Bodies, Ourselves* both describes and constructs, a movement that did not really exist in 1971.

The central chapters of the first two editions give an account of female maturation and accession to reproductivity and a general orientation to reproductive anatomy; the chapters on "Sexuality," "Venereal Disease," "Birth Control," "Abortion," "Pregnancy," and "Post Partum" march through an idealized life story of early sexual experimentation, decisions to become pregnant, childbirth, and motherhood. It was a normalizing story, with no divagations into lesbianism, menopause, or old age. Chapters on lesbianism and menopause were added in 1973; issues such as nutrition, exercise, and occupational health, in 1984; the current 2005 edition includes a chapter on old age. In all editions of the book, the text is generally ordered by its assumed sequence in the life of the reader, and that life is the story of her reproductive capacity. The text included the reader in a story of the reproductive life cycle that is seen as universally feminine. Such a narrative structure was intelligible and capacious, particularly in the editions from 1970 (eleven chapters) to 1984 (twenty-six chapters). The structural lines of the text blur in later editions, with their emphasis on self-care and comprehensive information.

From 1970 to 1984, the body was at once the protagonist and the antagonist of the narrative. Although the text asserts repeatedly that "we are our bodies," the body is also presented as opaque, tricky, and in need of management. Autonomy would not come easily; women were urged to decide things for themselves, but they were also warned that real choices could only be secured through collective action, as in these urgent and contradictory passages:

As we have begun to learn about our bodies and examine the available birth control methods we know that there is no ideal form of birth control. Collectively as women we have a lot of hard work ahead of us. If we really want control of our own bodies, we have to fight for it.[14]

We are trapped and defined in advance by the biological efficiency of the reproductive process: it is so easy to get pregnant. . . . When people are young, sexual feelings are surprising and newly intense. As a result, we become pregnant, married and unmarried, before we have a chance to develop fully as autonomous human beings.[15]

For psychological reasons as well it's important that you remain active and not let the pregnancy dominate your life for nine months. . . . Keep thinking about yourself and who you are/want to be in addition to the reality of being a pregnant woman. You neither begin nor end with that baby: you are a person apart from the child and need continually to think on that—for your sake and for the child's.[16]

A woman could only become autonomous through her control of her body, but the reproductive biology of that very body delivers her over to a life in which it is impossible to be "a person apart." Women are defined by their ability to make individual choices, to function "apart" from others, but only collective action can secure the means of making such choices.

By aligning the narrative of the female reproductive life cycle—a story, at least potentially, of restrictions—with the story of the growth of a movement—a story of achieving agency—the text brokered the contradictions that its readers faced. Autonomy, compromised by biology, would be redeemed by politics; the isolation of individual choice is buffered by the universal story of feminine embodiment. All editions of *Our Bodies, Ourselves* began and ended with a broad discussion of sexism, medicine, feminist consciousness, and organization. The collective's origin story, the "good story" of the 1973 introduction that every member of the collective delighted in telling me, connects the success of *Our Bodies, Ourselves*, the book that the reader holds in her hands, with the success of the women's movement. It thereby initiates the text's metalepsis. The reader is constructed not as someone who has purchased a commodity, but as a new arrival to an ongoing conversation: "It was exciting to learn new facts about our bodies, but it even more exciting to talk about how we felt about our bodies, how we felt about ourselves, how we could become more autonomous human beings, how we could act together on our collective knowledge to change the health care system for women and for all people. We hope this will be true for you, too."[17]

This metaleptic gesture was repeated, in various tones, in every edition. In 1984, when the initial materials in the book included all of the previous introductions and a new one written for the revision, the combined narratives covered ten pages. (The 2005 edition featured a letter from the Boston Women's Health Book Collective that told the group's story elliptically in four brisk pages, emphasizing diversity.) The good story of the collective's origin stipulated that the writers were much like the readers: ordinary women without medical training who had decided to educate themselves about their bodies. While the book itself, in its size, comprehensive scope, and impressive endorsements, claimed medical authority, the introductions unraveled these claims: the narrator of *Our Bodies, Ourselves*, the reader was assured, was someone like herself, and the work of the narrator in composing the book culminated in the work of the reader who sorted through it, compared it with her own experience, and discussed it with her friends.

The body and the self are agents, viewpoints, and speakers of the narrative; these ambiguities shape the text. The text insists, "What are our bodies? First, they *are* us. We do not inhabit them—we *are* them (as well as mind)."[18] But it enacts a radical separation between the body as object of knowledge and the self who, through reading, direct investigation, and intimate talk, claims that knowledge. Not that the body is passive or inert: its very mutability makes it hard to know: "The uterus changes position during the menstrual cycle, so where you feel the cervix one day may be slightly different from where it will be the next!"[19]

The body and the autonomous self connect at the nodal point of choice. Choice was a critical issue for second-wave feminists in general and for the writers of *Our Bodies, Ourselves* in particular. In these early editions, a reader could choose anything. She could, potentially, liberate herself from her own socialization and from cultural norms: "What we need to do is get rid of all the standards we've previously used to measure ourselves, our sexuality. By talking to each other, taking support from each other, we can set our own standards which will bear the mark of sanity and individuality."[20] Choice was so important for the collective, and their care to respect readers' choices was so intense, that the collective went out of their way to avoid prescriptive language. When they had to choose between writing in language that was not colloquial and writing in language that was prescriptive, they chose to avoid prescription. The 1973 edition, for example, includes a chapter titled "Considering Parenthood: Shall I Become a Mother?" Even in 1973, the use of "shall" to indicate future tense in the first person was rare, hypercorrect; "should" was a much more colloquial form. But two collective members remembered, more than thirty years later, that they had not wanted to say "should." "Should" implied a moral judgment, a recommendation of what the reader ought to do. As Ruth Bell Alexander put it, "We talked about the politics of 'should.' I kind of remember this discussion, that 'should' was a no-no word. And 'shall' is a future, opening-up-of-the-future word."[21] It is not surprising, then, that many of the book's narratives are organized around moments of choice. Women choose whether to continue pregnancies or to have abortions: "Whatever we decide, it is important for us as women to make an *active* decision, one which is ours, rather than passively slipping into one choice or another."[22] They also decide whether to nurse or to breastfeed: "When you decide how to feed your baby, whether to use breast or bottle, you may want to consider how that method fits in with the idea of sharing infant care."[23] Even birth, an involuntary process, can become a domain of agency: "If we are prepared and unanesthetized during childbirth, we are in touch with our entire self, mind and body, and we are working intelligently along with this inevitable biological process. We are in control. . . . We can feel more in control of ourselves as whole people, having used both our mind and our body, together, to see us through labor and delivery."[24] The self makes choices that transform the body in large and small ways, choosing whether to have pubic hair shaved before labor, or whether to use hormone-replacement therapy. At each of these moments the narratives of the reproductive life cycle and of the growth of a movement are sutured together: the woman who chooses her mode of participation in reproduction is potentially an autonomous political agent, since women who want to secure their choices will collaborate and organize. Since there is no inherent limit to what the self can learn about the body, the domain of choice can expand indefinitely with the reader's knowledge. By increasing that domain, the text of *Our Bodies, Ourselves* gets under the skin of the reader, metaleptically joining her to the consequential conversations of the collective.

The text presents itself, then, as a vector for contagious feminism. The story of how the collective became feminists is followed in all editions up to 2005 by chapters discussing what they learned as feminists. In 1973, for example, "Our Changing Sense of Self" connected the collective's history to an analysis of feminine subjectivity; it described the fears its members felt as they worked on the book, their struggles with internalized sexist values, and their rediscovery of activity, anger, and autonomy. The intimacy of this account consolidated the narrator's metaleptic link with the reader: the reader may have felt what the writers felt, or the text may induce her to model her emotions on theirs. The collective worked to make the connection between health education and politicization seamless through the 1970s and 1980s. The 1984 chapter on "Body Image" joined the text's conversation with its readers to readers' own conversations with their friends; these talks would lead to "form[ing] or join[ing] a working-women's organization; work[ing] on ways to pressure employers to accept a wider range of looks and dress."[25] Body education extended daily activities into both medical knowledge and political action.

All editions of *Our Bodies, Ourselves* featured a broad political analysis of health, healthcare, and the economy, beginning with Lucy Candib's "Women, Medicine, and Capitalism," which opened the 1970 edition and closed the 1971 edition. While this chapter offered a broad analysis, its suggestions for activity were very general—necessarily so, since feminist health organizations were thin on the ground. But by 1973, women across the nation were experimenting with gynecological self-examination; the predecessor of the National Women's Health Network was lobbying for action on DES in Washington; Jane, the lay abortion service in Chicago, was active; and some fifty women's clinics had opened.[26] No longer did the book ask women to create a movement from their circle of friends; a reader could be directed to a discussion group, an organization, or a healthcare provider. Ideally, she would move from an understanding of her own healthcare experiences to conversations that would demonstrate the social grounding of these experiences. She would see—either through the text's political analysis or through encounters with a growing movement—that the alienation she faced was structural, typical of conventional medical care in both the United States and the rest of the world, and she would engage herself in the transformation of these structures. Or, as Nancy Miriam Hawley said, "We all had bodies. This knowledge would provide power to every woman on the planet."[27] Women would move without interruption from body education (reading the book, taking a class), through individual actions (asking pointed questions of one's own physician, refusing hospital procedures during birth) to organized political activity (working in a clinic, agitating for abortion reform).

In 1973, the collective had decided that local action prompted by individual needs was the gateway to sustained politicization; in place of "Women, Medicine and Capitalism," they titled the final chapter "Women and Health Care." It gave an account of the American health-care system, followed by a practical guide to choosing healthcare and a discussion of ways to organize for change and develop alternatives. The change from an analysis based on political theory to one based on the readers' healthcare needs was a deliberate attempt to align the book more closely with readers. In editions after 1973, readers would find narratives both of small-scale actions that any woman could undertake and of the work of broader movements for global change. The nutrition chapter, for example, recommended cast-iron skillets, fresh vegetables, and campaigns against high prices in natural-food stores: "We need to make a united demand that our larger stores offer us healthier choices and carry more chemical-free foods. Such foods do not have to be more expensive than other foods. We should also demand that fruits and veg-etables not be prepackaged, so that we can examine their quality."[28]

While the collective's faith in a seamless trajectory from bodily edu-cation to political action would unravel as the movements of the 1960s receded, they continued to see the text as a metaleptic gesture establish-ing a relationship to responsive readers. Women would understand their own histories when they read accounts of bad medical practices in *Our Bodies, Ourselves,* and they would understand that their problems were not singular or idiosyncratic. They would become part of a movement to transform medical practice and perhaps join the network of distributed authors. Just as members of the collective began as "ordinary women" and became health resources, their readers would move from consuming the book to producing it. *Our Bodies, Ourselves* was presented to readers as a perpetually incomplete project, something for them to work on: "This book is a start in helping us to assume more responsibility for our health care, but we've only been able to touch briefly on the simplest aspects, the common medical events of a woman's life. The real toughies—the complicated diseases, the rare surgeries, death and dying—will have to be coped with and worked out individually over a longer time."[29]

In 1976, the collective began to augment the narrative of the repro-ductive life cycle ("the common medical events of a woman's life") with comprehensive health information, and subsequent editions included more and more information in chapters titled "Some Common and Uncommon

Medical Problems." The collective expected their own experiences and those of their readers to be the primary resources for this development, although in the event they relied on sympathetic experts and health advocates for information. The development of *Our Bodies, Ourselves*, ideally, would parallel the development of the women's health movement from an alternate source of care to a challenge to mainstream medicine. The spine of the book continued to be the sequence of chapters related to the reproductive life cycle; especially after 1984, this structure was complicated and then submerged in general health information.

Structuring Local Narratives

Individual chapters also presented local narrative structures to organize the complex stories that they had to tell. The idealized narrative of the conventional medical case history would not work for the collective's understanding of universal feminine embodiment as a common core of reproductive experiences, manifested in a wide range of individual variations. Medical narratives normally present a unitary, normative, "typical case," but the collective wanted to invoke a range of experiences and responses.[30] The forms they developed to tell such stories pulled readers into texts, sometimes by opening a broad range of alternatives, and sometimes by reversing the relations of power in a medical encounter to restore agency to readers. I am calling the first of these narrative structures "ramified," and the second "chiasmic." Ramified narratives organize multiple, disparate examples as alternatives, affirming them in branching structures that affirm a range of possible conditions, emotions, and therapeutic choices. To prepare for the 1976 "Menopause" chapter, for example, the collective organized a survey: nearly five hundred women answered questions about their experiences in menopause. Conceding that they had not taken a "scientific" sample, the collective mined these responses for anecdotes and used them to find the range of women's experiences with menopause. They organized the survey responses as a series of branching structures; each branch opened to further alternatives. Women could have no symptoms, or mild hot flashes, or debilitating hot flashes; some women needed treatment; others did not. Estrogen-replacement treatment helped some women, and not others. Some women found grandchildren a "delightful bonus"; others focused on a new personal autonomy. All these experiences and responses were affirmed; none was privileged. Similar ramified structures organized the chapters on responses to pregnancy, experiences in childbirth, and other events in the female reproductive life cycle. Ramified narratives need not break the frame of the text, but as the structure was deployed in *Our Bodies, Ourselves*, the multiplied alternatives metaleptically suggested that any variant experience that a reader brought to the text had already been spliced into the conversation, considered, and found normal.

If ramified narrative structures integrate individual variations into the narrative of the reproductive life cycle, narratives of chiasmic reversal stage stories of political transformation and suggest that the book would transform the reader. Chiasmus, a rhetorical figure, turns on a verbal inversion, understood as an "X," as in Mae West's, "It's not the men in my life; it's the life in my men." Chiasmus is associated with energetic argument, satire, and verbal exuberance. Often, the two halves of the chiasmic pair are joined by repeated words, but the repetition signals a reversal. One pair of terms (men/men) is an envelope for the other (life/life), forming a pattern that moves from the center of the phrase to the edges.[31] Chiasmus requires that readers attend to the text and actively take up the figure: its specular repetition moves a reader from the beginning of the text to the end, and then loops back to the beginning. Narratives which turn about reversal, complementarity, or mirroring can be called chiasmic: consider the New Testament parable of Lazarus and the rich man (Luke 16). At the beginning of the story, the beggar Lazarus longs for the crumbs from the rich man's table; at the end, Lazarus is in Abraham's bosom and the rich man is in hell. When the rich man begs Lazarus to cool his tongue with water, Abraham reminds the rich man that he had been well-off during life, while Lazarus had been in misery. He says, "Between you and us there is fixed a great abyss, and those who might wish to cross from here to you cannot do so, nor can anyone cross from your side to us" (Luke 16). This story illustrates the narrative work of chiasmus: it establishes a tight connection between two things, and it also places them in opposition to each other. The rich man is in hell *because* Lazarus lived a life of misery, but the rich man and Lazarus, in both halves of the story, are radically divided from each other by "a great abyss."[32]

Chiasmus was a popular figure in all the movements of the 1960s. It occurred frequently in the speeches of Martin Luther King; in "Beyond Vietnam," his sermon to the Clergy and Laity Concerned About Vietnam (May 1967), King developed a chiasmic relation between the use of military force in Vietnam and hardening resistance by the Vietnamese National Liberation Front. He extended this chiasmus to show that the ongoing war was corrupting the culture of the United States: military force abroad mirrored domestic violence and neglect. He advocated a "revolution in values" and promised that it would transform both America and the rest of the world:

And if we only make the right choice, we will be able to transform this pending cosmic elegy into a creative psalm of peace. If we make the right choice, we will be able to transform the jangling discords of our world into a beautiful symphony of brotherhood. If we make the right choice, we will be able to speed up the day, all over America and all over the world, when justice will roll down like waters, and righteousness like a mighty stream.[33]

The speech ended with this powerful invocation of reversal and transformation, of violence and destruction opening into universal harmony. The sound patterns, too, are chiasmic: *p*ending *c*osmic: *c*reative *p*salm; ju*st*ice *r*oll: *r*ighteousness *st*ream.

Chiasmus was a powerful, and frequently used, figure in second-wave feminist narratives. In *How Harvard Rules Women*, the writers discussed the intellectual passivity associated with Radcliffe students: "Working hard at tasks defined by others is the quality of a submissive creature, and we have always been taught to be more submissive than men. This in no way means that women do not become revolutionaries—indeed, our revolt is all the more profound and authentic when it does occur, because our entire lives have been spent, in a variety of subtle ways, in subservient capacities."[34] Or, in the more mundane context of the discussion of sexually transmitted diseases in a pamphlet titled "Women and Health," written by the Women's Health Ring: "Gonorrhea is very common, and can be especially dangerous for women. The only people who should be ashamed about VD are the doctors that don't check for it routinely, and people who have it but don't warn the ones they slept with."[35] In *Our Bodies, Ourselves*, chiasmus organized local narratives of resistance, of reversal of power. In the discussion of physical symptoms of menopause in the 1984 edition, the writers explained that doctors should not think of menopause as a disease:

The medical approach protects us from the normal discomforts and changes in outlook which accompany menopause and other transitions of the aging process. It leads us to believe that these changes are so painful or dangerous that we cannot get through them without drugs and/or surgery; that non-medical alternatives are ineffective, or that we are incapable of applying them systematically enough to benefit us. Many doctors do to menopausal women what they do to women in childbirth: they intervene in advance to prevent us from really *living* the experience of change.[36]

The narrative constructed a conventional medical view of the meno-pausal woman, and then chiasmically reversed it, moving control from the physician to the woman, urging her to locate herself within the process rather than vacating it or relinquishing it to the control of her doctor. The text performed a specular reversal of received medical practice, just as the Women's Health Ring's discussion of sexually transmitted diseases reversed the normal social vectors of shame and blame.

These chiasmic local stories enlist the reader in the structuring narrative of the rise of the women's health movement: when the reader becomes the agent of her own care, the process of politicization takes place as if by contagion. The text moves from exposition to provocation, so that the reader is never placed for long as a victim or passive recipient of bad care. Readers were invited, in various chapters, to imagine themselves as alone and neglected in childbirth, as embarrassed by healthcare providers when they asked for birth control, and as afflicted with scores of illnesses large and small. A reader might simply tune out these possibilities, becoming numb and disembodied; there is some evidence that readers of difficult texts do distance themselves from the imagination of pain and violation.[37] Such a disembodied reading was not what the collective sought. Instead, the text stood with the reader as she learned, anticipated her fear or disgust, and offered encouragement and reassuring humor. At the same time, the text invited the reader to step into the world of the collective, to repeat their self-education, to bask in their warmth, and then to replicate this experience with her own circle of friends.

Telling the Story of Sexuality

The sexuality chapter was one of the first parts of *Our Bodies, Ourselves* to be drafted. Here, the collective worked on ways of telling stories, of invoking the reader, and of keeping the multiple, potentially contradictory ideas of the book in play. The sexuality chapter connected the stories of the reproductive life cycle and of the growth of the movement; it drew readers into a metaleptic relationship with the writers. It demonstrates what kind of text the collective tried to create and how that text changed.

The history of the chapter is a history of accretion. The nub of the chapter, included in all editions, is a discussion of sexual feelings, masturbation, virginity, and orgasm. Sections on puberty and fantasies were added in 1973, and the material on orgasm was integrated into a longer section on lovemaking. By 1984, the chapter included information on anatomy and on alternate sexualities, including celibacy and bisexuality (lesbianism is discussed in a separate chapter, "In Amerika They Call Us Dykes"). The section on lovemaking discussed oral sex, anal sex, role playing, and sex games. All editions developed a political analysis of sexuality in discussions of stereotypes, objectification, and violence against women. In all of them, sexuality is articulated into the reproductive life cycle; we move, in 1973, from masturbation to loss of virginity to orgasm. This story connects to a very basic story of politicization: because the women's movement has assured women of their right to sexual pleasure, they are learning about orgasms. As the chapter developed through multiple editions, the story of the growing women's movement, powerfully reinterpreting women's sexuality to include a range of expressions and practices, becomes the controlling narrative, although there were limits to what the text could include.

A very early version of the chapter, a manuscript titled "Sexuality," appeared as an untitled document that apparently circulated among the close contacts of the nascent collective in 1970.[38] Both "Sexuality," the chapter published in the 1970 *Women and Their Bodies*, and this document began, "This paper was written by a group of us in Women's Liberation anxious to share our thoughts and feelings about sexuality with other women." The early "Sexuality" paper does not identify its writers and often refers to itself as a "pamphlet," as if designed for freestanding publication. "Sexuality" included readers metaleptically in its story of the reproductive life cycle by retelling the story of their lives. Instead of the conventional narrative in which girls move from innocence to initiation by a sexually experienced male lover, we read of girls whose full access to their sexuality and embodied pleasure was compromised by socialization and repression, of young women who, with the coming of the sexual revolution, were encouraged to express their sexuality, but only to increase male pleasure. Finally, we read of the awakening of feminist women to the value of sexuality as bodily experience, and their recovery of the freedom of childhood. Women's sexuality is presented chiasmically; what was lost will be specularly recovered. The reader is implicated in every episode of this story, which repeatedly invokes "our" experience: "By the time we're teenagers, we discover that there's only one norm for beauty. A commercial norm that sold products to us as we agonized over breasts, hair, legs, and skin that would not measure up. Again we are left with shame and anxiety. We have body smells and our feet are too big."[39] The narratives of the life cycle and of the growth of the movement support each other: it is the arrival of the women's movement that prompted readers to make their chiasmic crossing back to the freedom of childhood.

Information about sexuality was available in 1970, but little of it was addressed to women. The sexuality chapter takes on the masculine literature of sexuality chiasmically in an extended quotation and critique of Alexander Lowen's 1967 sex manual, *Love and Orgasm*.[40] The collective italicizes (with underlining) particularly dense expressions, and interrupts Lowen's text with irreverent comments: "The *problem* (?!) of orgastic potency in a woman is complicated (??!!) by the fact that *some* women are capable of experiencing a sexual climax through clitorial stimulation. Is a clitoral orgasm satisfying? (Is a penile orgasm satisfying?)"[41] The reader walked into a room where Lowen's book was being read aloud, accompanied with hoots, groans, and improper remarks, and joined a company of writers whose anger is expressed in irony, parody, and critique. Readers and writers both scribble in the margins of the received discourse about sexuality; both understand that "it will be a long time before our sexuality is written the way we know it."[42]

The final episode of this story is a ramified series of choices: "Out of the growing list of new options—men, solitude, work, friends, comes less of a need to bank everything on him. It makes it easier to consider having more than one love affair at a time, and easier to allow him the same option."[43] The writers of the chapter wanted to affirm the multiplicity of women's experiences; they avoided privileging monogamy over multiple partners, or celibacy over experimentation. Similarly, in the discussion of masturbation, various techniques of masturbation were presented as a ramified list, with the alternatives, all affirmed, suggesting the range of possible forms of sexual expression:

Some women masturbate by moistening their finger (with either saliva or juice from the vagina) and rubbing it around and over the clitoris. The amount of pressure and timing seems to vary among women. Some women masturbate by crossing their legs and exerting steady and rhythmic pressure on the whole genital area. A smaller number learn by developing muscular tension through their bodies, resembling the tensions developed during intercourse. Some ways of doing this are by climbing up a pole or a rope or even chinning parallel bars. Other techniques for masturbating include using a pillow instead of a hand, a stream of water, and electric vibrators.[44]

The paragraph continued for several more sentences. In this ramified structure, all the possibilities were given equal emphasis; any one of them could exfoliate into further choices (a pole or a rope or chinning parallel bars). The range of techniques and experiences was the point of the paragraph; the reader was encouraged to find herself among a range of possibilities, or to expand the list by adding techniques of her own.

In the early versions of "Sexuality," vaginal orgasm was the nodal point connecting the narratives of the life cycle and of politicization. Freud saw the vaginal orgasm as a sign of sexual maturity in women, and the collective found pernicious versions of this idea in pornography, marriage manuals, and conventional sex advice. The fetishization of vaginal orgasm derailed feminine desire, established a reign of guilt and confusion, and shored up masculine obliviousness. These discourses, which identified feminine maturity with masculine pleasure, gave way chiasmically to the frank talk of women, a discourse that introduced women to their full sexual expression.

Since sexual physiology was political, sexual relationships were seen as direct expressions of social relations: "'Sex' is about being a 'real woman'—being that ridiculous caricature of a person that this society tells us we had better become if we are to extract even the smallest amount of security, pleasure, and self-esteem from the world. It's a sexual achievement exam. You make love to your judge, and it's pass/ fail."[45] Sexuality determined sex roles, and so a revolution in sex roles would lead to a revolution in sexuality. Conversely, a revolution in sexuality could well lead to a revolution in sex roles. All bets were off, all bids open. Chiasmically, women were invited to move from being determined by their sexuality to using their sexuality as a vehicle for self-determination. The text recognized a kind of bedrock of biological constraint—vaginal orgasms are a physiological impossibility—but its investment is in the hope for sexuality without limits: "What we need to do is get rid of all the standards we've previously used to measure ourselves, our sexuality. By talking to each other, taking support from each other, we can set our own standards which will bear the mark of sanity and individuality."[46] (Lesbianism, named as "homosexuality," is listed among the many emerging choices, but the writers cautiously suggest that it might be caused by fear, however justified, of men.)

In 1970, the text offered a ramified narrative of multiple relationships and activities opening to women. Except for the very detailed section on masturbation, most of these options were drawn in broad strokes. By 1976, the text and its illustrations were both quite explicit. How many lovers were instructed by these images of "female superior with clitoral stimulation," "man stimulating woman's clitoris during coitus," and "self-stimulation during coitus"?[47] Here, and in the text's discussion of masturbation, the metaleptic gestures are bold and graphic. "Learning to Masturbate" invites the reader to explore her body, suggesting that she find a quiet, private space and relax. The writers set the scene: "Settle yourself into a comfortable spot. Put on a favorite record. Keep the lights soft, light a candle. Have a glass of wine or anything else that makes you feel mellow and easy. Think about the people or situations you find sexually arousing."[48]

The voice of the writer induced the reader to arouse herself; metaleptically, the writer has seduced the reader. As the scene develops, the

self-stimulation during coitus

Figure 3.3. Self-stimulation during coitus, *Our Bodies,*
Ourselves, 1976, p. 53. Drawing by Betty Dodson.

reader's hand became the instrument of the writer; the reader was the
passive recipient of the writer's caresses:

With some lotion or oil begin to stroke your body all over. Vary the pressure and timing. Let your sensations come. . . . Find your clitoris and focus
your attention on stroking it or your inner lips around it or the mons area
above it. . . . When feelings of sexual tension mount, experiment with what
you can do to increase them. Open your mouth, let your breathing be faster,
try making noises and moving your pelvis rhythmically to your breathing
and voice.[49]

The message of this passage is: "to experience orgasm, let go of control." The narrator of the passage encouraged the reader to cede control
of her body to the written text, which would tell her how to move and
prompt her to moan. That cession of control established a particularly
intense bond between writer and reader; the writer, an undemanding
and supportive lover, is not focused on orgasm as a goal, "If you do not
reach orgasm when you first try masturbating, don't worry. Many of
us didn't either."[50] The writer led the reader through the ramified possibilities of sexual experience as her metaleptic guide and companion.
The text reached outside its boundaries; an account of the writer's actions suggested the actions of the reader.

Other sections of the chapter play with similar violations of the textual boundary. Readers were invited to experiment and permitted to refuse: whether they took up the text's invitation or not, the text sanctions their reading. By 1973, readers were given advice about a wide range of sexual practices, illustrated with personal narratives. The range broadens in 1984. Although in the mid-1980s other feminist groups were embroiled in controversies about pornography, particularly sado-masochistic pornography, *Our Bodies, Ourselves* was open and permissive in its discussion of these practices, probably because the collective's own work had so often been subject to censorship. At each moment, like a considerate lover, the text reminds the reader to do only what she enjoys, to feel free to experiment, and to remember that "it's good only if we want to be doing it."[51]

This range of sexual practices demonstrated that "sexual equality begins in bed."[52] Readers who wrote letters in response to the sexuality chapter agreed, thanking the collective for their first orgasms, asking for validation of new experiences, or posing questions about sexual practices. Readers responded, perhaps, to the textual voice of the collective, tender and inquiring, curious and adept, interested in both scientific knowledge and the experiences of other women. This was, oddly, a *listening* voice, a voice that included without judgment other women's narratives. It offered a model to the reader: just as the narrator responds to the text's inset narratives without judgment, the reader should be open to the chapter's advice on sexuality.

That voice combined personal anecdotes and technical medical information, although sometimes the seams between the two discourses were prominent. Consider how the 1970 and 1971 editions described orgasm. After their hilarious critique of Alexander Lowen on the "problem" of female orgasm, the writers declared, "An orgasm is not a mystical experience. It is a physical experience, and here's a description of one."[53] What followed was a detached, clinical account of what happens to "the body" during orgasm, based on Masters and Johnson's four-stage theory of sexual response.[54] These stages were described as an observer might see them, rather than as an orgasming woman feels them: "The uterus also contracts rhythmically in wave-like motions but this isn't felt."[55] *Our Bodies, Ourselves* was not alone in treating Masters and Johnson as an authoritative account of women's orgasms, a scientific validation of women's experiences that was almost a substitute for personal narrative. For feminists, "Masters and Johnson" was shorthand for "yes to clitoral orgasm/no to Freud." Anne Koedt's influential "The Myth of the Vaginal Orgasm," for example, asserts: "Today, with extensive knowledge of anatomy, with Kelly, Kinsey, and Masters and Johnson, to mention just a few, there is no ignorance on the subject [of the vagina's lack of sensitivity]. . . . Rather than starting with what women *ought* to feel, it would seem logical to start out with what the anatomical facts are regarding the clitoris and vagina."[56] *Our Bodies, Ourselves'* description of the stages of orgasm may have been drawn from a short essay by Nancy Mann, "Fucked-Up in America," which included a summary of Masters and Johnson's four phases of orgasm. The collective certainly knew her essay, which was included in the New England Free Press edition of "The Myth of the Vaginal Orgasm"; they reprinted her list of nine reasons why a woman might not have orgasm without change or attribution in the sexuality chapter.[57] The objectified, abstract language of Masters and Johnson was a placeholder for the experience of orgasm. Their medical description of orgasm was a provocation, metaleptically inviting the reader to try these techniques at home.

In later editions, writers of the sexuality chapter were less enthusiastic about Masters and Johnson, less evangelistic about the clitoris, less ambivalent about fantasy, and more convinced of the value of communication between partners. But the very openness of the text created a different series of problems: How could the story of multiple sexual awakenings articulate to the story of politicization? When both sex and politics were generalized assertions of "what we desire" or "what we need," there was no conflict between them. But what if "what we desire" was a fantasy of domination? How, then, would the political story be brought to its happy ending?

The collective discussed the politics of the sexuality chapter repeatedly during the revision of the 1984 edition. For many of them, the chapter as written in 1973 and 1976 was among the best in the book: frank, revealing, full of good information and vivid examples. In notes on the 1976 edition, Wendy Sanford commented that although she wanted a "less heterosexually oriented" chapter, she felt that "basically . . . this chapter is good. The sections and categories are good. I'm not sure we need to change it a whole lot."[58] Sanford was not the only member to want more information about lesbian sexuality; Norma Swenson's proposal for the revision included plans for "a much-expanded section which looks at heterosexuality, both as a conscious choice and as an institution which our society has tried to make compulsory."[59] The group worried through various proposals for expanding and dividing chapters on sexuality, relationships, and lesbianism. Since the collective no longer assumed that their reader was heterosexual, or that she was usually involved in a sexual relationship, they normalized lesbianism and celibacy by integrating them into the narrative of the life cycle; women's relation to sexuality changed as they grew to maturity or aged. Many revision notes suggest that experimentation is normal and commendable for younger women, but that women in their forties, whether lesbian or heterosexual, are interested in committed relationships; Norma Swenson, often a contrarian, pointed out that, in later life, whether because of widowhood or divorce, stable relationships are less likely.[60]

In 1984, the sexuality chapter was more closely integrated with the structural narratives of the female reproductive life cycle and the growth of a women's health movement. These stories sometimes opened the text and sometimes closed it down. Sex was sometimes integrated with other life choices women make, and sometimes normalized (and trivialized) as youthful experimentation. Political analysis could show how sexual practices intersect with social forces, or reduce sexuality to a dreary set of prescriptions. Although members of the collective talked to each other about their own experiences—quite directly, by all accounts—as they revised this chapter, they were more concerned with writing than with sex.

In 1984, the collective wanted to "reach out" to readers, especially younger readers. While the metaphor of "reaching" suggests an extension of metalepsis, it actually expressed a recognition that the writers and readers were substantially different, that the text was not a permeable membrane between them but a real boundary. In a 1980 memo, Norma Swenson observed that it is hard to "recapture . . . the particular pitch of amazement, outrage, and determination-to-do-something" of the first editions: "It's not that we aren't sincere; we're just so much wiser now about why things are the way they are. To reach and to be meaningful to younger women (fewer of whom, by definition, will have seen our book and now will be getting the third revision instead), we will have to work against our own maturity, in a sense, our own experience and knowledge."[61] The collective thought that speaking to these younger readers would require recapturing their own younger (angrier, more emotional) selves—an effort that could only become more difficult with each succeeding edition. This effort also suggested that the metalepsis of the text would become difficult: if the reader was less wise than the writer, the boundary between them would become more difficult to negotiate.

In this chapter, I have spoken of metalepsis as a benign aeration of the text in which the reader was invited, solicited, and courted in various ways. Usually it was. Literary critics, however, also see metalepsis as imposing a narrative on both characters and readers, and the metaleptic logic of the sexuality chapter could also take up or exclude readers in ways they might not have chosen.[62] The 1984 edition discusses sex with multiple partners, role playing, and pornography cautiously, as if they were things that other people did, practices alien to writers or, presumably, readers:

We may distrust fantasies which seem to play into male pornographic images of women as submissive or masochistic, and imagine that, in a less sexist future, fantasies of dominance would come to us less often. Yet this is difficult to predict.[63]

A major concern is that the many *real* inequalities in our society create a risk that S/M won't be just play, and that one partner will actually *be* dominant, while the other feels forced to acquiesce. S/M can camouflage truly oppressive behavior.[64]

An article by Wendy Sanford, a writer of the 1984 "Sexuality" chapter and "editor and midwife" of that edition, offers some insight into this process. Reviewing a "Sex Issue" published by the women's journal *Heresies*, Sanford noted that the journal offered "welcome and familiar" discourse about sexuality—honest accounts of women's lives, theory built from narrative, attention to diversity of both experience and opinion. But she missed one of the central narratives of *Our Bodies, Ourselves*: "the mainline feminist attention to reproductive issues and to life cycle variations."[65] At first, she was put off by the reports from "the underside of sex—of sadomasochists, strippers, prostitutes, butches and femmes, women who enjoy pornography, faghags (women who are attracted to gay men), women into casual, recreational or experimental sex."[66] Reading these accounts had been an education for Sanford, who described herself as moving toward greater tolerance of sexual minorities. But her honest account of her own history clarifies that the "we" invoked by *Our Bodies, Ourselves* did not include sadomasochists, strippers, prostitutes, and other sexual minorities. The ramified narrative of sexuality did not reach quite that far. The collective's investment in a direct, intimate, identification with their readers, their commitment to telling a metaleptic story, also limited their address, since the collective identified some women as part of "us," and others as, well, "others."

The dynamics of distributed authorship helped the collective navigate such rough spots; "others" could become authors. In thinking about sexuality and disability, the collective, guided by their collaborators at Boston Self-Help, wrote, "Those of us with physical disabilities are feeling increasingly open and proud about being sexual people. Whether we get a physical disability during our life or grow up with it from birth, we too often find other people assuming that we are not sexual at all."[67] Disabled readers were included in the text's metalepsis; the need to attend to "the mechanics of bladder management" and questions about "making love with a limp" were treated with respectful intimacy. The openness of the text to readers whose sexual practices resembled those of the writers, or could be made to resemble them, sharpens the edge of its treatment of other sexual minorities. Those who were not interested in the back rubs or foot massages recommended by the chapter were excluded from the range of what women, modern and sexually enlightened women, do.[68] Here, perhaps, metalepsis imposed a narrative, as the text reached out to the reader, but not to the singular and desiring reader who came to the book from the "underside."

The Melancholy Text

Writing the 1984 *Our Bodies, Ourselves* was a paradoxical act. The collective enjoyed unprecedented material resources, a well-cultivated network of informants and writers, and time for discussion, planning, and research. But they faced a dispiriting political situation. Sandra Morgen's authoritative history of the women's health movement, *Into Our Own Hands*, characterizes the 1980s as the era of "Reagan, Retrenchment, and Operation Rescue."[69] The Reagan administration was much less supportive of community health efforts than the Carter administration had been; their reorganization of federal appropriations for health and human services reduced funding to the nascent women's clinics. Clinics were devastated by the federal budget cuts of 1981, repeated and deepened in subsequent years. Abortion providers faced harassment and violence, including arson, bombings, blockades, and vandalism. Although new activists entered the movement to respond to these threats, they faced diminishing resources and a defensive battle. Divisions within the movement also became pressing as feminist health workers, having developed a distinctive collaborative culture, recognized that their workplace was also markedly white and middle class. The Boston Women's Health Book Collective was affected, directly or indirectly, by all these challenges. Attempts to exclude the book from school libraries became more frequent; money had to be raised to pay staff who had been supported by government CETA funds. After 1984, it was no longer possible to imagine that the women's health movement would continue to grow in the face of repression and dwindling resources, that it would not face serious divisions, or that *Our Bodies, Ourselves* would introduce women seamlessly into a growing culture of health activists. As the figure of transformation, metalepsis assumed a fluid relation between interior and exterior, between the movement and the cultures that supported it. By the mid-1980s, this relation was not mobile; the border between movement activists and ordinary women was not open to casual negotiation. The conversation had become sober; the narratives were interrupted.

During the 1980s, *Our Bodies, Ourselves* began circulating as a book among other books, rather than as a gateway to a new experience of the body. Encouraged by the collective's success, other authors published women's health books. *Ms.* magazine sponsored *The Ms. Guide to a Woman's Health* by C. W. Cooke and S. Dworkin in 1979; Beth Richardson Gutcheon, who was associated with Planned Parenthood, wrote *Abortion: A Woman's Guide* (1975).[70] There were also independent efforts, like Kirsten Grimsted and Susan Rennie's *New Woman's Survival Sourcebook* (1975).[71] Even traditional "beauty books" gave a nod to women's health; Deborah Chase published the oddly titled *The Medically-Based No-Nonsense Beauty Book* (1974).[72] As *Our Bodies, Ourselves* was put to new uses, its meaning as a cultural object changed. The book that the collective had produced in 1984 was no longer the object it had been in 1973. Boston veteran activist Jackie King remembered keeping a copy of *Our Bodies, Ourselves* in the bathroom of her collective house during the 1970s. When women in the house wanted to meet privately, they congregated in the bathroom, and *Our Bodies, Ourselves* was a book they wanted ready at hand.[73] That battered newsprint *Our Bodies, Ourselves* was not the same object as a copy of the book saved on a shelf or carefully filed away as a memento. This is not to say that the book became insignificant: nothing could be more consequential than a young woman reading *Our Bodies, Ourselves* in her high school library, evading family censorship. By 1984, however, the writers imagined their readers as solitary consumers rather than as members of a group or class; the significance of addressing such readers as individual instances of a universal feminine embodiment necessarily shifted.

By 1984, the limits of the collective's commitment to universality had become clear. They had worked through emerging differences in sexual orientation among their members, were soon to be confronted with charges of racism from its staff, and had experienced the global inequalities of women's healthcare in their encounters with women activists in developing countries. A sharpening sense of the divisions among women—and a complementary sense of the ties among women and men—complicated the constructed identity of both writers and readers. In many chapters of the 1984 edition, these new understandings of division closed off the metaleptic action of the text. Some chapters, like "Sexuality" and "Anatomy and Physiology," built on the gestures of inclusion that had marked earlier editions. Others, such as the new chapter "Women in Motion," established very clear boundaries between readers and writers. For metalepsis to occur, for the text to exceed its frame, writers must understand themselves as sharing a common embodiment with readers. But if the reader's body is no longer seen comparable to the writer's, such gestures become thin. In the "Women in Motion" chapter, writer Janet Jones follows the landmarks of the *Our Bodies, Ourselves* style: the language is inclusive and nonjudgmental, and "we" is the pronoun of choice. But the chapter is a text written by a woman who exercises a lot to readers who exercise less. Sometimes, she invokes her readers as companions: "While we work to change this oppressive society into a humane one we can all live in, soothing our nerves through physical and mental activity is an important and necessary release, and gives us more energy to work for the changes we need."[74] Sometimes, she was a coach exhorting her charges: "Expect some stiffness. If you're really pushing your muscles they're bound to hurt the following day(s). But don't pamper yourself and stop. The best remedy is moderate exercise."[75] In both cases, there was a clear boundary between the world of the text, where women are active, physically fit, and confident, and the world of the sedentary reader. The text is closed; there is no metalepsis here.

The collective had suffered a paradox of their success. They represented a movement that had subsided, but their own success allowed them to continue. Melancholy was a response to this turn of events: no longer could the collective draw upon the historical agency of representation. And many passages in the 1984 edition, like many of my interviews with the collective (an optimistic and forward-looking group of women), are resonant with melancholy. While the overall tone of *Our Bodies, Ourselves* had been determinedly optimistic, after 1984 the collective's hope for change shifted from the U.S. women's health movement to global feminism; its direct engagement with readers was therefore mediated and displaced.

But there is a feminist critique of melancholy, and it is relevant to this moment in the life of the collective. Rosi Braidotti suggests that melancholia can repeat and perpetuate the ideological positioning of women as marginal and lacking. Conceding Freud's understanding that melancholia is an internalization of a constitutive loss, Braidotti rejects the "*fin-de-siècle* gloom" that presents the subject as continually constructed by both desire and its failure, and therefore necessarily melancholy:

I find the emphasis on the structurally aporetic and fundamentally failed attempt by the subject to affirm his or her libidinal intensity—this emphasis on lack and negativity—tainted with a comic touch of tragedy. Against the negative passion and the seduction of the aporetic, there has to be an alternative. Translated into nomadic language, I actively yearn for a more joyful and empowering concept of desire and for a political economy that foregrounds positivity, not gloom.[76]

Our Bodies, Ourselves is less contaminated with regret and self-justification than many other books rooted in that period. Yet, the 1984 edition is marked by a sense of belatedness, of being bereft, of things not having turned out so well, and that sense echoes in all subsequent editions until 2005. If metalepsis ruptures the textual frame, melancholy searches for fragments lost in the rupture. Daniel Heller-Roazen's *Echolalias: On the Forgetting of Language*, a study of language birth and language death, offers an illuminating analogy for such this sense of loss.[77] Heller-Roazen's study is relevant, since the melancholy of *Our Bodies, Ourselves* is that of speakers of a lost language, compelled to keep on talking, unable to find an audience for their most treasured ways of speaking. Consider this letter written by collective member Jane Pincus after a particularly difficult board meeting in 1992: "People spend no time either at the beginning or end of the meeting simply connecting in some way with each other. Maybe you all are used to the way you relate and don't mind it, but to me as an outsider the atmosphere seemed hurried, tense, hostile and impersonal."[78] She mourned a lost language. But Heller-Roazen argues that languages are continually emerging from their own deaths, evolving into new and vital forms at the moment when their traditional uses collapse. He gives the example of the Hebrew poetry of Islamic Spain, "It is perhaps no accident that the golden age in the history of Hebrew poetry, that of Islamic Spain, arose in the moment that the writers of the language let its native land fall definitively out of sight. Exile, in the end, may be the true homeland of speech; and it may be that one accedes to the secret of a tongue only when one forgets it."[79] Analogously, the writer who, in the 2005 *Our Bodies, Ourselves* takes the reader on a tour of her sexual anatomy, may have remembered the text's metalepsis by forgetting its original form.

Appropriate as it might have been for Pincus to express her alienation, we may not need to mourn, any more than the last speakers of Latin would have been sad to meet the first speakers of Romanian, or than modern Israelis (with all the contradictions that implies) mourned when they began once again to speak Hebrew, adapting the syntax of Yiddish—another language that survived its premature elegy.[80] Ancient

Hebrew, like ancient Latin, died more than once so that it could survive. We can see texts as holding various historical layers of language in a kind of simultaneous suspension, rather than in neatly defined sedimented layers. All the history of the text is available at once to readers, but writers only preserve the history of the text by forgetting it, by writing in the language available to them rather than invoking the memory of a past textual practice. The dialogue between readers and writers always invokes the past and relocates its resources in the present. Writers may be melancholy; language is not. Since this book has included many pages that reconstruct the feminist world of the 1970s and 1980s in painstaking detail, it may seem late in the game for me to suggest a program of amnesia, and that is not my intention. What can be forgotten, however, is the sense of the past as a lost homeland of emancipatory agency. The practices of the 1960s seemed, to those who engaged with them, to be magically efficacious, but the texts associated with those practices should not be fetishized. They should be read, with all the tools at our disposal, remembering them as labors of language.

While the collective's own story properly foregrounds what was distinctive in the text when it was produced—the integration of personal narratives, for example—what may be most significant to us now is the text's ordinariness, its participation in everyday contemporary discourses—its use of homemade and do-it-yourself publication practices, for example, or its deployment of narratives of reversal and change. The text speaks to us of choices made imperfectly, under pressures of time and circumstance, of writers who did what they could with the knowledge that they had at hand; such a reading therefore contradicts any story of magical efficacy and transformation. To read *Our Bodies, Ourselves* without melancholy is to ask, in Michael Warner's terms, "the question of how, by what rhetoric, one might bring a public into being when extant modes of address and intelligibility seem themselves to be a problem."[81] It is to continue, and to make available for the present, the text's metalepsis.

4   What Is This Body That We Read

FOR THE WRITERS OF 'OUR BODIES, OURSELVES,' the book's title was a triumphant proclamation that embodiment was the central, collective truth of women's experience. Their title can also be read as a series of questions: How can we understand our bodies as selves? What is the relationship between women's bodies (seen as capable of being owned, as "their" or "our" bodies), and women as reflexive subjects ("ourselves"). Is the body the subject? Did the subject come into being as she came to know the body? How was the body gendered, as it certainly is in all editions of *Our Bodies, Ourselves*? Was the subject necessarily plural? The body that the collective constructed was aligned with their metaleptic text and anticipated some central concerns of contemporary feminist theory.

Readers came to *Our Bodies, Ourselves* because they relied on its frank, detailed depiction of women's bodies and their experiences; from the beginning, the collective worked on ways of describing the body that countered conventional medical representations. Those texts and images offered representations of a body divided into parts, depersonalized, and idealized. Moreover, representations of the body, personalized or not, were not easy to come by in the early 1970s, and access to them could be restricted. The writers of *Our Bodies, Ourselves* represented women's bodies, as much as possible, as wholes, and for them, segmentation was depersonalization. *Our Bodies, Ourselves* presented women as a norm, rather than as deviations from a male standard. The collective avoided representing a single idealized woman and showed a range of possibilities for women's bodies. The text strove to offer frank and detailed information, rather than euphemisms or silence.

Readers of *Our Bodies, Ourselves* found its visual and textual representations of the body novel. Images of the body were plentiful, clear, and explicit. They presented women as integrated, active, and situated; rather than seeing a floating body part on a blank background, readers saw pictures that situated internal organs within living bodies, recalling the striking images of Vesalian anatomies. Finally, the text of *Our Bodies, Ourselves* fostered an investigation of the feminine body that drew the reader's attention to the sensation of investigating herself. Women learned about anatomy, but they also learned what it felt like to touch themselves and to manipulate structures so that they could see interior organs. Just as the text metaleptically broke its frame, its representations of the body led the reader to study herself, noting her own reactions to looking, to touching, to feeling her own hands and eyes upon herself. Technically, sensations produced by the actions of a body itself are called "reafferent," and the doubled, reflexive logic of reafference was consonant with the doubled relation between text and reader in metalepsis.

Feminist studies of science have demonstrated that representing women's bodies is a powerful cultural practice, consequential both for women's self-understanding and their public role. Such representations also shape how science understands its relationship to nature.[1] We experience our bodies as constructions mediated by a range of cultural practices, including medicine, and we experience medicine, not only through our experience as patients, but through its representations in fiction, film, and journalism.[2] If our bodies do not appear to us as skin bags enclosing organs that float in fluids, but as tightly packed assemblages of organs and systems, it is because our experience of the body has been shaped by high school or college biology classes, anatomical diagrams in newspapers, and simulated images of the interior of the body on television medical dramas. Medical images, freely available in mass media, offer us visual experiences of the body that provoke both the pleasures of satisfied curiosity and anxieties about illness, death, and simple materiality. The dissemination of bodily images is therefore deeply affected by the media ecology of a culture: for us, images and texts present medicine that is both knowable and unknown. We may visit the Visible Human Web site to inspect whisper-thin sections of any body part; we may consult Med Line's enormous database of medical articles, taking advantage of a resource formerly available only to hospitals and medical schools. Any of these sources of knowledge also measure our ignorance, demonstrating how much of our bodies are unseen and dimly understood.

Our Bodies, Ourselves and Media Ecology

For the writers of the first editions of *Our Bodies, Ourselves*, representations of the body were much less ubiquitous than they are in the twenty-first century. Newspapers did not routinely include science sections, and articles on medicine were sparingly illustrated: science and medicine, as opposed to their political and cultural implications, were scarcely considered "news." Medical knowledge could be restricted to medical professionals: the Countway Library of Harvard Medical School was off limits to anyone but medical students and faculty. Members of the collective, even if they were students at Harvard, borrowed credentials from friends to sneak into the library; one member, a social worker, sometimes claimed that she was collaborating with a physician on an article.[3] In many ways, nineteenth-century conventions of privacy and decorum still affected how the body was represented in media and popular culture. Even though stories such as the thalidomide scandal and the development of oral contraceptives were widely reported in the 1960s, they were usually presented as social and political issues, as if the technical details were beyond most readers. Participants in the first women's health classes were struck by the images that they saw there; Joan Ditzion's recollection is typical: "The woman who was talking, she had actually a diagram of a woman's vagina, vulva and all. And it was like, never having a seen, you know, a picture. . . . And so the idea, that was a really important, the whole idea of clitoris, you know women's sexual anatomy was like—whoa!"[4]

Conventional representations, whether in mainstream medical texts, anatomy books, or popular medical articles, showed a male body, and women's bodies were presented as deviations from this norm. Medical images generally showed depersonalized body parts or schematic outlines, dislocated in time and space, and almost always faceless. Representations of bodies were especially squeamish when it came to sex. Anatomy textbooks commonly left the clitoris out of their diagrams of female genitals or did not label the organ.[5] The writers of *Our Bodies,*

Ourselves contested these conventions by taking the female, rather than the male, as a norm. Organizing the text as a narrative of the reproductive life cycle, a distinguishing characteristic of female embodiment, supported this focus. While a shift from "male as center" to "female as center" is sometimes seen as a hallmark of liberal or cultural feminism, in the representation of biology it has more subtle implications, as Elizabeth Grosz has shown:

> If women are to be granted a position *congruous* with but independent of men, the female body must be capable of autonomous representation. This demands a new use of language and a new form of knowledge capable of articulating femininity and women's specificity in ways quite different from prevailing alternatives. Biological sciences, for example, would have to be drastically modified so that distinctly female processes are no longer considered passive a priori or by definition, in opposition to the activity attributed to men's biological processes.[6]

Our Bodies, Ourselves was a text in search of just such a new language, beginning with direct inventions in early editions. There, a female-centered view might be constructed by simply leaving men out, just as an early women's meeting might make its strongest political statement by excluding them. Later editions, particularly the 1984 *The New Our Bodies, Ourselves*, are more articulated. Women's biology is connected with social and emotional issues; women's health problems are connected to the vicissitudes of living in a female body, rather than being presented as variations on a male model. The 1984 chapter on "Alcohol, Mood-Altering Drugs and Smoking," for example, pointed out the special risks for women who smoke and drink, the social stigma associated with women's use of alcohol, and the emergence of programs for women such as Women for Sobriety. But the chapter on food in the same edition, while generally helpful, says nothing about women's distinct nutritional needs, although it acknowledges their cultural responsibility for feeding families and the pressures on them to diet.

While the collective faced a thin and undeveloped field of medical representations of women, the political discourse of second-wave feminism was deeply occupied with the question of how women were represented. "Images of women" was a favorite topic for consciousness-raising groups, and the alternative press struggled constantly with questions of what was a respectful image. We have already seen that the collective, for example, rejected mounting an exhibit of "many cervices" because they did not want to show women "in parts" (Chapter 2). The isolated body part was part of the medical repertoire of representation that the collective wanted to leave behind; as Paula Doress-Worters said, "We also had some criticisms of the way some of the technical information was given in medical textbooks. For example, their idea of protecting someone's privacy would be to present the picture or drawing of organs with no head, whereas our idea was that we didn't want these disembodied women. We wanted, you know, if we had a drawing, the drawing to have a face. So we just wanted to present the image of a whole woman."[7] This preference for representations of a whole, personalized body, common to second-wave feminism, was expressed in the women's press and feminist theater.

The collective accepted this preference, taking it as an expression of their desire for integration and autonomy. They found an exemplary expression of the preference for images of whole bodies in the lyrics to "Our Faces Belong to Our Bodies," a song included in every edition of *Our Bodies, Ourselves* from 1973 to 1998. The lyrics read in part:

Our faces belong to our bodies
Our faces belong to our lives.

Our faces are blunted.
Our bodies are stunted.
We cover our anger with smiles.

. . .

Our power is changing our faces, our bodies,
Our power is changing our lives.

Our struggle is changing our faces, our bodies.
Our struggle is changing our lives.[8]

"Our Faces Belong to Our Bodies" was sung at the beginning of each performance of the New York feminist group, the It's All Right to Be a Woman Theater, during the early 1970s. Both the women's theater performance and the text of *Our Bodies, Ourselves* responded to similar political impulses to see women's bodily self-exploration as politically consequential. During the first verse, a woman stood onstage, touching her hair, her face, her arm; when she touched her breasts or her genitals, a kazoo warned her off. These actions parodied a taboo against investigating one's own sexuality: feminine narcissism was encouraged, but sexual reafference was forbidden. As the song continued, the audience picked it up and echoed it, until at the last verse, the performer was presented as liberated and supported by other women.[9] The song, and the performance that accompanied it, expressed a belief that women who explored their bodies would also express their emotions, leading to liberation. And liberation was seen as a connection between "body," especially the sexual and reproductive body, and the "face," the public, expressive presence of the individual. In *Our Bodies, Ourselves*, the song lyrics were usually printed just after the introduction, on the same page as the collective's group portrait. "Our Faces Belong to Our Bodies" was presented as a kind of theme song for the book because of the collective's commitment to the close connection between showing the whole body and understanding a whole person. When I asked Paula Doress-Worters about the longer personal narratives included in the 1973 edition, she replied, "It was sort of like not wanting to have women without heads. We wanted the story to be contexualized, especially talking about a relationship because you can't really explain a relationship in two sentences."[10]

Canons of Representation

Feminists in the 1960s and 1970s valued images of the female body that, like "Our Faces Belong to Our Bodies," integrated body with face; the expressive body, direct gaze, and facial focus of these images recalled conventions of male portraiture.[11] *Our Bodies, Ourselves* maintained a steady focus on the face: the book portrayed unified subjects associated with bodies that were never morcellated. Even if, in a given section, not all of the text's illustrations show the whole body, the sequence will begin with an intact body and include the face. Diagrams of genital organs in the 1976 anatomy chapter begin with an image of the reproductive organs in a standing body; the discussion of suction abortion opens with a photograph of a woman having an abortion, focused on the faces of the woman and her supporter.

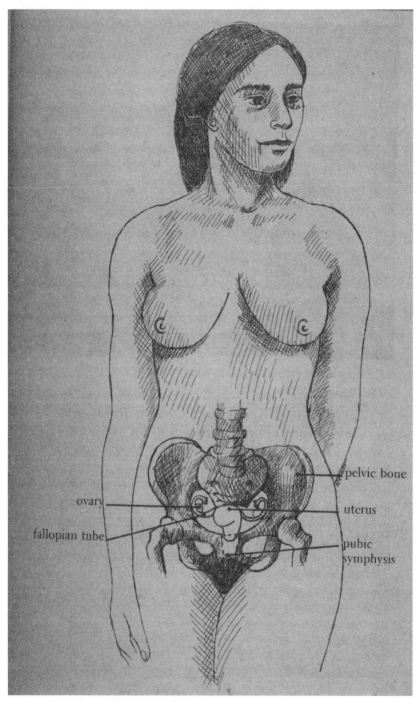

Figure 4.1. Showing the whole body, *Our Bodies, Ourselves*, 1976, p. 25. Penguin UK. Drawing by Nina Reimer; Boston Women's Health Book Collective.

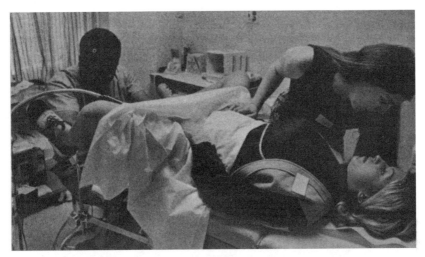

Figure 4.2. Abortion patient and caregiver, *Our Bodies, Ourselves,*
1976, p. 229. Boston Women's Health Book Collective.

The "many, many cervices" of the rejected women's health fair display would have complied with another of the collective's aims in representing the body: to show a range of physical types, rather than a single
idealized norm. And in fact, the collective overcame its aversion to the
representation of segmented parts to include a picture of "some hymen
variations," beginning in 1973.[12] The image, six line drawings of hymens,
was drawn for the collective by Nina Reimer. But the group was as interested in socially marked variations as in demonstrating the range of
anatomical possibilities. Their collaboration with Boston Self-Help, an
activist group of disabled women, encouraged them to integrate information on disability into a range of chapters in the 1984 edition. The
chapter "Women in Motion," for example, includes disabled women, fat
women, older women, and institutionalized women, emphasizing that
"each person is different," insisting both that movement is the right of
every woman and that everyone has "the right to remain physically in-
active" if they choose.[13] In representing sexual anatomy, the collective's
understanding of universality supported a matter-of-fact tone: in 1984,
the text identified organs and structures as "the vestibule," "the clitoris," and "the urethra."[14]

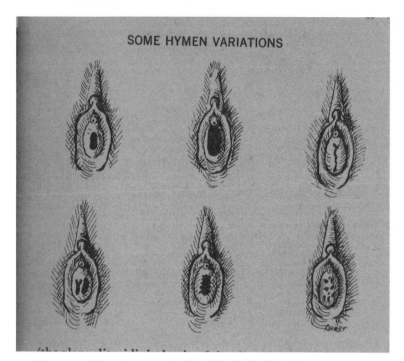

Figure 4.3. Some hymen variations, *Our Bodies, Ourselves*, 1973, p. 15. Drawing by Nina Reimer; Boston Women's Health Book Collective.

The collective struggled with the relationship between their commitment to a universal female body and their desire to account for variations in women's experiences. The pivotal concept of choice moved the reader from an abstract, universal body to the particular, varied bodies of individual women. Universal embodiment grounded universal rights to cultivate the body, to choose forms of care and experience, but these universal rights only become effective when women's differing circumstances are mitigated. In the chapter on "Women in Motion," the text recognized that living in a crime-ridden neighborhood makes it hard to take walks, so poor women need extra security; being disabled makes it hard to use public pools, even though swimming is good exercise, so accessible pools should be built; being in a mental hospital makes it dangerous to "let out how you feel in a physical way," so these institutions should be reformed.[15]

If variation and difference appear as forms of deprivation, marking women by the activities from which they are excluded, the rhetoric of choice redeems these deprivations. The woman whose body has been marked by conventional culture with a sign of difference has been inscribed as limited or deviant. In *Our Bodies, Ourselves,* difference was a reason to offer compensation and accommodation: "When we are face to face with survival, any kind of real health care for the body and soul—sufficient and nutritious food, regular exercise and good times—appears to be an extravagance. So the challenge is how we can all join together to fight not just the cutbacks but the prevailing government attitude which says scraping by is enough. We need bread *and* roses. Nothing less will do."[16] This connection between universal rights and individual accommodations was not without its own problems: to articulate the connection between female embodiment and social location established a boundary between the writer who asserted universal rights for others and the reader whose difference might be accommodated. The text was sealed off; metalepsis, the figure that draws readers into the text, was blocked. Nobody, after all, tells the undergraduate at Yale or the young attorney that she is entitled to roses, let alone bread. The reader is offered political representation rather than being invited to mutual exploration. Paradoxically, the collective's acknowledgment that women of color might need special support to undertake new experiences of emancipated embodiment also marked these women as different, in-need-of, lacking—exactly the markers that the group would have resisted for themselves. The conventions of showing whole bodies and of representing a range of variations were contradictory. Both of these practices complied with common rhetorical practices of the women's liberation movement, but they also enacted assumptions—of bodily wholeness, of female universality—that would be questioned by later feminists. They also cohered uneasily with the collective's insistence on individuality: "Our bodies are unique because they—us—will never occur again."[17]

The issues raised by the collective's choice of textual registers were equally complex, although less contested. The collective balanced a rich range of vocabularies in their representations of the female body. They took pride in deploying the technical vocabulary of medicine. They drew on the political and cultural vocabularies of the women's liberation and New Left movements. But the collective had to invent supplements to these registers: they wanted a lexicon for the female body that was not crude, sentimental, or technical, and they had to work hard to find one:

> Sometimes when we want to talk or even think about sex we need words and we face the annoying dilemma—what words should we use? For many of us there are no words that really feel right because of the attitudes and values they convey: the clinical, proper terms—vagina, penis, and intercourse—seem cold, distant, tight; the street, slang terms—cunt, cock, fuck—seem degrading or coarse; euphemisms like "making love" seem silly and inexact. . . . We feel awkward, and this awkwardness convinces us that even if sex is a natural way of expressing ourselves, we have no natural way of talking about it.[18]

Of course there could be no "natural" way of talking about the body, since the body always comes to us through multiple layers of cultural mediation. It may have seemed, in 1976, as if a natural language could be invented. Shere Hite, for example, proposed that "orgasm" be used as a verb.[19] The collective liked this neologism, and it appeared in some sections of the text, but never became colloquial. A sentence like "some women can orgasm twice or more in quick succession" would be followed by "Knowing that 'multiple orgasms' are possible has made some of us feel that we 'ought' to have them, that we are sexually inadequate if we don't."[20] Even if the collective believed that orgasm was something that a woman does, ordinary language kept on suggesting that orgasm was something she had.

The Body Political

The collective's conventions for describing the body presented a series of political problems. What is a "whole" woman, and what does it mean to represent a woman's whole body? When does the representation of variation become a fetishization of racial or age differences? Can a book intended for a mass audience disseminate the particular forms of speech that mark membership in the women's health movement? Nowhere were these questions more fraught than in the description of the clitoris; nowhere was the collective's practice more inventive than in their continual re-creation of that organ.

Psychoanalytic theorist Jacques Lacan has offered an influential theory of how we represent the body to ourselves; this theory is use-

ful in thinking about a bodily object as intensely imagined as the clitoris. Lacan talks about two kinds of bodily knowledge: we come to
our first sense of ourselves as separate beings when we see the illusory image of the outline of our bodies, usually in a mirror, in Lacan's
mirror stage. But we also experience the body not as a whole, but as
a discontinuous series of boundaries, sites of both pleasure and pain,
places where the body touches and is touched by other objects—objects
that can be lost. Lacan names these places as apertures of the body: the
mouth, the eyes, the anus, the genital organs.[21] We know a mirrored
self, triumphant and nicely bordered, in a different way than we know
the libidinal self, inchoate and fluid, that takes in the mother's breast.
The libidinal self draws complex and varied boundaries, sometimes
including its objects and sometimes nostalgically searching for them.
In neither case do we encounter a real body: the body is emphatically
not what we see in the mirror; our nostalgia for complete infantile satisfaction is a longing for something that we remember but have never
experienced. Both these forms of knowledge are saturated with desire:
for wholeness, for a particular object, for a particular localized experience, for a particular objectification of our own bodies.

While the collective valued images of the whole body, they could not
learn without dividing the body into parts and examining them in turn;
conversely, their emphasis on women's bodily experience as fluid and
mobile encouraged them to think about the body in terms that recall
Lacan's libidinal self. The narrative of the reproductive life cycle could
organize these two approaches to representing the body: various body
parts swim in and out of prominence, and they are alternately represented
as bounded objects and as vectors of sensation. When writers of *Our
Bodies, Ourselves* took on the task of making an organized, accessible map
of the body in the chapter on anatomy, focusing on the genital organs,
they were not making a street map of Cambridge. In undertaking this
project of representation, they claimed to be knowing subjects, subjects
for whom the body is transparent, regular, and highly functional. The
speaker of *Our Bodies, Ourselves* knows the body, owns the body, is the
body, and is completely at home in it. When the text is metaleptically
opened, as it often is in the anatomy chapter, she encourages the reader
in experiencing a similar relationship with her own body.

This integration was presented as a remedy for that unmediated experience of the lived body eloquently described in the 1971 edition as "disgust":

Nearly every physical experience we have as a woman is [so] alienating that we have been filled with extreme feelings of disgust and loathing for our own bodies. Every part of our body is an area of real or potential disgust to us— armpits, faces, vaginas, buttocks, stomachs, breasts. The slightest so-called "imperfection" is a source of very private anxiety and fear that we dare not communicate to each other because we are taught to think we are the only ones who feel these things. And the objectified disgust we have for ourselves we feel towards other women and we are filled with disgust at the thought of her (our) body under the clothing (armpits, vagina, etc.).[22]

The speaking "we" of this passage was positioned as a seeker of knowledge, delivered from an experience of disgust that divided the body into parts, each of which was then open to masochistic rejection. Her avowal was both remarkably frank and quite politically incorrect, a refusal of sentimental celebration or comfort. To members of the collective, this language seems strange today; when I read this passage to Jane Pincus, she responded, "Really? That's odd. Is that possible?"[23] While the main argument of the text presented the female body as a universal, privileged, whole, in this passage bodily experience reflected the speaker's disgust with her own body. The other woman is indeed just like me; we do share the same body; both of our bodies are objects of "anxiety and fear." In openly discussing their experience of shame and alienation, the collective was not alone. Such admissions were much more common in the earliest days of the women's movement than they would become in the mid-1970s. Meredith Tax, for example, one of the leading writers in Boston Bread and Roses, wrote in *Woman and Her Mind: The Story of Everyday Life*: "The self-consciousness we are filled with! It is so painful, so physical. We are taught to feel that our only asset is our physical presence, that is all other people notice about us. The most minute blemish on a total person—a pimple, excess weight, a funny nose, larger than average breasts—can ruin a day, or years, with the agonies of constant awareness of it."[24]

Later in the 1970s, such language would become rare: feminists wanted to model affirmative self-esteem in their public statements. But at the beginning of the second wave, confessions of disgust and unease relieved writers and reassured readers. Such language could be found in Simone de Beauvoir's *The Second Sex*, a book that was for a long time the only serious, extended text on women's oppression available to members of the U.S. women's movement.[25] De Beauvoir's book was used, for example, as a central text by the Chicago Liberation School for Women and was a transformative book for more than one member of the collective.[26] Consider de Beauvoir's evocative account of young women's insecurity:

But, above all, the lie to which the adolescent girl is condemned is that she must pretend to be an object, and a fascinating one, when she senses herself as an uncertain, dissociated being, well aware of her blemishes. Make-up, false hair, girdles, and "reinforced" brassieres are all lies. The very face itself becomes a mask: spontaneous expressions are artfully induced, a wondering passivity is mimicked. . . . The body is no longer alive, it waits; every gesture and smile become an appeal.[27]

This language resonated with many women in the late 1960s, although many of them, including the collective, disagreed with de Beauvoir's rejection of the feminine body as the ground of women's alienation from themselves: "Woman, like man, is her body; but her body is something other than herself."[28]

It was not easy to sort out how a woman could experience her body as at once universal and isolated, at once a source of furtive disgust and an object to be displayed. This difficulty is felt as a pressure in the language of the text; pronouns waver, as in "We think we are the only ones who feel these things." Solitary, isolated shame is precisely an emotion that no "we" can ever have, just as there can be no natural object that is designated as "her (our) body," the target of disgust. The subject's desire for autonomy is directed toward the body. And so knowledge of the body is liberating. Knowledge of the body is also knowledge of the socialized body, and therefore a source of anxiety and shame. The critical appraiser who finds flaws everywhere therefore enacts not only her body's distance from an ideal of beauty, but her own failure to achieve autonomy. The speaker of the text convicts herself of both deviations from the norms of conventional beauty and of a reluctant compliance with those norms. Her critical gaze marks at once bodily flaws and her failure to ignore them. The body is divided into zones of noncompliance, points of divergence from an ideal of beauty and charm, and zones of compliance with those ideals that mark the subject as dependent, as fashioned for others. Paradoxically, this shaming appraisal is also experienced as an idiosyncratic experience, a form of individuality that reverses cultural norms: what is individual about you is your loathing of the specific imperfections of your body; nobody else feels this way. Disgust is perhaps an appropriate reaction to such entanglements, named later in the text as "the nowhere identity we have been forced to subsist on for so long."[29]

Such an assertion, of course, simply reframes the question of the subject: Who is it who is aware of feeling this disgust? What kind of subject is constructed in this complex report of a complex reaction to the feminine body? De Beauvoir answered that question with a challenge: the body, for women, is not the self, and the woman must transcend her body. But the writer of the "nowhere identity" passage, with her tangled response, her avowal of raw anxiety and disgust, has both refused transcendence and taken a critical step away from the identity she describes—she has, in fact, objectified her response. Her writing transforms and redeems the feminine body, so that the loathing it prompts is transferred to ideological formations, cultural norms, and alienating practices that inscribe the body, judging and rejecting it. Such a displacement of disgust clears a space in which the body can be opened up, displaying organs that cannot be readily judged and bodily processes that know no norms of appearance. Our culture of surfaces has not established norms for a "nice" liver or the "right" fallopian tubes; the interior of the body, at least for young and healthy women, is a region free of judgment. It can serve as a ground of positive universality; it is the place where women's bodies may not all look the same, but all work the same.[30] That working body provoked wonder, as in Jane Pincus's response to the diagram of how the cervix opened during childbirth, a simple set of nested circles: "I found that the most amazing diagram in the world to look at. That's where we all come from!"[31] While the conventional experience of the objectified body led to concealment and isolation, investigation of the body's interior encouraged a regime of self-care and transformation of the body; communicating the results of these investigations opened new space in a refashioned public sphere.

Publicity overcame shame: the narrative of the growth of a women's movement corrected and mitigated the shock of investigating a body one did not entirely approve of. It also prompted the reinvention of a classic program of self-care that any nineteenth-century women's reformer would have approved: nutrition, outdoor activity, and sensible clothing. "We want to become physically healthy, strong, and enduring through exercise, proper eating and training (like karate) and proud of our bodies. Pride because we feel good ourselves, not because we look good for others."[32] Readers of *Our Bodies, Ourselves* are encouraged at the end of the anatomy chapter to discuss such questions as "How does our self-concept integrate a sense of our physical and mental selves? (conquering mind-body separation)" and to see them as political.[33] Their investigations are rooted in the history of the women's movement, in the philosophical preoccupations of midcentury America, and in the traditional discourses of Marx and Freud.

Speaking of the Clitoris

Once the body is claimed as both the full expression of the knowing subject and as an object of knowledge, both the self and the body are doubled: the self is the known object, and also the vehicle of knowledge; the body is the objectified domain of knowledge, and therefore emphatically not the knowing subject. *Objectified* was a resonant word for second-wave feminists, who considered sexualized or stereotyped images of women to be objectifying, a way of constructing the "nowhere identity." Images of body parts, particularly eroticized body parts—breasts, legs—were held to be on their face objectifying; second-wave feminism protested against the part object. (A part object, of course, need not be a body part: the mother herself can be a part object, experienced as a substitute for the impossible object of desire.) Such divisions and objectifications are not mistakes or accidents. Although the collective projected an ideal of integration and autonomy, their own textual practice demonstrated that all understandings of the subject are split and doubled, and that there is no desire, no action, no pleasure without radical division. The text's discussion of the clitoris is both an investigation of the interior of the body and a demonstration of the division of the subject.

The 1971 New England Free Press edition of *Our Bodies, Our Selves* presents the sexual organs in general and the clitoris in particular as androgynous:

The embryonic gonad (sex gland, from the Latin "gone" or seed) is "indifferent"; that is, it will become male or female depending on the chromosomes and hormones present at the time.[34]

The gonads have a dual function in both sexes.[35]

Sex organs of fetus at 8 weeks when differentiation first occurs. [36]

The clitoris is homologous with the penis, and has analogous functions of erection and orgasm. . . . The hollow areas in the man's penis and in the woman's clitoris are called corpora cavernosa (literally, hollow bodies). . . . Like the penis, the clitoris is composed of shaft . . . and glans.[37]

These quotations from the "Anatomy and Physiology" chapter are followed by a second description in the "Masturbation" section of the "Sexuality" chapter: "To masturbate you have to know something about your body, and in particular about your clitoris (klit'-o-ris). This is a small round ball of flesh located above the opening of the vagina, and it is the center of most sexual stimulation. It functions like the penis in the man. When it's rubbed up and down rhythmically, you get excited. The clitoris is where *all* female orgasms happen, whether by masturbation, intercourse, or fantasy."[38] A third description of the clitoris as the source of women's orgasms is given in a later section on "Orgasm."[39] Finally, the chapter "Some Myths About Women," gives a general account of sex role socialization that insists, "since female satisfaction depends on some clitoral stimulation a woman must have some sense of her sexual self which is real and different from a man's for her to ask for or want this experience."[40] The repeated insistence that readers find and acknowledge the clitoris reflects both the light editing of the early editions of *Our Bodies, Ourselves* and the importance of the clitoris to each of the women who drafted individual chapters. In these descriptions, the clitoris guarantees both androgyny and autonomy. It signifies both the illusory nature of sexual difference (it is, after all, just like the penis) and the radical difference of women from men. The clitoris defines women's autonomy: because of the clitoris, our sexuality is not oriented to male satisfaction in intercourse; because of the clitoris, we can express and explore our own sexuality. The clitoris is the sign of a primal equivalence between men and women, of the difference of the knowing female subject, and of her sexual autonomy, an autonomy that is quite practically insured by anatomical knowledge. The clitoris was therefore divided and contradictory in its gender coding: it was both male (paradoxically, the collective echoes Freud's analysis of the clitoral orgasm as phallic), and female. This double coding economically mapped multiple understandings of gender on the new territories of the body; it cohered with feminist interests in androgyny.[41]

The collective's account of sexual and reproductive anatomy was an audacious reclamation of biology as an argument field for feminism. For de Beauvoir, biology condemned women to immanence; the first chapter of *The Second Sex*, "Destiny: The Data of Biology," states the problem that the rest of the book resolves: women's lives are determined by biology, and they can only overcome this limit by transcending biological destiny. Freud's argument that "anatomy is destiny" had seemed to fix women forever in immature narcissism. To refunction the clitoris is therefore to remake destiny and to realign anatomy as a political resource. Either women are a lot like men, because our clitorises are a lot like penises, or quite different from them and independent of them. Either way, knowledge of the clitoris subverts the axiom that women's social role is focused on their sexuality; sexuality is redefined as an autonomous practice. Anatomy becomes a rhetorical resource for the women's movement just as history is a resource for movements for national and ethnic liberation: both serve as records of oppression and as catalogs of strategies and practices of resistance. Women are encouraged to survey, investigate, and occupy the body: "We emphasize that you take a mirror and examine yourself. Touch yourself, smell yourself, even taste your own secretions. You are your body and you are not obscene."[42]

What representation of the body, then, is offered by the 1971 edition of *Our Bodies, Our Selves?* It is a body deeply divided, split into the material, abject ground of a contagious disgust and the shifting location of that disgust in a knowing agent; it is a body experienced as a series of external zones of possible degradation; it is a body that is internally undifferentiated and unknown. The text investigates that body, mapping the territory of internal organs and establishing correspondence to external, palpable structures. The exterior of the body remains the domain of ideology, oppression, and division; the interior is claimed for nature, liberation, and universalizing knowledge. The palpating hand, the seeing eye, belong to an agent of anatomical knowledge who will understand the unseen interior. The clitoris is presented in these early editions as an organ that connects the interior and the exterior of the body. The collective assumed that for most readers, the clitoris would be as mysterious as, if far more interesting than, the spleen. Most readers of *Our Bodies, Ourselves* would not have seen images of the clitoris; it was not a visually objectified body part; there were no standards for a beautiful or ugly clitoris. The new research on the clitoral orgasm was evidence at once of the ignorance of male-dominated professionals who promoted illusory vaginal orgasms and left the clitoris unlabelled in their diagrams; of the possible rectifying effects of science, instantiated in Masters and Johnson's research; of the evanescence and insignificance of sexual differences; of the profound sexual difference between men and women. The clitoris told all these stories, and it told them efficaciously.

The territorial metaphors that structured the discovery of the clitoris have not escaped previous critics. Donna Haraway, in "The Virtual Speculum in the New World Order," connected self-examination to colonial exploration: "More than a little amnesiac about how colonial travel narrative work, we peered inside our vaginas toward the distant cervix and said something like, 'Land ho! We have discovered ourselves and claim the new territory for women.'"[43] Kathy Davis has usefully pointed out that the practice of the collective, rather than supporting colonizing exploitation, sponsored both a feminist epistemology and a collaborative international practice.[44] But it is also worth looking closely at the metaphors Haraway identifies—of vision, exploration, and discovery. Haraway, uncharacteristically following a line of thought in feminist studies associated with Carolyn Merchant, equates vision with domination.[45] But the investigation suggested by the collective was not a speculative gaze into untouched, virgin territory. Vision and touch inform each other; reader and writer cross multiple boundaries. What is investigated is no "new found land" to be claimed and converted, but an interior space always somehow known, always available, but under prohibition. It would only be an act of colonization for a woman to see her own cervix for the first time if the cervix had been, all along, the ancestral homeland of the gynecologist. (And I suppose that, in a way, it was.) The form of visual pleasure this space affords is not that of conquest; the reader, taking "that first tentative look," might well be an incarnation of that "modest witness" that Haraway's book celebrates.[46]

The collective's investigation of the body in 1973 and 1976 told quite different stories. No longer a celebration of androgyny, the chapter on anatomy and physiology was completely rewritten, taking the shape it would hold until 2005. The clitoris' station at the border between the interior and the exterior of the body became more explicit. In the 1973 edition, the writer stands aside from her own disgust and dissatisfaction with the body, quotes it, and performs it as a deformation of consciousness that is quickly being cast off. What takes its place, as in the 1971 edition, is anatomical knowledge: "Until we began to prepare this material for a course for women, many of us didn't know the names of parts of our anatomy. Some of us had learned bits and pieces of information about specific body functions (menstruation, for example), but it was not permissible to find out too much. The taboos were strongest in the areas of reproduction and sex, which is why our book concentrates on them."[47] Again, anatomical knowledge is knowledge of names, a partitioning of the bodily spaces that had been indeterminate and inchoate. Although the text is much more modest in its deployment of technical terms than the 1971 edition had been, anatomical terms still occur frequently. In both 1973 and 1976, the collective points to palpable structures, presented as reference points in the reader's act of direct investigation. The text invites the reader to move, to feel specific joints, to distinguish the outer and inner lips, to locate the vagina in relation to the anus, and finally to identify the clitoris. The text's staging of self-examination, a literal form of self-knowledge, is also and at once its most direct intervention in the lives of its readers. Whether or not the reader actually performed the self-examination suggested in this passage, the book's positioning of the reader as philosophically detached investigator is enormously powerful. That investigator's attention is drawn to previously unknown submerged provinces of the clitoris.

In the 1976 edition, that solicitation, printed on the page illustrated with the photograph of "Esther's vulva," begins: "The following description deals first with the outer organs and then with the inner organs. It will mean much more if you look at yourself with a mirror as well as at the diagrams." And then, in a footnote, it continues, "You can squat over a large mirror or sit on the floor with your legs apart and use a hand mirror. Make sure you have plenty of light and enough time and privacy to feel relaxed. This is really body education!"[48] The reader who accepted the book's invitation could draw on both the photograph of a woman standing over a mirror and a labeled diagram of the external genitals. Members of the collective, the text admitted, were "not as familiar with [our sexual organs'] appearance as . . . with other parts of our bodies. We found that it was helpful to use a mirror to see ourselves."[49] The text led readers through an examination of the external genitals, proceeding, in the style of a good anatomy book, from upper to lower, from outer to inner. But, unlike any conceivable textbook description, this account assumes a deeply interested and personally involved reader: "If you are not sure of the location of your clitoris, feel your genitals until you hit upon the most sensitive spot. This is pretty sure to be the clitoris, since it is richly supplied with nerves."[50] The text reveals the reader to herself, explaining that the elastic walls of the vagina usually touch each other, that "Women are not a series of holes."[51] The text reaches through holes of its own making, showing writers to readers and readers to writers; it becomes a transparent window through which everyone understands their embodiment in all its variations, as a kind of open secret. The secrets of the body surrender to direct experimentation: "When you feel your own vagina with your fingers you can also tell that the outer third is sensitive when you touch it."[52] The method of experimentation is reafference: your own fingers will tell you which structures are sensitive. The collective's invitation to explore embodiment enacted the universal female bodily experience that was for them the bedrock of feminist commonality, the unfailing basis of common action: many members of the collective would have agreed with Wendy Sanford's observation that "there is some authentic core of experience that you can get to via experience of the body."[53] Reafference was also an induction into a style of reading that was engaged, aware of the consequences of knowledge for one's own body, and in dialogue with the writers.

By 1976, the clitoris had become an extensive and complicated organ; it is no longer a tiny ball of flesh, but a system of both interior and exterior structures that can be identified and manipulated:

Let the hood slide back over the glans [of the clitoris]. Extending from the hood up to the pubic symphysis, you can now feel a hardish, rubbery, movable cord right under the skin. It is sometimes sexually arousing if touched. This is the *shaft* of the clitoris. It is connected to the bone by a *suspensory ligament*. You cannot feel this ligament or the next few organs described, but they are all important in sexual arousal and orgasm. At the point where you can no longer feel the shaft of the clitoris it divides into two parts, spreading out wishbone fashion, but at a much wider angle, to form the *crura* (singular: *crus*), the two anchoring wingtips which attach to the pelvic bones. The crura of the clitoris are about three inches long. From the fork of the shaft and the crura, and continuing down the sides of the vestibule, are two bundles of erectile tissue called the *bulbs of the vestibule*. These, along with the whole clitoris and an extensive system of connecting veins throughout the pelvis, become firm and filled with blood (pelvic congestion) during sexual arousal.[54]

The reader has become the writer; the investigator was fully identified with the object of investigation, so that structures that could not be seen or felt were located and understood; the territory of the genital organs has became animated with the events of arousal and orgasm. The clitoris of the 1976 edition had become a mobile organ; it distinguished the body as feminine on its surface, but a woman who wanted to see it needed time, privacy, a mirror, and good light. Her inspection would teach her to divide the external organ into parts (hood and glans), but she would be encouraged to investigate structures she could not see. She would find some of the interior portions of the clitoris by touching them and by being aroused, a state she would learn to clinically name as "pelvic congestion." (In that act, she meets herself as both sexual object and sexual agent.) As the collective said in the 1973 preface, "Learning about our bodies in this way really turned us on."[55] Other, more subtle, parts of the clitoris could only be appreciated indirectly, from the text's description, from its illustrations, or from the reader's experience of arousal and orgasm. If, in 1971, readers discovered the clitoris as if it were an unknown organ, in 1976 they found an organ that was itself gemellated into a series of parts. Each of these parts was named and articulated into a new morphology—*"crura* (singular: *crus)"*—so that the reader could move from the surface of the body to its interior. Visible structures gave way to palpated structures; palpated structures gave way to names. The whole organ and each of its parts was known by a reader who was at once a cool-headed observer and a woman engaged in transgressive autoerotic investigations.

This description expands and complicates the part object of the clitoris, but it also presents the clitoris as a representation of, or substitute for, the integrated whole body. The earlier editions of *Our Bodies, Our Selves* focused on the visible organs of the vulva and referred to internal structures by simply listing their names. In its movement from surface to interior, the 1976 edition offered the possibility of wholeness and integration: this is a known body, and its surface has been redeemed by the subject's knowledge of its interior. Knowledge neutralizes the specular image of the body: the body is not just what you see, but more especially what is unseen but known. The body has become whole, and one.

The clitoris is invested with the power of this knowledge. Lacan points out that the phallus must be imaginary, since it is experienced as "an organ in glorious, monadic isolation, rejecting any tie or relation (whether complementary or antagonistic), in favor of the sole alternative of being or not being."[56] In the 1976 *Our Bodies, Ourselves*, the clitoris is not only gloriously isolated, but capable of both being and not being: it is palpable and visible, but also hidden, known only through textual mediation. This text draws on a particularly rhetorical imagination—the body is reorganized through the agency of Masters and Johnson's popularized scientific discourse. In *Our Bodies, Ourselves*, political difficulties are translated into highly overdetermined images that promise a relation of the investigator to the self that is both scientifically detached and erotically engaged. The book and the body become representations of each other, each promising that connection and autonomy need not be mutually exclusive.

Self-Reflection and Reafference

While the collective proposed anatomical investigation as a search for integration and wholeness, the text that they produced was an ingenious performance, prompting women to redraw the boundaries that divided and split the feminine self. Women who had been caught in the specular act of constantly performing femininity and savagely rejecting this performance were offered a new way of viewing the self. Self-regard would not be a matter of accepting and rejecting body parts, but of investigating the body, moving from the visible to the invisible, and of simultaneously experiencing the body as a site of pleasure and arousal. The woman who learned from *Our Bodies, Ourselves* was, presumably, released from the constant review of the body; instead, she knew herself, bodily, as an investigator. I have been calling this sense of self-reflection "reafference," a term that refers to the nervous system's ability to distinguish sensations that an organism produces from external stimuli. Our capacity for reafference lets us know when the voice we are hearing or the touch we are feeling is our own.[57] While the doubled relation of reafference was most vivid in the section on the clitoris, it also shaped discussions of exercise, childbirth, and menopause. "Body education," the collective's term for this activity, was not simply a way of teaching women facts about the body. The body was changed by being investigated: it became capable of orgasm, or of lifting weights, or of giving birth without medication. The experience of investigating and transforming the body reorganized the reader's experience of corporeality—that experience metaleptically crossed the boundary of the text. The division between investigator and object was reinterpreted, by the collective and presumably by the reader, as wholeness, integration, and heightened self-awareness. While this interpretation overlooked the division at the heart of the experience of the body that the text sponsored, it was not delusive. Sensory experiences have a property of unity, and no edge separates the reader's experience of naming from her experience of doing, so that both the text's invocation of wholeness and the reader's understanding of her experiences as integrated suspend and buffer the profound divisions that the text enacts. The reader's experience of integration does not establish the subject as an isolated individual: the body, the investigation of the body, and the reader's understanding of that investigation are all understood as socially located and deeply conditioned.

Body by Marx, Body by Freud

The embodiment that *Our Bodies, Ourselves* imagined for its writers and its readers was not stable. This was not a book that needed or aspired to theoretical consistency. Instead, acts of investigation and transformation were modulated in various chapters and successive editions, opening a range of possibilities for self-understanding. In imagining different forms of subjectivity and embodiment, the collective drew on the sources available to them: in the early editions, these included Marxism and psychoanalytic theory.

These authorities may seem odd for a second-wave text; Robin Morgan's "Goodbye to All That" and Naomi Weinstein's "Psychology Constructs the Female," central documents of the movement, roundly reject Marx and Freud.[58] Neither Marx nor Freud was quoted directly in any edition of *Our Bodies, Ourselves*; neither is mentioned in the minutes of the collective. However, both Marxism and psychoanalysis were common, if disputed, points of reference within Boston Bread and Roses and in other New Left and women's liberation organizations. Both were widely understood to have elaborated a theory of subjectivity and embodiment, but to be in need of political revision: Marx, to take gender into account; Freud, to take class into account; both, to correct for misogyny. Both Marx and Freud were seen as rough indicators of the ways in which the body is modulated by practices of power: the collective used them to worry at the same questions that later scholars would address through Foucault or Butler. Second-wave feminists, including women in Bread and Roses, saw Marx and Freud as models of how collective experience and bodily subjectivity could be understood and misunderstood. Sometimes, that dialogue was hostile, barbed: Marx was blamed for the New Left's misogyny; Freud, for the sad spectacle of female domesticity. Sometimes, Freud and Marx appeared as theorists whose work could be broadened and extended to provide explanations of gender oppression and liberation. But whether or not the dialogue was hostile, these thinkers and the practices associated with them were the ground on which feminists worked to define a new understanding of embodiment: there are no feminist pamphlets titled "Accounting Constructs the Female," and Robin Morgan bid good-bye to a series of Marxist groups, not to the League of Women Voters.

Feminists worked with and against the formulations of Marxism and psychoanalysis current in intellectual and academic circles in the late 1960s. In New Left study groups and socialist schools, not to mention university courses, feminists would have encountered both the economic

Marx of "Value, Price, and Profit," and the early Marx, especially the collection known as *The Economic and Philosophic Manuscripts of 1844*, which explores the relations among labor, alienation, sensory activity, and the worker's experience of labor.[59] The psychoanalytic theory available to second-wave feminists was equally distinctive: they read, or at least referred to, Freud, but most activists were more familiar with such figures as Eric Fromm, Herbert Marcuse, and R. D. Laing. In these works, division and self-alienation was not (as in Lacan) inevitable for any subject, but a trauma inflicted on a naturally integrated subject by repressive social and familial structures.

Both Marxists and Freudians understood the body as a direct record of oppression that cut off the subject from sensory experience, integrated activity, and immediate, somatic expression of emotion. The essay on "Estranged Labor" in the 1844 *Manuscripts*, for example, discussed objectification: "The worker can create nothing without *nature*, without the *sensuous external world*. It is the material on which his labor is realized, in which it is active, from which and by means of which it produces."[60] Marx went on to say that the estrangement of the worker in the object he creates—expressed as impoverishment and dependence— meant that "the more values he creates, the more valueless, the more unworthy he becomes; the better formed his product, the more deformed becomes the worker."[61] These sentences, of course, were not on every lip in 1969, but others that echoed their themes were. Posters for the 1969 Harvard student strike, silk-screened on large newsprint sheets, included phrases such as:

Strike to seize control
Of your life strike to
become more human str
ike to return paine hall
scholarships strike be
cause there's no poetry
in your lectures[62] (line breaks in original)

The project of becoming "more human," and the hope for more poetry in the world echo Marx's claim that, "The transcendence of private property is therefore the complete *emancipation* of all human senses and

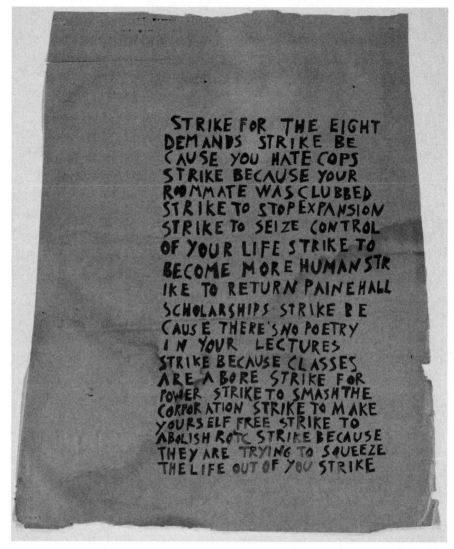

Figure 4.4. Harvard strike poster, 1969. Top width: 14"; bottom width: 16.5"; height: 20". Candib Papers, Schlesinger Library, Radcliffe Institute, Harvard University.

qualities, but it is this emancipation precisely because these senses and attributes have become, subjectively and objectively, *human*. The eye has become a *human* eye, just as its *object* has become social, *human* object—an object made by man for man."[63] Feminists would cringe at the repeated universal "man," but they would also adapt Marx's method of connecting embodied life to broad social dynamics and of placing individual actions within the context of history and culture. Marxism suggested to them that everything about our bodies—how we see, how we work—could be transformed. Whether or not they studied Marx, activists in the women's movement would have encountered representations of the body as formed by its social activity, as degraded, deformed, and blunted by the oppression of class society, and as open to transformation in a new social order.

Psychoanalysis provided the women's movement with alternate rhetorics of the body. Shulamith Firestone's *The Dialectic of Sex* was one of the earliest full-length books of feminist theory; her chapter on psychoanalysis is titled "Freudianism: The Misguided Feminism."[64] After a satirical account of American culture's love-hate relation to Freud, she concludes: "Freudianism is so charged, so impossible to repudiate because Freud grasped the crucial problem of modern life: Sexuality."[65] Other second-wave writers found R. D. Laing's theory of schizophrenic families and events convincing: Boston activist Meredith Tax, soon after her account of bodily shame, invoked Laing to explain women's reaction to objectification. Tax held that women respond to oppression by making a radical split between body and mind, leading them either to devalue their bodies or to glorify them.[66] For her, this split accounted for feminine interest in appearances, feminine socialization, and the ways in which women are "stupefied, made *stupid*, by the roles they are pushed into."[67] Tax's essay was published as a pamphlet by the New England Free Press, included in *Notes from the Second Year*, and reprinted in the influential anthology *Radical Feminism*.[68]

The discourses associated with Marxism and psychoanalysis gave members of the collective a political vocabulary for talking about the body, for understanding embodiment as a specifically feminine experience. Both Marxism and psychoanalysis made the body transparent: its specific structures and functions were translated into metaphoric interpretations, and thus they were lost to perception. A penis that has become a metaphor for male entitlement is no longer a penis. In both Marxism and psychoanalysis, and frequently in the feminist documents of the late 1960s and early 1970s, the feminine body is a negative space: the surface on which oppression is inscribed, the reified object with which a woman manages her objectification, the mystified substitute for an integrated whole person. It is not surprising that cultural feminists, later in the 1970s, countered this abstraction with representations of the female body as productive, natural, and mysterious.

The women's movement parsed the analytic statements of Marxism and psychoanalysis programmatically. Their work would be to show how the body was shaped by social relations and to change both the body and the culture it inhabited. The project began with an investigation that raised the transparent, abstracted body into materiality, naming its parts and describing its functions. This investigation, it was hoped, would initiate the reader into integrated self-understanding. Instead of a "stupefied" experience of the body as an external object, a source of guilt and anxiety, the collective proposed an attitude of curious exploration, punctuated with wonder, moving from the exterior of the body to its internal organs. Instead of passively receiving information from a physician, women would investigate themselves and learn things that their doctors could never know. New knowledge would support a general refunctioning of the body; no longer the ground of oppression, it would become the guarantee of a new gender identity and the ground of a new sense of self-worth.

The collective described this self-worth with terms like "wholeness" and "overcoming division," terms drawn from writers like Laing and Fromm. The investigation they proposed required a complex splitting and realignment of the subject; the experience they sponsored was not one of seamless integration but of reafferent self-reflection. This investigation affirmed female embodiment as the basis of a political identity as well as the mark of gender oppression. If other Boston feminist groups, like Cell 16, saw the feminine body as in need of transformation—women needed karate classes, for example, to make them stronger and more assertive—the Boston Women's Health Book Collective advocated a transformation of the afferent system. Women's bodies would not visibly change, although they might become healthier; what would be transformed was women's understanding of themselves as spectators of the body. Instead of exigent judges, they would become investigators. Instead of searching for surface flaws, they would discern the subtle workings of interior organs.

For activists in the women's movement and for the collective in particular, both the "objectified" experience of an oppressed female body and the transformed experience of the known and awakened body were conditioned by power. Contemporary readers are likely to frame this understanding in terms drawn from Foucault, surely the leading late twentieth-century theorist of the body and power. For such readers, the continual invocation of external compulsion in *Our Bodies, Ourselves* seems dated—"we are told" and "we are taught" appear on nearly every page of these early editions. Contemporary cultural theory has accepted Foucault's analysis of power as constituting the subject through disciplines of the body, rather than as something exercised over a previously existing autonomous subject. Or, as Judith Butler put it: "Power that at first appears external, pressed upon the subject, pressing the subject into subordination, assumes a psychic form that constitutes the subject's self-identity." For Butler, "turning back upon oneself" is not a reafferent process that offers emancipation; it is implicated with self-consciousness, with the Nietzchean bad conscience.[69] It was exactly this bad conscience, of course, that *Our Bodies, Ourselves* undertook to rectify. Rather than constructing an interiority based on guilt and self-reproach, the text sought to soothe the reader's monitoring of the surfaces of the body, prompting her instead to investigate its interior spaces. The anatomical knowledge that comes to light in these investigations is secondary to the reader seeing herself as an agent who produces knowledge of, and sensation in, her body. Self-examination reinscribes the body that had been relentlessly sexualized within the socially powerful (and less overtly sexualized) registers of science. It then recruits the reader to a feminist critique of medicine that consolidates and generalizes her reinscription, so that she redirects the constituting power that had established her feminine subjectivity in relation to her objectified body. Such a reading subject is both expressive of and excessive to her own constituting act of subordination. The early editions of *Our Bodies, Ourselves* imagined a subjectivity that opened every kind of bodily experience—orgasm, menopause, childbirth—to reflection and transformation. Although these writers anticipated a Foucauldian world, they did not inhabit it in Foucauldian terms.

This, at least, was the plan. There were moments in the text when the divided subject was simply a vehicle for a new level of judgment, when feminist consciousness was recuperated to something like Nietzschean self-consciousness. The identification of the body with the self was, for the collective, an achievement of feminist consciousness: "our bodies, ourselves" was a fact that they had triumphantly created.

We are our bodies. Our book celebrates this simple fact.[70]

Knowing that we're coming to feel our bodies as ourselves feels great![71]

This assertion of agency against an external power could, however, implicate the writers in subtle forms of bad conscience:

How can I explain it? It gets to you, it is you! We have this notion that mind and body are separate—but how can you feel good in the head, really, if your body's like a limp rag? Before, my body would embarrass me—do clumsy things, because there wasn't a lot of muscular control, or it wouldn't do much at all. Now that I exercise, I'm happier about my body, it acts and reacts in ways that please me—it's stronger, more real, more energetic.[72]

This opening of the 1973 "Women in Motion" chapter constructs relationships between "the body" and "me" (or "you"). The body is identified with the self, but insecurely and partially. The self is embarrassed by the body, or pleased with the body; her embarrassment and pleasure are linked in a narrative of self-improvement. The chapter echoes a basic trope of advertising: "I used to hate my x. Then I used product y, so now I'm happy with my x." This speaker expects to control her body, and she seems puzzled when it fecklessly goes off on its own, doing clumsy things, or failing her when she needs it. Her body can be more or less "real." The mind complicates the relation between body and self, since it haunts them both, and is the source of feeling, emotion, and judgment. The mind readjusts the relationship between self and body, approves of the transformed body. It is, somehow, not quite the body: the body begins below the neck. Reafference, in this case effected through movement and exercise, establishes the mind as an honest broker between self and body. As the agent of reafference, the mind monitors the self's investigation and transformation of the body. Whether reafference mitigated a bodily bad conscience or established a new relationship between the subject and embodiment, the circuits it established had to be rewired when difference emerged as a central theme within the women's movement. The reader was no longer understood as a generic woman seeing herself in "that first tentative look." She was positioned as a member of a certain group of women, with specific racial and class experiences, considering her own embodiment. For the collective, this modulation enacted the melancholy loss of a particular self that had briefly offered the promise of both agency and full self-representation. As the collective discovered that its own political conscience was vexed by issues of race and class, reafference became self-reproach: to look at one's body was no longer simply to replace the sexualized body with a domain of wonder, but to find a body marked by privileges of race and class, a body that had to be worked up into universal femininity through a series of accommodations. The collective's acknowledgment of race and class was necessary and productive; there was no way for them to continue their work, let alone to build ties with international women's groups, without accounting for their own position. But, like the metalepsis that opened the boundaries of the text in early editions, reafference did not survive this relocation. The lost universal feminine subject is both a sign of the collective's initial errors, the mark of its implication with the oppressive structures of race and class, and a sign of utopian possibilities it has lost. That universal feminine subject was both hated and loved; it became a spectral feminine self, global and endlessly differentiated. In the real world of the text, that feminine body is marked by wrenching divisions of privilege and oppression, divisions that must be repudiated; only as a future creation of global feminism can it be beloved. Thus, the earnest avowals of a passage like this one, from the 1998 edition:

Learning to accept and love our bodies and ourselves is an important and difficult ongoing struggle. But to change the societal values underlying body image, we need to do more than love ourselves. We need to focus our attention on the forces that drive wedges between us as women: racism, sexism, ableism, ageism, and our national obsession with size and shape. To truly create change, to create a world in which all women can make choices about our appearances for ourselves and not others, we must incorporate all women into the heart of how we see ourselves. From this expanded horizon of sisterhood, we may begin to value the lives of women who previously meant nothing to us.[73]

It is a little chilling to see the writers of *Our Bodies, Ourselves* characterize themselves as in need of political education to value the lives of women; the impossible embodiment that this passage imagines reinscribes the collective's initial rejection of the split subject into a rejection of all forms of social division. The utopian hope and universal energy remain, but not the joyful appropriation of the body's interior, and certainly not the liberation from self-consciousness.

The multiple vocabularies that the collective used and the complex political project that they undertook shaped their understanding of the body in other contradictory ways, beginning with the title of their book. The change from *Women and Their Bodies* to *Our Bodies, Ourselves* is part of the story the collective tells about itself, but the smaller change from *Our Bodies, Our Selves* (1971) to *Our Bodies, Ourselves* (1973) passed without comment. When asked about it in interviews, collective members remembered a change, but not who initiated it or why. *Our selves* and *ourselves* are quite different words: the *our* in *our selves* is possessive, suggesting an impossible relationship between a preexisting collective *we* and a group of individual, but linked *selves*. *Ourselves* is an intensifier—*we ourselves will do this* work—or a reflexive—*we defend ourselves*. (A Google search of all six reflexive pronouns—a crude but interesting measure of frequency—shows that *ourselves* is the least common of them. Of the 84 million odd instances of *ourselves* that turned up in a recent search, roughly 1.9 million are variations of the phrase *our x, ourselves*—conscious or unconscious invocations of the phrase *our bodies, ourselves*.) The title *Our Bodies, Ourselves* has several senses: our bodies are really ourselves; we are most ourselves when we are our bodies; our bodies are both the subjects and the objects of this book. The reflexive pronoun evoked the text's performance of reafference, the experience of the body investigating itself—or, more properly, of women investigating themselves.

That self-investigation could be both pressing and vexed, as in this description of a divided body from the 1973 edition:

Sex has to do with the body—that alien part of us residing below the neck that has needs and responses we don't understand. But our feelings reside in our bodies. Fears make their presence felt by our pounding heart, our chest caved in, our stomach turning. Joy is tingly—our head feels a little light, our fingers and toes sort of shimmer and the rest of us feels warm and all in one piece. For some of us anger feels like a pounding in the head, hands tighten and clench, and so on. When you feel these feelings, or any others, try to stop and feel them in your body—below the neck as well as above it.[74]

Emotions are internal objects, even internal agents, expressed in a bodily language that the reader is encouraged to learn. Bodily sensations are modeled on the structures of language: they form a shared system of significance, since we all have the same pounding heart, the same shimmering toes; that system also admits variation, since some of us have a pounding head. The subject includes both a "self" and a "body," but she is inhabited by various other entities: feelings that "reside" in her, but also the part of herself that might "try" to feel the bodily expressions of emotion. Emotion is an anima, a spirit inhabiting the body that "makes its presence felt" from time to time, but is otherwise silent and inaccessible. This reafferent self is to be sought out and cultivated: "It's one way of getting more in touch with you."[75] The body—at least the body "below the neck"—is the self, but can only be understood as the self by a transformed consciousness. Investigating the body is a joint project of reader and writer: the first draft of the manuscript includes the invitation, "We hope you learn something from this paper. If you already know more than we do, we hope you write it down."[76]

The transformed body would support the reader—as it had supported the writers—in a practice of autonomy. In the early editions, feelings of dependence and inadequacy were associated with bodily shame, with inactivity: "There were many factors that affected our capacity to act. For one, the ideal woman does less and less as her class status rises. Most of us, being middle-class, were brought up not to do very much."[77] Productive activity, as well as vigorous physical labor and play, were associated with masculinity; women would take on these modes of embodiment, practicing androgyny:

We tried to incorporate within us the capacity to do more "male" product-oriented activity. Our motivation to write this book falls into that category. . . . We became more and more motivated to work hard on our ideas—to refine them, to clarify them, and to present them in a form that would be accessible to other women. . . . Along with our more task-oriented activity comes a new sense of wanting to succeed. . . . This ties in with our new sense of pride—feeling proud of what we do.[78]

Masculine pride in activity and achievement was balanced by a feminine commitment to collaboration, to self-care, and to pleasure in work. Since choice was a central concept for the collective, it is not surprising that autonomy was expressed as the ability to choose—to adopt or refuse masculine modes of embodiment and activity, to focus on work or relationships: "We realized that we could survive on our own and that until we felt confident of our ability to feel like separate people and take on the freedom and responsibility of being adults, we were not free to live with one another out of choice."[79] Autonomy, individual self-sufficiency, and embodied activity supported a new collective identity, an identification with a newly constructed universal womanhood. The collective modeled that identification: "We are both a very ordinary and a very special group, as women are everywhere."[80] Autonomy was the basis for both collective rights and individual participation in collectivities. As the first sentences of the 1976 "Abortion" chapter read, "One of our most fundamental rights as women is the right to choose whether and when to have children. Only when we are in control of that choice are we free to be all that we can be for ourselves, for children we already have or may have in the future, for our partners, for our communities."[81]

Pregnancy: Autonomy and Its Limits

Individual autonomous agency and group identity were both tightly compacted in reproductive politics. Pregnancy, the prevention and termination of pregnancy, childbirth, and the postpartum period were all crises of autonomy, junctures where a woman was called upon to exercise agency through repeated acts of choice. They were also demonstrations of universal femininity, showing that bodies "all worked the same." This dual sense was most fully expressed in the 1984 *New Our Bodies, Ourselves*, when the collective had the time and resources to express its understanding of embodiment, and when they were coming to terms with identity politics. The chapter on pregnancy in that edition was cowritten by Jane Pincus, a founder and the overall editor of that edition; Norma Swenson, who came to the collective in 1973 after years of experience with the International Childbirth Education Association, having served as president of that organization; and Mary (Bebe) Poor, an expert in public health with a focus on maternal and children's issues and a longtime collaborator with the collective. A close reading of these chapters and an analysis of notes that led to their composition, generously made available by Jane Pincus, shows the complex linkages between agency and universality that the collective was constructing, linkages connected to issues of reafference. The chapters on pregnancy and childbirth were the longest and most detailed in the central section on childbearing in the 1984 edition. The pregnancy chapter is profusely illustrated with dramatic photographs of pregnant women and drawings that show the progress of pregnancy. Pregnant women are photographed naked and clothed, surrounded by family and friends; the drawings by Nina Reimer follow the collective's conventions of showing the whole body, including the face. The chapter is rich in personal accounts; the ramified structure of the narrative includes many women's voices, often reporting divergent experiences or desires:

We're having a home birth with a very fine midwife. The more I learn, the more I'm sure that's what I want.

I chose the hospital because I wanted the whole experience to be separate from the rest of my life, and I felt safest there.[82]

The rivers of text that characterized the first three editions of *Our Bodies, Ourselves* have been broken up and articulated: medical information is often summarized into tables, such as the one titled, "Tests During Pregnancy"; historical sidelights are presented in boxes.[83] Parts of the chapter are designed as "takealongs" that a reader can carry to prenatal appointments: a list of questions for caregivers, a list of interventions for labor pain. Other portions of the text are boxed and written in capitals: the boxes warn women against the lithotomy position or advise them not to worry about weight gain during pregnancy.

The text of this chapter continually invokes the autonomy of the pregnant woman: "Though your pregnancy will have much in common with other women's, it is yours and unique (and each pregnancy you go through will differ from the others)."[84] Elsewhere, the text speaks of "an autonomous labor" as a goal of pregnancy.[85] Autonomy, as elsewhere in *Our Bodies, Ourselves*, is organized by women's choices, although the book is frank in recognizing that choice has both geographic and temporal boundaries. Choices are most commonly available in "a narrow, concentrated band in suburbs and edges of cities," and they are thin on the ground in inner cities or rural areas.[86] In the world of this text, choices are made by individuals, each reflexively for herself, but they are secured by collective action. The reader is urged both to exercise her own powers of choice and to work with others to expand their range:

If you do have real choices where you live, learn as much as you can. Ask yourself, what is most important? Where and with whom will you feel most secure? You are the only one who can decide.

When we understand these limits [on choice] we can work for the changes that make *real* choices possible.[87]

The events of pregnancy posed particular problems for this approach, since reproductive events are open to intentionality in limited ways, but offer deep experiences of agency. If agency is defined by choice—as it certainly was for these writers—how can it be expressed by carrying a fetus, which offers few points of decision? If agency is understood as autonomy—as it certainly was for these writers—how can it be expressed in a process directed and conditioned by the needs of another? These contradictions were worked out in the text in two ways: by encouraging women to align themselves consciously with the physical processes they were undergoing, often through some reafferent process of self-monitoring, and by encouraging them to resist medical interference with "normal" reproductive processes. The opening paragraph of the "Pregnancy" chapter expresses compactly the connection between reafference and resistance to medical interference:

Prenatal care means caring for yourself. We no longer believe that it is enough just to "see the doctor regularly" or "leave it all to the doctor." When you visit your practitioner (doctor or midwife) every month and then every week, s/he is simply monitoring the care you give yourself. When you have conditions which require watching or medical attention, you especially need to care for yourself to keep in top shape and minimize complications. Caring for yourself means that your good mothering has already begun.[88]

Self-care is the alternative to the system of medical monitoring: to take up the regime of self-care is to cultivate reafference; "caring for yourself" exfoliates into a range of reflexive activities that bring the reader to terms with the complex, divided, pregnant body: "It is essential to eat well during pregnancy. Think of it as eating for yourself—when you are healthy, most likely the baby will be healthy, too. And think of it as eating for three—you, your baby, and the placenta which links you together, through which your baby receives all its nourishment."[89] Conventional medical care, described in later chapters as forming a "climate of doubt," is seen as a parody and reversal of the attentive mother's self-monitoring. Rigid external guidelines for weight gain during pregnancy or the length of time a woman is permitted to labor erase her autonomous individuality; by comparing her to an artificial average, they make it impossible for a woman to have "her own" pregnancy and labor.

In these passages in *Our Bodies, Ourselves*, Pincus, Swenson, and other members of the collective both anticipated and corrected twenty-first century theories of embodiment, particularly those proposed by Elizabeth Grosz. The body found in this text is, with all its contradictions, very close to that projected in Grosz's *Volatile Bodies*: "Human bodies have irreducible neurophysiological and psychological dimensions whose relations remain unknown and . . . human bodies have the wonderful ability, while striving for integration and cohesion, organic and psychic wholeness, to also provide for and indeed produce fragmentations, fracturings, dislocations that orient bodies and body parts toward other bodies and body parts."[90]

Our Bodies, Ourselves assumes a divided, looped, reafferent subject who is the investigator of her own body, or who segments her body into invisible parts that mapped uncertainly onto its visible surface even as she invokes experiences of wholeness. The body that the text advocated was natural and organic, but the body they constructed was much more complex. The writers affirmed that their experiences brought them closer to other women, to women different from themselves whose "bodies worked the same." This body, offered to readers in *Our Bodies, Ourselves*, was both divided and integrated, both individual and collective, and it anticipated feminist theory by some forty years. Grosz's understanding of "double sensation," the body's perception of itself through its own touch on the skin, as the basis of ego formation is a localization and thinking through of the reafferent experiments that *Our Bodies, Ourselves* invited its readers to undertake. While Grosz sees all "double sensation" as modeled on touch, the discussion of the clitoris in the "Anatomy" chapter of *Our Bodies, Ourselves* suggests that touch and vision reinforce each other in the subject's movement from the skin surface to internal organs.[91] While Grosz sees investment in body parts and judgment of them as necessarily entailed in the subject's investment in her own ego, *Our Bodies, Ourselves* offers a model of ego-formation in which the subject invests in her own understanding of the presumably normal functioning of her invisible, but partially palpable, internal organs. The collective propagated a benign hysteria, an attempt to realign the imaginary anatomy of a generation.

While the project of the Boston Women's Health Book Collective anticipates, to some extent, Elizabeth Grosz's theoretical work, it also offers an alternative to her Deleuzean account of the feminine body. *Volatile Bodies*, like much of Grosz's subsequent work, was directed to a project of reclaiming the body as the ground of ego identity, offering a corrective to the Cartesian subject, split between the mind and an abjected body. Grosz's reader comes to a new way of acting through a new understanding of her subjectivity. The reader of *Our Bodies, Ourselves* is prompted to a course of action that will lead her to understand herself differently. This distinction is subtle, since the acts that *Our Bodies, Ourselves* sponsors include reading, talking, and looking at pictures—actions that are sometimes seen as inconsequential. Attention to the texture of this activity offers an alternative to the reification of flow and viscosity in *Visible Bodies*; Grosz writes as if agency and the bounded object were incompatible, as if individuals could find new ways of being only in the absence of definable structures. *Our Bodies, Ourselves* offers an alternative: structures are explored; new boundaries take the place of commonsense conventions; flows and movements are monitored reafferently.

In other ways, Grosz's theoretical project corrects and supplements what is contradictory in *Our Bodies, Ourselves*. The rhetoric of second-wave feminism could treat the body as an object owned by an autonomous subject who exercised rights over it: "Get your laws off my body," was an early pro-choice slogan. *Our Bodies, Ourselves* sometimes used this language to support a program of feminine autonomy, extending it, in the 1984 pregnancy chapter, to describe the relation between a woman and the developing fetus. This language was at odds with the text's sense of the body and the subject as continuously linked in complex reafferent loops, in reflexive relations of causality and mutual implication. The collective wrote about a porous body, but they thought they were asserting the monologic sovereignty of the choosing self over the body, seen as an object of possession. Grosz demonstrates that the body is not available for possession.

In discussing textuality in *Our Bodies, Ourselves*, I have named the text's relation of reader to writer as metaleptic: the text continually breaks its frame, reaches outside of itself. A similar relationship is invoked in the term "reafferent": the text invites a woman to investigate herself, to perceive herself as being investigated, and to assume the identity of the investigating subject. In both metalepsis and reafference, identity is split and spread over a number of locations: it is located in the text, in the text's excessive movement outside itself, in the bodily sensations prompted by the text, and in the self-understanding of the subject as occupying the newly understood body and its internal spaces. The movement of the investigating subject mirrors and repeats the movement of the mobile text. The collective insisted that the act of writing a book refunctioned their own gender identity: it gave them access to satisfactions that had been seen as particularly masculine, and it connected them to forms of feminine embodiment that had seemed alien. The gendered body produced by this book is not the simple binary body of the reproductive life cycle, although the collective was certainly interested in that narrative. It was a wandering body, both bounded and surprising: temporarily stabilized in a text or a diagram, it could emerge at any moment into a practice of vision, of "that first tentative look." The body was investigated in total privacy, but the investigated body took its place in an expansive and potentially transformed social order. The reading subject, who takes up the book in anxiety and confusion, is offered many ways of being at ease. She can appropriate the voice of the text; she can find in its pages a workable objectification of her body; she can align herself with its project of communal transformation.

All of these positions, of course, express the possibilities of a particular time and a particular social formation. Nothing that the collective wrote was intended to endure forever, or to work for all women everywhere. It is quite likely that *Our Bodies, Ourselves* and its characteristic figures no longer offer a release from anxiety, no longer model a form of embodiment that is new. This very thinning-out of the text is, in many ways, a sign of its success: just as we take it for granted that health information for women should be freely available, we understand our own embodiment as an experience to be investigated. But what has also changed for us, in the years since the first editions of the text, is the development of a new medical practice, more scientific and also more corporate. Did the early editions of *Our Bodies, Ourselves*, confronting a professionalized medicine that was not yet corporate, offer any models for understanding these practices?

5   Taking on Medicine

Origins

Members of the Boston Women's Health Book Collective (BWHBC) tell different stories about their earliest engagement with conventional medicine. One story, told in the 1973 preface to *Our Bodies, Ourselves*, begins with the workshop on Women and Their Bodies at the 1969 Emmanuel Female Liberation Conference. There, women decided to collect information on local doctors so that they could recommend those who treated women well. This "Doctor's Group" circulated questionnaires; when they collated the results, they found that one woman's sympathetic physician had been another woman's insensitive nightmare. They concluded that, since the search for an individual accommodation was fruitless, they should teach themselves what they needed to know to promote their own health and initiated the health course and the health books. This story is certainly true, but it is only one version of the collective's origin. It is attested by Jane Pincus's private papers, which include copies of the questionnaire that the group circulated asking for women's experiences with their doctors and for their recommendations. The leaflet reads in part:

When we go to doctors we are in the most literal sense committing our bodies to them, entrusting them with decisions about both bodies and minds which we should at the very least take part in making.

Going to doctors is a private act: we hear of someone, we go alone and we are treated in isolation. . . . We've got to get beyond the mystique of the doctor as the ultimate authority over our bodies and minds, and we need to think more clearly about what we should expect of him and what we need to do ourselves.[1]

The questionnaire was a first step to compiling a list of doctors that could lead to collective action against abusive individual doctors and medical institutions. Like the student evaluations of university teachers just coming into use, often outside official university channels, the questions posed by the Doctor's Group offered women a chance to talk back, to judge the professionals who so often had judged them. The intent of the questionnaire was not simply to reward the good and expose the bad, but to bring into the public sphere what had been a private relationship, to open the examining room to collective understanding and action. This origin story is reflected in the earliest editions of *Our Bodies, Ourselves*, which focus on the relationships between individual women and their physicians. Advice about talking to doctors was plentiful, as were anecdotes of disastrous conversations.

Another story about the collective's origin is told in the documentary record, which shows that the "Doctor's Group" project was not abandoned for study and health classes. Women in the collective continued the project of sorting out the good docs from the bad while they were offering the first, transformative, health class. The Boston *Women's Liberation Newsletter*, a jumbo fold-out circular set up for wall posting, carried announcements for meetings of a "Doctor's Project" through the summer, fall, and winter 1969.[2] These announcements ask women to fill out questionnaires and to help compile results.

In a third story of the collective's origin, the survey of doctors was never a compelling project. When Vilunya Diskin and Paula Doress-Worters spoke with me together about the first years of the collective, Diskin began to tell the story of the "Doctor's Group"—and who better to do so, since she was listed as their public contact?—when Doress-Worters interrupted: "It wasn't called 'The Doctor's Group.' I know you always say that. It was called 'Women in Control of Our Bodies,' and the two focuses were on birth control and childbirth."[3] These three stories express the collective's desires at once to enter the house of medicine and take it over, and to remain firmly outside of it. Their ambivalence worked itself out most profoundly in their writing: it would shape the complex negotiations of medical discourse that marked *Our Bodies, Ourselves* from the earliest editions through the major revision in 1984. The language of *Our Bodies, Ourselves* transformed medical discourse into something colloquial, metaleptic, and mobile. It entered the medical register, took it over, and also maintained critical distance from it.

Members of the collective saw themselves as both good scientists and critics of science. They insisted on their right to medical knowledge and made their own raids into the territory, seizing both the language and the understanding of the body that characterized medicine in the 1960s. This moment of the collective's project is expressed in the 1970 and 1971 anatomy chapters, bristling with technical language, deploying embryological evidence, presenting a body of cavities, organs, and tissues, each clearly named and demarcated. Women are urged to adopt this powerful objectification of the body in order to "overcome objectification."[4] Knowledge of anatomy would give women tools to combat the imposition of medical knowledge, would dismantle the doctor's right to proclaim what was happening in the body of a female patient. Knowledge of medicine, particularly knowledge of medical vocabulary, was a practice of power: "We have been ignorant of how our bodies function and this enables males, particularly professionals, to play upon us for money and experiments, and to intimidate us in doctors' offices and clinics of every kind."[5] To claim medical language was to claim autonomy and agency: as Wendy Coppedge Sanford, longtime editor of *Our Bodies, Ourselves* put it, using technical language was "a matter of pride."[6] In later editions, medical terminology was less prominent; the text also reworked the characteristic syntax of medical writing.

The collective further proposed a project of correcting medicine, of bringing women's particular modes of embodiment and their experiences of reproductive life to bear on medical knowledge. This correction required, first of all, a demystification of the physician, one of the last bastions of traditional authority in the late 1960s. Lucy Candib, writer of the chapter on medicine and capitalism, understood demystification as corrective to undue deference: "Left wing people had all this great criticism of government and but had totally conventional ideas about doctors. And that would blow me away, because the doctors thing was just as bad as the war thing and they hadn't figured it out."[7] The collective castigated conventional medicine as "bad science" that could become better by listening to women.[8] One attempt to correct this bad science was the collective's research project, the Menopause Survey of 1973. They reasoned that doctors viewed menopause as a health problem because they saw only those women who had troublesome symptoms. A survey would uncover a broader, more positive, range of experiences: "Most research has been done on 'clinical samples'—that is, on the minority of women who have chosen or been forced to seek medical care because of the severity of their symptoms. Consequently we know very little about what menopause is like for all the women who never seek medical help."[9] The collective distributed menopause questionnaires to two thousand women of all ages, asking about their symptoms, response to medical treatment, and experience of menopause. Responses gave them the "privilege of hearing the voices of many women talking about this experience which society presents so negatively"; the majority were neutral or positive about the experience of menopause.[10] The 1973 and 1976 editions summarized the collective's results. While they would never organize another substantial research project, successive editions of *Our Bodies, Ourselves* emphasized the need for woman-centered medical research: "Most nonreproductive medical research is done only on men and the results are applied to women. Such a process is . . . far from 'scientific.' Despite the fact that women make up the greater number of patients, most research, in nutrition and drugs, for example, is conducted on men. One result: women do not know the real benefits and risks of drugs they take."[11] The collective was generous in reporting on other women's clinical projects. West Coast women's clinics began to teach and practice menstrual extraction: the uterus was emptied through a sterile tube, giving women control over their menstrual periods and also a technique for very early abortion. (Many physicians considered menstrual extraction dangerous, and women's clinics generally taught the practice only to stable groups who could take proper precautions.) In some early editions of *Our Bodies, Ourselves*, menstrual extraction was discussed in general terms and presented as a promising example of feminist clinical research: women who investigated their bodies, the book suggested, would produce better, safer medicine.

All editions of *Our Bodies, Ourselves* emphasized that medical care in the United States is highly stratified by race and class; the 1984 edition gives detailed information on race, class, and medicine, and extends this analysis to a discussion of global issues in women's healthcare. Beginning in 1984, *Our Bodies, Ourselves* began to express a broad feminist critique of the central authority of medicine: "Our critique of medicine has taken on a new dimension. We see basic errors in its fundamental assumptions about health and healing. Although conventional medical care may at times be just what we need, in many situations it may be bad for our health because it emphasizes drugs, surgery, psychotherapy (especially for women) and crisis action rather than prevention."[12] Characteristically, the collective initiated this critique by proposing a term new to their readers: "healthism," the medicalization of women's lives. In the introductory chapter, they argued that instead of relying on medicine to keep them healthy, women should be encouraged to see what they could do for themselves and each other.[13]

From the Politics of Medicine to Medicine as Politics

By embarking on a broad critique of medicine, *Our Bodies, Ourselves* opened ground that would be explored by later feminist theories of the body and other political theories of embodiment and subjection. The collective realigned the relations among science, politics, and embodiment, undertaking a particular kind of textual work and writing these connections in a new way; its work intersects with Giorgio Agamben's theory of embodiment and politics. Agamben focuses on the *homo sacer,* the representative of "bare life" who stands outside the relations of citizenship but constitutes them by exclusion. Agamben argues that, in the Athenian polis, "bare life," the experience of *zoe*, was not of interest; the city-state was only concerned with a "good life," the significant civic engagement of the citizen. Language marks the difference between "bare life" and "the good life." Agamben writes, "There is politics because man is the living being who, in language, separates and opposes himself to his own bare life and, at the same time, maintains himself in relation to that bare life in an inclusive exclusion."[14] For Agamben, modernity brings "bare life" within the ambit of political power by regulating individual bodies. The *homo sacer* begins as a criminal who, under Greek law, could not be executed but whom anyone was allowed to kill, and ends as the modern subject, "born free," the bearer of rights and citizenship. Surely the process is even more complex than Agamben admits: the "man" who enjoyed citizenship in the polis was not a generic human being, but quite specifically a male citizen; the process of associating citizenship with bare life was also a process of uncoupling citizenship from masculinity. Today, the carrier of bare life is often a *femina sacra*, a woman whose engagement with biomedicine strips her of autonomy. Language practices "separating and opposing" subjects from their embodiment are central means of disseminating sacred life into feminine bodies.

Since democratic citizenship does not simply release the subject into autonomy, but rather integrates him into the many-sided relationships of domination that characterize modernity, opening citizenship to women did not end male domination. In both the United States and Britain, the nineteenth century saw a long process of dissociating masculinity from citizenship and of associating it instead with science.[15] Science offered a repertoire of values and practices essential to democracy: disinterested research, willingness to set aside tradition, merit-based competition. Medicine was critical to that process: the medical concepts of infection and contagion provided a rationale for the regulation of bodies; the endlessly replicated relationship between doctor and patient brought each individual into a regularizing relationship with ideas of normalcy and health.

For most of the nineteenth and twentieth centuries, the cultural roles of doctor and patient were coded as male and female, although many women practiced medicine and many men consulted physicians. Physicians regulated women's speech about their bodies; women were positioned as the reluctant objects of regulation. Physicians valued women's silence as a sign of the general submissiveness that should mark all patients; they celebrated it as an expression of feminine modesty; they regularly sought to violate it in the interests of accurate diagnosis. In the consulting room, whether she wanted to remain silent (but was induced to speak), or wanted to discuss her illness (but was required to limit herself to replies to the doctor's queries), a woman's speech was constrained. Thus, the Code of Medical Ethics adopted in Philadelphia in 1847 counseled women against allowing "feelings of shame or delicacy to prevent their disclosing the seat, symptoms, and causes of complaints peculiar to them."[16] Thus, Charles Meigs, the Philadelphia physician, routinely praised women's reticence in his lectures to students: "I confess I am proud to say that in this country generally, certainly in many parts of it, there are women who prefer to suffer the extremity of danger and pain rather than wave those scruples of delicacy which prevent their maladies from being explored. I say it is fully an evidence of the dominion of a fine morality in our society."[17] Meigs connected feminine silence to the manners of "this country especially"—masculine citizenship, no longer defined by women's invisibility, was now guaranteed by feminine silence; feminine embodiment was a domain of knowledge and regulation.

The twentieth century had seen its share of challenges to these arrangements, but when the women of the collective entered public life, physician's authority had been reinforced by a postwar affirmation of professional expertise. During the baby boom, pregnancy and childbirth were highly regulated and medicalized. The *Better Homes and Gardens Baby Book* (1943, 1946, 1951, 1963), a popular health guide for pregnant women in the postwar period, urged early prenatal care, not as a health measure, but as a way of saving the doctor's time: "Serious complications, which might have been avoided by early diagnosis, are a much greater drain upon your doctor's time and strength, and upon hospital and nursing resources, than routine examinations and a normal delivery."[18] Physicians regulated pregnancy and birth; the reader was promised that the doctor would "manage your life so you'll remain comfortable and happy."[19] While the book passed over childbirth in silence, it recommended that mothers trust (but not bother) their doctors to direct care of the newborn: "If there are any nursing or feeding difficulties he'll know just what to do."[20] While this text is more structured than Dr. Spock's— there is a section titled "Discipline Begins at Birth"—it illustrates the mid-twentieth-century understanding of medical care for women as an exercise in the doctor's careful management of his patient's diet, schedule, hygiene, and mental attitude.[21] The role of the patient was to comply, to ask intelligent questions, and to avoid wasting the doctor's time; the role of the doctor was to correct the mother's ignorance and indulgence. These roles were seen as politically consequential: "The future of our nation depends on a coming generation that will be healthy, vigorous, and intelligent."[22] The authority of the physician shored up institutions of citizenship and subjection; the Boston Women's Health Book Collective challenged those institutions.

Their first problem was lack of information: when *Our Bodies, Ourselves* was first published, the popular press did not routinely offer stories about medicine. Media coverage of the birth control pill, for example, focused on the significance of the pill or on public reaction to it, but rarely gave details about how it worked. The *New York Times* printed some 444 articles on birth control pills between its report, in 1954, of a speech by John Rock predicting that a birth control pill was likely to be developed soon, and May 1969, the date of the Emmanuel Conference. These articles focused on the political and social implications of the birth control pill: Would it end overpopulation? Poverty? Would the Catholic Church oppose it? It was not until January 1966 that one of Jane Brody's first articles for the *Times* gave a physiological account of how birth control pills worked.[23] A somewhat more detailed account was published in the *Times* Sunday magazine in 1966, but even the most devoted follower of America's newspaper of record would not have found an explanation of how the pill worked as simple, detailed, and readable as the one given in the 1970 *Women and Their Bodies*.[24] No wonder the production of birth control manuals was a cottage industry at college campuses, beginning with the McGill *Birth Control Handbook*, in its fourth edition in 1970; similar manuals were produced at Boston University, the University of Colorado at Boulder, the University of North Carolina, the University of Washington, University of California at Berkeley, North Carolina State, and Yale. The pamphlets were short (twenty to sixty-four pages) and cheap (between ten cents at Boston and a dollar at Yale).[25] Other mass media did better than the *Times*: *Good Housekeeping* would publish regular updates on the pill, and readers of *Mademoiselle* in 1961 could have found an early article on the subject by Ellen Willis.[26]

The BWHBC collected information from conventional sources, but insisted that women should not take it at face value. After recommending some inexpensive pamphlets produced by Tampax, Ortho, and Planned Parenthood, the first edition of *Women and Their Bodies* warned women to read critically: "Don't forget that Ortho and Tampax are capitalist organizations, pushing their own products for profit; nevertheless, their educational departments put out some excellent stuff. Planned Parenthood pushes population control and birth control pills."[27] While the first editions of *Our Bodies, Ourselves* focused on the relationship between a woman and her physician, the text recognized that this relationship was mediated by other institutions and organizations. The discussion of birth control pills placed the physician in the context of government regulatory agencies and of drug companies:

The drug companies' cover-up of the hazards of the pill was evident in the patient pamphlets which distorted or denied known risks. Now after the pill has been in use for ten years in this country the FDA is finally urging doctors that they disclose to their patients the warnings, adverse reactions and counter indications. Most doctors, in fact, do not take the time to discuss with their patients the counter indications or inform them of all the other possible birth control methods available.[28]

These sources of information were to be compared with, and judged against, women's own experience. The discussion of birth control pills in the 1970 edition exemplifies how complex the category of "experience" was. The reafferent and metaleptic rhetorics of *Our Bodies, Ourselves* placed a woman's experience of her body in the context of many other self-investigating bodies; the individual body was expanded and dispersed: "Instead of relying solely on doctors we must rely on ourselves, our feelings, our experiences and those of other women."[29] In invoking "our experiences," the collective was not suggesting that women intuit whether the pill was good for them, or that they should take it and see how it felt. "Experience" did not invoke an intuitive, unreflective hunch, but a deliberate process of discernment, education, and critical reflection on many sources of information, including conventional medicine. The text specified issues that women should consider, including benign cysts, family history of cancer, fibroid tumors, possible loss of sexual desire, and the danger of depression. A woman who carefully investigated all of these contraindications would still need to talk with family members, consult her physician, and gauge the warning signs of anxiety and depression. These activities would increase her autonomy and enable her to make an informed decision; they would also integrate her into the clinical style and language of medicine. If a woman decided, after investigation, to take the pill, *Women and Their Bodies* recommended that she have a long conversation with her doctor, and that she research the chemical composition of the specific pill she was prescribed: "Insist that your doctor discuss with you the composition of the particular brand he is prescribing."[30] In this text, the reader's self-education balances the physician's reluctance to describe possible side-effects and the drug company's policy of minimizing them. The reader is learning to see her body and to read her body with medical eyes. Even if the language she uses to describe what she sees is quite different from conventional medical discourse, she writes herself into that discourse on terms that seem to be her own. This practice of mediating experience, the collective felt, was its distinct contribution to women's health. As early as 1973, when the collective discussed its relationships with other women's health groups and tried to define what distinguished their practice from that of women's clinics, Ruth Bell Alexander observed, "They're doing healthcare, self-help. We demonstrate the process of how we arrive at thoughts and discoveries."[31]

In *Our Bodies, Ourselves,* the body became a source of knowledge through prolonged reflection and study, a practice that established the reader as autonomous, as a citizen of modernity. The reader whose experience was shaped by a particular appropriation of medical language became a complex subject. Her body was seen as a source of intuitive and reliable knowledge, connected to her "self," and yet oddly compartmentalized. A woman accessed this bodily, experiential knowledge when she refused to be controlled by either medical institutions or her own propensity to worry. She legitimated her own body's self-sovereignty, and she participated in the authorizing discourse of the culture.

In early editions, the body's intuitive knowledge is sometimes invoked as "natural" and presented as an alternative to biomedicine. For example, the 1973 edition's discussion of fetal heart monitors suggested that they might be causing the fetal stress that they record. Fetal heart monitors were seen as at once unscientific and unnatural: their effectiveness has never been carefully studied, and they interfere with the natural rhythms of labor: "We feel certain that if these unnatural procedures were used less frequently there would also be a decline in fetal and perinatal mortality and morbidity."[32]

But often, it was not at all easy to decide what was "natural." These difficult cases posed a rhetorical problem: If they could not resolve a medical problem, how could the collective write a book that was both honest and reassuring? Writers might report their confusion, sharing their anxiety with readers and framing it politically. After listing the new female contraceptives under development in 1970, the writers noted, "Some of this research is frightening and confusing. We don't want contraception to become one more area in which we are intimidated and frightened into doing things we're not sure of or don't want to do."[33] The language of the text implicitly compared a decision to use contraception to the decision to engage in sexual activity, transposing the reader's anxiety about medical research into a familiar narrative of female anxiety about male sexual pressure.

The logic of reafference also enabled the writers to compare experiential to scientific knowledge and mobilize both discourses for a critique of medicine. It was not enough to affirm intuitive bodily knowledge; the body must not only be known but also be seen as knowing. In an audacious extension of this rhetoric, anxiety was framed as an experience inherent to the uncertainty of embodiment, rather than as a personal failing. Even confusion, therefore, was a resource: the reader was invited to see herself worrying and to recognize herself as a woman who must make consequential decisions based on incomplete information. These practices of discussion, research, and reflection broadened the reafferent system that characterized the representation of the body in *Our Bodies, Ourselves*. Both medical and experiential discourses were mediated, for better and worse, by the emerging languages of feminism: a woman who experienced vaginal orgasms had a lot of explaining to do in her consciousness-raising group. Women were invited to investigate their own bodies directly, but then to collate what they learned from other women, from medical texts, and from conversations with their caregivers.

The reafferent circuit developed branches and correcting loops; it became porous to both feminism and conventional medicine. If there has ever been such a thing as unmediated experience of the body, it was not that of the women who, prompted by *Our Bodies, Ourselves*, looked at themselves carefully, who touched and investigated themselves ("the finger becomes an eye," in the words of one of Jane Pincus's informants), read, looked at diagrams, and discussed what they saw.[34]

Elizabeth Grosz suggests that radical theories of embodiment can develop in one of two directions: by understanding the body as a surface on which "social law, morality, and values are inscribed," and by investigating the body as the location for lived experience. In *Our Bodies, Ourselves*, these two approaches emerge as the body of lived experience, which knew what it needed, and the inscribed body, which women would learn to read through reflection and self-education.[35] Grosz is skeptical about any possible synthesis of these two approaches; she observes that they correspond to the location of the body "as a kind of *hinge* or threshold: it is placed between a psychic or lived interiority and a more sociopolitical exteriority that produces interiority through the *inscription* of the body's outer surface."[36] For the writers of *Our Bodies, Ourselves*, synthesis was never a question: they needed both approaches to the body, and they fully trusted neither of them. If the body was a surface inscribed by medicine—and in such practices as fetal heart monitoring, the inscription was quite literal—then they wanted to be able to read the inscription. The "lived interiority" of the body, alternately, offered access to the dynamics of subordination, to their own formation as female subjects. Both these processes were politically consequential: the body that was colonized by medicine, the body of the subjected citizen, could be reinscribed through feminist practices. Both ways of understanding the body were seen, particularly in early years, as potentially reversible through a reafferent practice of writing.

The Register of Medicine

The work of writing *Our Bodies, Ourselves* presented itself to the collective and its readers as a political task, a personal struggle, and a project in medical research. It was all these things, but it was also, and most particularly, a labor of language. The collective encountered the language of medicine, consumed it, and slowly transformed it. Even when they could not change medical relationships or medical practices, they could translate medical writing into a different register, transforming the medical text, surely one of the central technologies of medicine's scientific practice. In order to analyze this labor of language, I will use the theory of scientific writing as a practice of knowledge that was developed by Australian linguists M.A.K. Halliday, Robert Veel, and J. R.

Martin.[37] Halliday and his associates are functional linguists, examining language use in its social and interpersonal context. They see scientific writing as a language practice invested with enormous social power, and they describe it as a register of English, a marked variety of language use characterized by a defined semantic range. Or, in Halliday's words, "Registers [unlike dialects] are not different ways of saying the same thing; they are ways of saying different things."[38] The "things" discussed in scientific registers are processes, actions, events, or qualities that have been turned into objects: "water condenses" becomes "condensation of water;" "hormones regulate menstruation" becomes "hormonal regulation of the menstrual cycle." These nominals can be modified, connected with similar objects, and integrated into further chains of nominalization, so that we have "rapid condensation of water," and then varieties of rapid condensation, not to mention the causes and effects of rapid condensation. Halliday names the shift in function that creates such objects a "grammatical metaphor," and he considers the play between syntax and meaning that it creates to be both the mark of mature sciences and one of their most significant linguistic resources. Some grammatical metaphors are so distilled and condensed that they cannot readily be "unpacked" into their constituents; such a metaphor becomes a technical term, a new thing, "a virtual entity that exists as part of a theory."[39]

Grammatical metaphor and the related resources of the scientific register—for example, the construction of taxonomies, effacement of persons in the text, and heavy postmodification of nominal groups—enable scientific writing to abstract powerfully. Typically, readers learn to make sense of the register of science in secondary and undergraduate science courses, after encountering approximations of it in elementary school, and continue to develop fluency in it throughout their careers. The linguistic resources developed in scientific writing are adapted to other registers that direct and coordinate social activities, including those of government and the social sciences. Scientific writing supports the construction of powerful concepts, allowing writers to work with those concepts and transform them, to take advantage of the rich resources of language for "the formulation of difference and relationship, for the making of categorical distinctions."[40] The scientific register effects and supports hierarchical relationships in the work it organizes: the depersonalized abstraction it sponsors is a habit of mind learned only slowly, and at some cost.

A short example, drawn from Jay Lemke's "Multiplying Meaning," in Martin and Veel's *Reading Science*, may make these points more clear. Grammatical metaphor condenses events that are actually dispersed in time and place into a single entity that can cause other events, as in this discussion of glaciers in a school science text: "In high mountain areas, large thicknesses of snow can collect. This is compressed by its own weight and hardened. The compression of the snow can cause it to form into large bodies of ice. The weight of the snow and ice causes the ice to move slowly down the valley."[41] The text both creates and normalizes the cause-and-effect chain: thicknesses compress; compression forms ice; ice moves. Lemke remarks, "The role of human observation and reasoning in construing 'natural' relations is completely effaced."[42] The preference for passive and middle voice in scientific writing—one of the most commonly noted features of the register—reinforces elision of the role of human observation, since clauses are organized around nominalized processes: "the compression of the snow can cause it to form into large bodies."

Halliday observes that scientific texts are often organized taxonomically, presenting categories of objects, and so dividing the world into discrete units. Sometimes, in a "register metaphor," taxonomy becomes argument: a taxonomy of the forms of pollution produced by human beings becomes evidence for the proposition that "human beings are making the air dirtier and dirtier" in this excerpt from a science textbook: "Human beings are making the air dirtier and dirtier. As the demand for energy has increased, more and more harmful gases have been produced as a result of burning fossil fuels, such as coal, oil and gas. Two of the principal air pollutants are sulphur dioxide (SO_2) and nitrogen oxides (NO_2) which are the main causes of acid rain."[43] In this passage, the taxonomic list of pollution does not demonstrate that the overall level of air pollution is increasing, but that list will be taken as persuasive by many readers.

The Medical Register Transformed

Members of the collective wanted to change the language of medicine, particularly as it was addressed to them in the consulting room. Their first tactic was to learn it. The 1970, 1971, and 1973 editions of *Our*

Bodies, Ourselves are a bravura display of technical language. As the collective explained in 1971:

Understanding the medical terminology means we can now understand the things the doctors say. Knowing their language makes medical people less mysterious and frightening. We now feel more confident when asking questions. Sometimes a doctor has been startled to find us speaking "his" language. "How do you know that? Are you a medical student?" we heard again and again. "A pretty girl like you shouldn't be concerned with that."

But we are.[44]

The redistribution of medical knowledge seemed, in 1971, to be an effective claim to medical authority.

But the metalepsis of *Our Bodies, Ourselves*, with its gestures of inclusion and performance, was at odds with medical language. And conventional medical discourse did not cohere with the collective's intellectual goal: the mutual correction of the disciplinary knowledge of medicine and the direct language of an experience of the body. Today, in spite of their awareness of current antiessentialist body theory, the women of the collective still believe that there is a core of authentic bodily experience that can be accessed through continual collective reflection.

The collective responded to these problems by transforming the medical register, beginning in the 1973 edition, where it was spliced into a more metaleptic discourse. A discussion of the breast, for example, relied on a pamphlet by the San Francisco Women's Health Center that began "with what we can see" and read the surface features of the breast as signs of internal structures—a characteristic metaleptic figure that invited the reader to map the interior of her body onto its surface. The collective moved to the conventional medical register in the next paragraph, which described various tissue types to be found in the breast: we read of a "great increase in sex hormones" during puberty that causes the glandular tissue in the breasts to increase, and of "variations in the amount of glandular tissues"; both phrases are conventional grammatical metaphors.[45] The first paragraph drew the reader into the text; the second transformed the breast from a palpable organ to a set of nominalized processes.

The writers of *Our Bodies, Ourselves* constructed a style that was fully absorbed by neither inscription nor experience; the text laminates Grosz's categories together. In the 1984 childbirth chapter, this juxtaposition is especially marked. Jane Pincus and Norma Swenson, the principal writers for this chapter, prepared for the revision by consulting with one another, reading in the medical literature, and interviewing dozens of women, including women who had recently given birth, midwives, medical workers, and family members. They also drew upon their own experiences—Pincus had kept a detailed journal of her pregnancies—and upon searching discussions with other members of the collective. Since, in the early 1980s, members of the collective had finally secured the resources and time to produce the book they wanted, Pincus and Swenson used these resources to torque the medical register, to reshape it to the ordinary speech of mothers and midwives, and to construct a new way of writing medicine for *Our Bodies, Ourselves.*

We can trace how that style developed by seeing how the writers used a conventional medical source. One of the books Pincus consulted was *Biology of Women*, a book by Ethel Sloane.[46] *Biology of Women* is a comprehensive guide to women's physiology, health, and hygiene; first published in 1980, it is currently in its fourth edition. The very existence of this book was a tribute to the work of the collective and the women's movement: no such text had been available ten years earlier. Sloan acknowledged that the women's health movement had shown that "there is nothing mysterious about medicine and human structure and function; it is all knowable, if a woman understands the medical jargon."[47] Sloan developed *Biology of Women* as a textbook for women's studies courses, an alternative to both the patronizing books written by male physicians and the less detailed, more political, books produced by the women's movement. True to the mission of giving women a medical vocabulary, *Biology of Women* deployed a medical register. Pincus took four full pages of careful notes on the pregnancy chapter, keeping track of page numbers meticulously in the margin. In the text of the childbirth chapter, Pincus carefully translated Sloane's medical register (itself a marvel of clear adaptation) into the metaleptic style of *Our Bodies, Ourselves.*

Even though both *Biology of Women* and *Our Bodies, Ourselves* are designed for general audiences, they approached the task of adapting medical information quite differently: *Biology of Women* offered readers accommodations to help them take in conventional medical writing; *Our Bodies,*

Ourselves transformed those conventions. One example is the discussion of smoking during pregnancy. Sloan summarized the research detailing the health risks of this practice, ending with the admonitory figure of a pregnant woman who stopped smoking because of first-trimester nausea only to resume later in pregnancy, and who thereby demonstrated "appalling disregard for her own health and that of her unborn child."[48] Sloane's text is organized by nominals; we read of "amount of growth retardation," "lower maternal weight gain," "decrease in fetal weight," "the level of fetal carboxyhemoglobin," "high levels of carbon monoxide," and "the development of brain cells."[49] Pincus's notes for this section of *Biology of Women* read: "*Smoking*: amount of growth retardation is directly correlated to # of cigarettes smoked.—premature & small babies. Presence of excess carbon monoxide in mothers blood. Both smoke inhaled and 'sidestream' smoke dangerous."[50] While the central relationships among smoking, carbon monoxide, and fetal growth that Sloan had discussed are accurately reproduced in Pincus's notes, this fragmentary text is much less nominalized and entirely free of moralism. The parallel passage in *Our Bodies, Ourselves* reads: "*Smoking*, on the other hand, has consistently been shown to have detrimental effects on fetuses. Heavy smokers (more than fifteen cigarettes a day) have a higher rate of miscarriage, stillbirths, premature and low-birth-weight babies. If you can't stop smoking altogether, then reduce the number of cigarettes you smoke, and eat well."[51] Here, the reader is moved into the text ("if you can't stop"); the advice, while still urgent, is much less moralized. And the relation between smoking and low birth weights is organized as a relationship between people ("heavy smokers") and those affected by their actions, rather than as a ratio between the rate of smoking and a rate of abnormal births.

In *Biology of Women*, smoking does not affect women, fetuses, or babies; it affects the rate of growth. The issue most likely to interest a woman reading the passage—"premature and small babies"—is syntactically demoted to an illustration of the effects of growth retardation. The text elaborates the characteristic causal chain of the scientific register: the number of cigarettes smoked affects the amount of growth retardation because of the excess carbon monoxide in the mother's blood. The woman reader becomes a location for "excess carbon monoxide," or rather, her blood, "the mother's blood," carries the chemical that effects a change in growth rates. That change, not the pregnant woman or the fetus, is the focus of Sloan's passage. There is nothing sinister in this structure: it is intended to give the reader control of a useful idea. Nonetheless, it cannot be read without powerful acts of abstraction and displacement.

The corresponding passage in *Our Bodies, Ourselves* did deploy elements of the conventional register, but with a difference. *Our Bodies, Ourselves* used the technical term, "low-birth-weight babies," in place of the vernacular "small babies" in Pincus's notes. The passive voice, often considered a mark of conventional medical writing, also appears: ("smoking . . . has consistently been shown").[52] But the overall organization of the passage foregrounded persons: the reading woman, the pregnant woman, her fetus, her baby: "*Smoking*, on the other hand, has consistently been shown to have detrimental effects on fetuses. Heavy smokers (more than fifteen cigarettes a day) have a higher rate of miscarriage, stillbirths, premature and low-birth-weight babies. If you can't stop smoking altogether, then reduce the number of cigarettes you smoke, and eat well."[53] "Heavy smokers," were defined precisely by the number of cigarettes they smoke, constructing the group that will be metaleptically invoked in the final sentence. The text, which called out to those readers, offered strong direction without the "shoulds" that the collective so disliked. Instead, the text described consequences and offered alternatives. (Later editions, responding to more alarming research, were more directive and dire in their warnings.) These changes are subtle, perhaps, but they amount to a refunctioning of the medical information drawn from *Biology of Women*: no longer is medical knowledge a system in which one term relates to another. Instead, the information gestures toward the reader, places her in relation to possible stories about herself, her fetus, and her baby, and summons her to a place of choice.

Politically motivated and deeply democratic, this transformation was also specifically a labor of language. Neither the politics of the text nor its popular audience account for it. *The Ms. Guide to a Woman's Health* (1981), a book addressed to general audiences that was certainly shaped by the feminism of the 1970s, presented the topic of smoking during pregnancy in the register of conventional medicine:

Recent studies have shown that babies born to women who are heavy smokers are smaller in size and more likely to be premature. The incidence of early abortion (see #121), bleeding during pregnancy, abruption placenta (see #157c), placenta previa (see 157b) and premature rupture of the membranes (see #138) is higher in heavy smokers. (Ref. 9, 10) Women must cut back to less than one pack per day during pregnancy; and preferably stop the habit altogether, both for their own and their baby's health.[54]

Predication is from "studies," rather than from "smoking"; the focus of the passage is on the correspondence between rates rather than on the effects of smoking on women, fetuses, and babies. The list of effects is given in technical language—readers are encouraged to seek definitions of the possible complications in other sections of the book, and so enter a series of relationships among taxonomic terms rather than a narrative about their own health. The final sentence is a blunt imperative: women must cut back. The information is the same, the political intent is the same, but the text has created a different reader, and a different relationship to medical information.

While the 1984 *Our Bodies, Ourselves* worked hard to refunction medicine, it also looked critically at some of the values implied by earlier editions. An early draft of the "Introduction to Childbearing" in the 1984 edition ended by advocating "efficient mobile medical emergency units so we could have our babies more naturally and inexpensively at home." In a marginal note, Pincus suggested that the passage not use the word "naturally." She wanted "another word that doesn't have 'hippie,' anti-technological *old women's roles* connotation."[55] The collective had moved from an easy identification of the integrated experience of feminine embodiment as "natural" to a realization that their own embodiment included technological innovations, and that it must move beyond traditional roles. Elsewhere in the preliminary documents, Swenson and Pincus argue that there is "no such thing as 'natural childbirth,'" since "all births are culturally conditioned, including the culture of preparation (all methods)."[56]

While neither Pincus, Swenson, nor the collective made a conscious plan to refunction the register of conventional medicine, they did think about issues of syntax and word choice. Should the pronoun corresponding to "pregnant woman" be "we" or "you"? (The writers went back and forth a few times before settling on "you.") Should the text refer to a baby or a fetus? A doctor or a physician? These decisions, based on many interactions among Pincus, Swenson, their informants, and their readers, refunctioned the medical register. The writers' approach had been shaped by conversations with informants, who often told birth stories, recounting either their own experience of hospital or home birth, or the general contours of the births they managed as midwives or caregivers.

In the text of *Our Bodies, Ourselves*, inset personal narratives speculate that women may even be able to control when their labor starts. In one story, a woman is told by her midwife to "Just have the baby," goes home, makes love, and thinks about it: her waters break. Another reports that a woman who wanted to be assisted by a particular midwife "managed to time all four labors" to fit the midwife's twelve-hour shifts.[57] These narratives organized medical information by placing the reader metaleptically within the text's narrative structure. They also collected the sensations of "bare life": movement, swelling, pain, embarrassment, bad temper, but also breath, energy, and rhythm.[58] For Pincus and Swenson, these stories shaped a rhetorical and political exigency: "How to help women make sense out of the experience? By making peace and making war."[59] They argued that although women who thought that they could be in control of their pregnancy and birth experiences were right, in a way, they were also "trapped" by their own misunderstanding of how tightly their bodily experience had already been laced into systems of medical technology and training.[60] To see themselves as socially situated would release them from abjection and guilt and would support both effective resistance and a sense of bodily empowerment.

In drafting the chapter, Pincus began with notes from her interviews. For example, Pincus's account of her conversations with birth attendants reads:

Dangerous things: Don't let you eat or drink. Give IV's, "Back or side; propped up." Make you dependent, then after taking away, give back. Monitor; threatens: "a lot safer for your baby."

Desires vs. safety rather than desires *being* safety. What we want are not peccadilloes, but help to make our childbirth safer.[61]

In an early draft of the birth chapter, Pincus wrote, "How often are things set up so that it becomes a matter of our desires *versus* safety, rather than: Our desires create the conditions for safety. How many of us are told

'You don't want an IV, a fetal monitor? That is selfish of you. If you don't accept them, your baby will be harmed.'"[62] In revision, Norma Swenson added, "The risk of these procedures are rarely researched and always presumed to be 'worth it.' The current cesarean epidemic (almost 1 in 4) cannot be justified after expert evaluation, yet it continues."[63] Their elliptical, conversational notes developed oppositions between women's experiences of birth and medical norms and expectations: medicine saw women's desires as obstacles to safe birth, as "peccadilloes"; medical workers enforced control over childbirth by asserting their knowledge of what is "safe for the baby." Pincus's text transposed these oppositions into a narrative that located knowledge in the laboring woman, whose desires are assumed to include a desire for safe birth, but who faced ill-informed assumptions about the relation between medical intervention and safety. In working up the interview material, Pincus and Swenson developed a discourse that realigned medical knowledge by moving from personal narrative to political reflection.

In the final text, medical language was smashed up and transposed into a series of fluid narratives in which women made sense of their experiences, shared them with others, and did the best they could in the face of uncertainty. Many of these narratives were ramified to accommodate plural subjects and multiple resolutions. The inset personal narratives were quite long and were organized to present a range of experiences and perspectives. Organizing the text into narrative templates of varying structures and complexity disrupted the basic structures of the medical register: In this new style, nominalization became difficult; once created, nominals could not easily become subjects of sentences. The narrative form worked against taxonomies; systems of abstract nouns are not easily incorporated into stories. The metaleptic staging of the reader within the text resisted the medical register's effacement of persons. Whether the information that writers worked with was drawn from medical texts or from interviews, the narrative template led them away from the abstractions characteristic of the medical register and helped them to combine medical information, personal experiences, and political reflection in new ways.

The collective was not using narrative just to amp up the emotional resonance of the text: they wanted to use narrative to get at the biomedical system. At the end of the childbirth chapters, the writers reflect on the ways that women evaluate their own experiences: "Even with our knowledge we are sometimes unable to find a language adequate and powerful enough either to express our wonder and sense of accomplishment or our frustration, anger, and outrage."[64] The speaker of the text foregrounds the thinness of the medical register; she contains the difficulty of knowing what to say, the untranslatability of women's experience of childbirth. The ramified text goes on to describe various ways of responding to negative experiences, gathered together at the end of the passage, where the narrators—and by extension, their readers—are absolved of blame: "And worst of all, inappropriately, we blame ourselves—'My body just didn't work right'—instead of seeing clearly how the system undermines our knowledge and self-sufficiency; instead of saying to ourselves, as one mother did, 'Whatever the luck of the draw for your labor, be assured that you have done the best you could on that day for your baby.'"[65] The reader is invited to reflect on what may have gone wrong as a way of healing her birth experience, of strengthening her resolve to do things differently, or of inspiring activism: to make peace, and to make war. We might contrast the judgmental tone of *The Ms. Guide to Women's Health*, which includes such statements as:

When you are in labor, keep your mind firmly fixed on one idea—that the stronger the pain is, the closer you probably are to giving birth to your baby.[66]

It is a relatively simple matter to avoid extreme anxiety during labor: use the nine months you are given to prepare for it by reading and learning relaxation exercises during labor.[67]

If no one can get to you fast enough, and you are alone when your baby is born, *don't panic.*[68]

Any woman who is interested in breast-feeding should do it; and if she isn't interested, she should try to be.[69]

Implicit in all these directives is an understanding of the individual woman as responsible for her own mental state, able at will to relax, avoid panic, or excite her own interest. In *Our Bodies, Ourselves*, childbirth was sometimes presented as an act of self-definition, but the choices entailed required both expert and communal support: "Childbearing is *your* experience—you, not anyone else, are having your child. If you want to give birth in a climate of confidence you must know it is possible, create it, seek it out, surround yourself during pregnancy with friends and practitioners who feel positive about childbirth."[70] The "climate of confidence" permits a woman to "accept that it's really happening."[71] It also encourages her to "let go trying to keep . . . control"; by understanding labor as a process with its own time, its own pace, the woman identifies with her own laboring body.[72] That body is immediate; the woman can attend to nothing else, at least during contractions. Labor is simultaneously porous to a woman's subjectivity—slowing if the woman becomes tense or upset, but quickening if she aligns herself with the process—and opaque to her understanding—the laboring woman cannot herself tell how quickly labor is going, how dilated she is, or how the baby is doing. To identify with this process seemed transcendent: one woman remarked, "I felt godlike—a miracle worker."[73] The chapter quoted midwives who felt that a positive birth experience increased a woman's courage and ability to make changes. The body's mysterious interior remains unknown, but the woman's unverbalized knowledge of her own laboring body becomes as potent a source of self-transformation as the anatomy lessons presented earlier in the book.

If labor was an alien process that could be contained by identification, the baby was even more difficult to assimilate. As we have seen, the woman's self-care during pregnancy was framed as her start to "good mothering." The chapter offered vivid examples of women who experienced the developing fetus as both occupying their bodies and as demonstrating their embodied power. In the "Childbirth" chapter, the baby was assimilated to the female subject as a possession: "Right after birth, hold your baby close. S/he's your own; you have waited all this time and labored hard."[74] A later chapter, "Postpartum," would work out a more complex set of identifications, relationships, and dependencies between women and their babies, but in these chapters on the crises of pregnancy and childbirth, the baby was nearly a side-effect of the mother's bodily transformation, of her self-creation as a laboring woman, and of her alignment with her own involuntary processes. The woman who understood her own pregnancy and birth process dramatically represented the possibilities of a reafferent monitoring of one's own body: she could take care of herself; she would understand herself; she was equipped to resist medical manipulation.

The routine interventions of obstetrics—fetal monitoring, invasive testing during pregnancy, anesthesia—were seen as alienating substitutes for a woman's self-understanding and the experienced eye of her birth attendant. These interventions were benefits to doctors, rather than to mothers or babies, or expressions of ritual misogyny. The text spoke of Caesarians being "so dear to the medical heart."[75] It characterized the shaving of pubic hair as "one part of the male medical ritual of depolluting, purifying women."[76] And it quoted Sheila Kitzinger's description of the episiotomy as "ritual genital mutilation."[77] Medical intervention during childbirth was seen as a dramatic attempt to take women's bodies away from them, to deprive them of both autonomous agency and of the chance to encounter their bodies as resistant, ungovernable, and "natural."

Medical Treatment

The medical register is one of the most important resources of the profession, and in chapters like "Anatomy and Physiology" and "Sexuality," the collective offered readers access to that discourse. But readers also wanted advice about birth control, or pregnancy, or childbirth; the Boston Women's Health Book Collective therefore had to come to terms with issues of medical treatment. Early editions of *Our Bodies, Ourselves* explained common medical treatments, established standards of care, and cautioned women against ineffective or excessive treatment. By 1984, the collective began to place these questions in the context of their critique of medicalization and their growing interest in alternative healthcare. The collective collated reports from readers, critically reviewed the available medical research, and considered such issues as fairness, responsibility, and respect for women's autonomy in its evaluations of treatments. These evaluations combined the genres of political polemic, textbook anatomical description, technical research review, and personal narrative. In 1984, the collective also decided to make recommendations to readers based on its research and experience, leading to extensive revision of the birth control and childbirth chapters and the development of a new chapter evaluating new reproductive technologies.

The 1984 birth control chapter was a departure from the collective's policy of avoiding "shoulds." This chapter was one of the few in the book attributed to a single author, Susan Bell, although the text is voiced through the usual collective "we." Bell had encountered the early texts of feminist science studies, including Emily Martin's *The Woman in the Body*.[78] Martin's book, in particular, led Bell to question the "cafeteria style" of her earlier chapter, and so in 1984 Bell was considerably more combative.[79] In the 1973 edition, the obstacles to birth control had been framed as local obstructions: repressive laws, the high cost of contraceptive materials, the attitudes of partners. With care, self-education, and persistence, a woman could bypass them, find a birth control method that worked for her, and use it safely. But in 1984, the obstacles to safe birth control were systemic, powerful, and deeply structural. The "population control establishment" set the agenda for developing and distributing contraceptives; reproductive health was lower on their agenda than limiting undesirable births. Scientific medicine "views us as ignorant and incapable of taking an active role in controlling our fertility," while pharmaceutical companies seek higher profits from contraceptives.[80] The chapter protested against contraceptive research and practices that discounted dangers to women's health or compromised their autonomy, connecting them to dangerous practices such as sterilization abuse. The chapter also attacked the Moral Majority's campaign against sex education, the FDA's refusal to test the long-term safety of the pill, and "paternalistic and condescending" physicians.[81] The reader of this chapter inhabited a world in which no healthcare provider was especially interested in her desire for safe, convenient birth control, the desire that presumably brought her to the text. The book recognized that the reader might face personal obstacles to good birth control: her partner could be unsupportive, or she might feel sexual shame, or denial, or romanticism, or ambivalence.

In contrast, writers of *The Ms. Guide to a Woman's Health* were triumphant in their discussion of birth control:

No single scientific breakthrough has altered our lives so momentously as the discovery and mass use of safe, effective contraceptive methods. . . . Birth control was really the first liberator of women. All our other efforts at liberation are its spin offs.

When a woman chooses to practice birth control, she is not just making a decision about her personal life and her health—she is making a judgment about what is best for her economy, her political system, her soul, and the very destiny of her species.[82]

While *The Ms. Guide* saw a woman's choice of birth control as a transformation on economic, spiritual, and political levels, *Our Bodies, Ourselves* saw it as a fraught decision, crossed with dangers and dissatisfactions, requiring careful study and discussion. The collective recapitulated the arc from knowledge to correction and critique: women must learn about birth control on their own, since doctors are not reliable sources of information; women must monitor their healthcare providers; they must work for improvements in current methods. Beyond that, the text urges a reflective practice that helps women understand and transform their experience; "By talking together we can also get a better handle on our more subtle resistances to using birth control."[83] As so often in *Our Bodies, Ourselves*, these discussions ideally lead to political action. The reader who came to *Our Bodies, Ourselves* to find out whether low-dose birth control pills might be a good option for her, then, has been summoned onto a large stage, where her own hesitation and shame or her partner's awkwardness are connected to worldwide population policies and the norms of scientific research. These connections are not fanciful: fragile, individual bodies are repeatedly laced into the systems of a multinational healthcare industry and big science. No individual can make their healthcare decisions solely on the basis of these political relationships, but to ignore them would repeat the presumption of the doctor who explained that "if you tell them they might get headaches, they will get headaches."[84] The collective always believed that knowing more was better than knowing less.

The conceptual focus of the birth control chapter was the collective's advocacy of barrier contraceptives:

The Collective favors certain methods of contraception over others and has chosen to place them first. Most of us who use birth control choose a diaphragm, cervical cap, or foam and condom, because they are both effective and safe. We have become increasingly discouraged about the Pill and IUD after receiving hundreds of letters from women who have been harmed by those methods. Research also documents Pill and IUD risks. We believe that the Pill and IUD are dangerous enough to warrant their use as methods of "second choice" rather than "first choice," and so we describe them toward the end of the chapter.

As you read, you will, of course, form your own opinions and make your choices. No one method is likely to satisfy us through all our fertile years.[85]

This approach modified the collective's initial commitment to choice: in 1971 and 1973, like the writers of the McGill *Birth Control Handbook*, they considered opposition to the pill to be opposition to women's access to convenient, woman-controlled birth control, so they urged women to be cautious and learn the risks, but not to rule out the pill.[86] But from 1984 until 2005, all editions included some version of the paragraph endorsing barrier methods, and this position was reiterated in many public appearances.

The 1984 endorsement was controversial. Judith Rooks, reviewing *The New Our Bodies, Ourselves* for *Family Planning Perspectives*, complained that "this valuable book is seriously flawed by a disturbing lack of balance and objectivity in the chapter on birth control," and suggested that the collective was biased against the pill and the IUD.[87] It was also an interesting speech act. It began as a conventional testimonial: members of the collective use barrier methods themselves. They cited personal communications from women to the collective, letters that have discouraged them from continuing to recommend the pill. Finally, the text summarized the growing body of medical research on the dangers of the pill and the IUD. Once again, the category of "experience" was highly mediated. Personal experience was the warrant for opposing the contemporary medical view that the pill and the IUD were safe choices, but personal experience included "hundreds of letters" and a careful review of current research. The collective presented their position as a move in a conversation: they had listened to readers, and now they were reflecting readers' experiences back to them.

Early editions of *Our Bodies, Ourselves* had rigorously avoided telling women what to do, abstaining from even colloquial uses of "should." By 1984, the collective had reevaluated the limits of choice as a central, life-defining act and began to focus more on healthcare systems than on individual autonomy. The final chapter of the book recognized that the uneven delivery of medical care limited women's choices.[88] It argued that women should not blindly trust healthcare providers, "since medical professionals offer false reassurances much more often than we'd like to think, we *must* be as critical as we can, get all the information possible and ask friends and family to help us in doing this."[89] Their growing distrust of conventional medicine led the collective to recognize the limits of choice. The urgency of this perception led the collective to station itself as an alternate medical authority, to recommend the choices that they had made, after study and reflection, to other women. This decision was also hedged and recuperated into the life-cycle narrative that so powerfully structured the book. They conceded that "no one method" would work for women throughout their childbearing years.[90] They suggested that the pill might be a viable choice for women who were "just starting to have intercourse," who might progress to barrier methods as they became more comfortable with sex and sexual communication.[91]

In their discussions of particular birth control methods, the writers combined racy vernacular with complex discussions of anatomy and physiology. This text never forgot that it was talking about sex: there were complaints that various spermicides "taste terrible" or were "drippy."[92] The woman using birth control was regularly invoked as a social being with ordinary problems: she might live with her parents, or she might have trouble buying condoms. That woman's body appeared in detail: in diagrams and directions for inserting the diaphragm ("You should then reach in to make sure you can feel the outline of your cervix through the soft rubber cup"); in the explanation of fertility awareness ("Some women can take a sample [of cervical mucus] and stretch it between two fingers"); in the discussion of the relation between the pill and cervical cancer ("if a woman has cervical dysplasia [abnormal cells in the cervix], the Pill may cause that dysplasia to become cancerous)."[93] As these examples suggest, details could be presented colloquially or in technical medical language; either phrasing could open metaleptic identifications to readers. The movement among vocabularies, registers, and forms of knowledge brings light and motion to a chapter whose ostensible point is all about limit and difficulty: it demonstrated that while we may not have good birth control, we could know a lot about the birth control that we have. The openness of the text and its willingness to risk its own opinion suggest that the knowledge of the writers can become the knowledge of the reader.

Alternative Health

The 1984 *Our Bodies, Ourselves* explored alternatives to conventional medicine in "Health and Healing: Alternatives to Medical Care," a new chapter written by Pamela Berger, Nancy Miriam Hawley, and Jane Pincus. Although the collective had always been critical of biomedicine, their previous forays into alternative treatments had been sporadic. The new chapter on alternative medicine demonstrated the implications of the collective's critique of medicalization and their shared search for an alternative concept of healthcare. The chapter discussed how to evaluate alternative medicine providers and described the available therapies, including meditation, massage, yoga, chiropractic, movement therapy, and psychic healing. The writers gave a positive account of the holistic philosophy they imputed to alternative medicine: an emphasis on the whole person, on the importance of environmental factors, and on the patient's own ability to heal. They warned against dependence on alternative healers, the incipient professionalization of alternate healthcare providers, and restricted access to alternative care. The chapter's advice on evaluating practitioners recalls earlier discussions of choosing a physician; its critique of conventional medicine reflects the collective's emerging position on medicalization. The evolution of this chapter can be traced from initial decisions by the collective to include it in the book; this chapter demonstrates how the women of the collective worked to take into account the changes in healthcare during the 1980s.

In October and November of 1980, during the early stages of work on the 1984 edition, the group debated whether to redo the book—some of them were a little tired of it—and began to sort out the general shape of the revision. As part of that process, each member wrote an essay about her own healthcare practices, responding to a series of prompts. Some of these responses appear as personal narratives in the alternative medicine chapter; taken together, they show how women in the collective worked out individual accommodations to medicine and how they thought about these practices.[94] The first prompt for these essays was "How do I integrate different healthcare models in my life?" None of

the collective members was willing to claim an "integrated" approach
to their own health:

I'm not sure I do (!). Never gone to a chiropractor. . . . Done talk therapy and
get massages, take baths, hot, for tight achey muscles, once in a while experiment with herbs. Haven't been too sick—What I need to do is *sleep*. . . .

I don't integrate health care models. I learn about different modes—never
trusted doctors much. Am interested in chiropractic, herbal, massage.[95]

Collective members assimilated the prompt to the narrative conventions
of consciousness-raising and told stories of their early family experiences
with healthcare. A collective member who grew up in a household divided on the merits of Christian Science reported "chronic conflict . . .
a whole childhood full of tugs and pulls." (Later, this member explained
to me, "What is built into me was a skepticism that I think the average
person in American society does not have. . . . I was not immune, but I
was skeptical."[96])

For some writers, the question opened issues of social responsibility, "What am I responsible for? Do I go to family or friends? Then,
social consciousness level: in a vision of a good society, what would be
a good model? Not what I'd do, but what would be utopian." Another
was "ashamed to be so conventional."[97] Members of the collective most
commonly mentioned basic health practices: waiting, resting, hoping
a problem would go away. Many admitted that they would more readily seek a doctor's advice for one of their children than for themselves.
Almost all distrusted doctors, but named a specific situation (broken
leg, diabetes) where "allopathic medicine" was in order. While almost
all were wary of practices that felt mystical, like psychic healing, many
members were interested in chiropractic or massage. For the collective,
these alternative therapies were both options outside biomedicine and
ways of transforming it. One member observed that "all the stuff about
alternatives filters into the medical system. Learning ourselves helps us
become a little more independent of the iatrogenic [disease-producing]
medical system." Another speaks of working hard "to escape the clutches
of the conventional system."[98] In these written conversations, accepting
conventional medicine is seen as passivity; exploring alternative treatment has transformative potential.

The essays on personal practices helped the collective to develop a concept of healthcare that is patient centered and oriented to vitality and energy rather than the absence of disease. Health is preserved by a varied program of self-care, including nutrition, rest, exercise, and limited interventions by both conventional physicians and alternative healers. All these health practices are connected to both psychological well-being and broader issues of social concern and care. Alternative therapies and other strategies of self-care, quite conventional in themselves, are understood as moving the feminine body outside the regime of sanctioned care. Experimenting with these therapies constructed an alternative to both the "*femina sacra*" whose subjected materiality was the mute object of biomedicine and the "good patient" who intelligently consumed conventional medicine. But stabilizing these experiments in a written text was quite difficult.

In an early draft of the alternative medicine chapter, the writers broadened their focus from doctor-patient relationships: "In earlier editions of *Our Bodies, Ourselves* we accepted much of the traditional medical system's way of thinking about disease and health. If something was wrong in our bodies, we thought it could be 'cured' with medical care that was accessible to all, and administered with respect. . . . In this 'curing' process we asked that our doctors be trained in the necessary communication skills and that they take more time to listen to our concerns."[99] The collective felt that it was important for women to move beyond the doctor-patient dyad and to choose among the healing modes. At this early stage of writing, their investigation took the writers far afield into discussions of systems theory and of self-organization that would be cut from the published text.

In this early draft, stress was named as a cause of specific diseases and symptoms. This discussion recalled ideas of the body as a finite reservoir of energy, using such terms such as "wear and tear," which would have been familiar to readers of nineteenth-century health reform literature. In the draft, stress was not the body's friction with its environment; stress was political. Government policies caused stress, while alleviating stress made political resistance more effective: "But our contribution to the political efforts to control this madness can be more directed and efficacious if our individual lives and actions are not

206 Taking on Medicine

disoriented by stress."[100] Stress acted on the subject (junk food or restrictive abortion laws) and was also part of the subject's interior life (desire to exercise or to have sex). "Stress" organized a discussion of social forces and norms, but it also held individuals responsible for dealing with them. Jane Pincus commented on the draft's description of the Type A personality, noting that writers "must warn against blaming the victim here if you leave this in."[101] But since the very idea of the Type A personality explained illness as an effect of personal traits, it could not be explained without blame.

Stress was, in the 1980s, one of the categories that disseminated "bare life" among political subjects: it linked embodiment and political power, but resolved this linkage therapeutically, through "stress reduction." The collective was appropriately skeptical of corporate stress-reduction programs for employees; they thought that it was good to get time off at work, but warned of "the dangers of social control associated with companies becoming too actively involved in our lives outside of work."[102] Various editors suggested cuts or augmentations in the section on stress, but the logical problems it posed were simply not solvable within the conceptual framework of the 1984 *Our Bodies, Ourselves*. The section on stress was cut, and a one-page discussion of the subject was included at the end of Wendy Sanford's introduction to the book.[103] Stress had become the unmanageable counterpart of reafference: it was something that the subject did to herself; it was a process that sustained and augmented itself. Stress demonstrated both the boundaries of the self and their permeability; it complicated the collective's understanding of autonomy without opening the discursive resources afforded by the logic of reafference.

The draft included references to healing as an unmediated, mystical force, and these references were also cut in the final text. The writers excised such anecdotes as one woman's experience of "no separation between [herself] and a Universal force."[104] Not all members of the collective were comfortable with this quasi-religious language, which presented a connection between individuals and larger forces as a basic fact of organic life rather than a social concept or program. Many accounts of treatment modalities were shortened, and sections on healthcare policies and on the history of alternative medicine were also cut, as was a discussion of psychotherapy (discussed in its own chapter).

Like many other recommendations of *Our Bodies, Ourselves*, their advocacy of alternative medicine would become medical common sense. In the final text, the writers were cautious and reserved in their accounts of specific therapies: their recommendations are similar to those currently offered on the National Institutes of Health website. Like the NIH, the collective counseled research, discussion with all healthcare providers, and informed use of alternative treatment modes. This chapter also resembled the early editions' chapters on birth control: it presented a cafeteria of treatment modalities and left readers to choose among them. The alternative medicine chapter indicated the limits of the collective's appropriation of biomedicine and also the limits of their rejection of it. Their traditional means of investigation—discussion, conversation, interviews with resource people—were not enough to make sense of this new body of medical information. Alternative or complementary therapies were counterparts to other emerging means of treatment: the array of drugs, tests, procedures, and surgeries characteristic of contemporary biomedicine, constantly changing and deeply located in complex medical institutions. These institutions could not be taken in as experience; global in their influence and widely distributed in research capacities, they exceeded the boundaries of even the most seasoned and astute of observers.

New Problems, New Ways of Writing

Although it certainly contained useful information, the chapter on alternative medicine can be seen as a compromised attempt to find a new logic for the collective's transformation of medical discourse. The more consistently the collective applied the logical structures that supported their therapeutic recommendations to these new modalities, the more they ran the danger of blaming women for their illnesses, telling readers what to do, and inviting the intrusion of large social institutions into the details of daily life. Rather than creating an alternative to the *femina sacra*, the text of this new chapter proposed new strategies for consigning her to a state of perpetual emergency. In the 1970s, it had been a radical political act to connect women's ignorance of sexual anatomy to their oppression, or to suggest that women should make their own healthcare decisions. By 1990, these ideas had become truisms: no patient could negotiate managed care without careful research and self-education. Bodily life was no longer defined as private, but rather was regulated, researched, performed, and highly politicized.

Subsequent editions of *Our Bodies, Ourselves* have struggled with these contradictions. Some textual features retained their force—the metaleptic presentation of the body and the transformation of medical discourse, for example. Others had become normalized as obligatory features of medical popularization: ramified narratives, multiple inset anecdotes. As the outlines of a new system of medical economics emerged, it has not been easy to find a rhetoric that simultaneously differentiates and connects individual medical problems and structural issues of access to care. The collective's deepening connection with global feminism has broadened the range of issues begging for inclusion in *Our Bodies, Ourselves*. The text that emerged from these pressures in 2005 was not entirely recognizable to longtime readers of the book, or indeed to all members of the collective. Some of the new chapters—the revised anatomy chapter, the chapter on gender identity—were fresh and inventive. Others seemed flat and conservative.

The difficulty of successfully revising *Our Bodies, Ourselves* demonstrates the audacity of the early editions, which set a high standard for success: the transformation of the reader's experience of her own embodiment. That project was undertaken with limited resources by a small group of women who learned to distribute the work of writing to a broad network of healthcare advocates, to write about the body in new ways, and to turn medical writing inside out. It was supported by readers who were eager to enter the text, both in response to its metaleptic invitation and as correspondents or informants. *Our Bodies, Ourselves* invented languages, narrative forms, and rhetoric that produced new identities and new practices; this work of writing, brought to birth in the social movements of the 1960s and 1970s, continues to be productive in a new century.

Postscript

THIS BOOK EXPLORES how medical information is written, presented to lay audiences, and read—questions central to the rhetoric of science. *Our Bodies, Ourselves* is an excellent venue for considering these questions, since it has been embedded in a sustained movement to change women's health practices. Reading and writing are consequential actions, but their consequences are usually subtle; *Our Bodies, Ourselves* is robustly connected to the world of embodied action. Women read the book and looked at their genitals or asked their doctors inconvenient questions. For forty years, as the health care system changed, *Our Bodies, Ourselves* helped readers negotiate the shifting balance of information between patient and physician.

My book is also a rhetorical history of the Boston Women's Health Book Collective, a group of political women whose project of writing remains central to their identities. Just as *Our Bodies, Ourselves* is a very human text, marked by both inconsistencies and brilliant passages, theirs is a very human story of intellectual and social work. In writing this book, I studied the work of living writers, women deeply engaged with their project, women whom I had admired from a distance for decades. On my first visit to their archive in 2000, I opened the spiral notebook in which the collective kept the minutes of their meetings from 1971 until 1973.[1] I knew this book: I knew its slick cover, its musty paper. I had written in ones just like it during the late 1960s and early 1970s, taking my turn keeping minutes for a socialist school, a feminist study group, and any number of other political organizations. The collective's spiral notebook, like the ones I remembered, had been filled with doodles, lists of dishes for a potluck, complaints of boredom, and multiple plans for ongoing projects. I fell into that notebook and, with it, into the collective's writing and into this project. I was happy to spend time in the archive, and very happy that members of the collective were willing to be interviewed. It was surprising that, for so many of them, the work of writing was ancillary to that of doing research, or speaking in public, or organizing health care initiatives. Clearly, there was something vital to learn here about sustaining a writing project without buying into various cultural myths of authorship. I was also a little uneasy: these women cared about how they were represented in public, and I was—well, I was a kind of a wiseass, expert at pulling at the seams in texts, really interested in the representation of the clitoris. I eventually decided that, since I was not a member of this group and could not do their work for them, I should do the work that was my own and try to read their text with the same joyful seriousness that suffused the pages of their book.

That decision carried me through my own writing until the time came to bring this book to publication, when the ground shifted. As the collective approached the fortieth anniversary of the book's first edition, they became more invested in their own legacy. They responded to other scholarly publications about their work with detailed lists of corrections and comments—and to me, those lists were a little scary. They offered to fact check my own manuscript. I talked to the social scientists who had helped me over my worst errors early in the project, and they advised me to stay objective and keep control of my text. I talked to feminist researchers in rhetoric who favored a more collaborative approach: they advised showing the collective the whole text and working to produce a book that satisfied everyone. I compromised by choosing sections of the text that discussed individual women, or sensitive junctures in the collective's life, or health care issues that seemed private, and sending these short passages to various members of the collective. I did not want my book to be hurtful to the women who had been so generous to me, but I wanted it to be my book.

The responses were absorbing, and a little daunting. I found that I'd made many errors (and I worry about others lurking undetected). I'd misspelled names and mixed up dates. Some things just looked different from my perspective than they did to the women I was writing about:

for me, women who had given birth within six months of each other had had their babies at the same time, but for these women, six months was a real difference. Almost all readers were tickled by how "academic" or "intellectual" their work sounded. I was glad to provide amusement and to have the chance to correct errors, but other responses were more challenging. I often ran up against the collective's belief in its egalitarian process; any statement that one woman's work was "central" or "very important" was likely to be contested. And, for some of my readers, "fact checking" meant "finding things I don't agree with." Pages would return to me laced with comments, objections, and alternate wordings that I really didn't like. Some readers wanted to see what I'd done with the comments and engaged in another round of editing and suggestions; they were puzzled when I took a pass on a third reading.

As writers of *Our Bodies, Ourselves*, of course, these women had gone through many more than three rewrites. For years, I had been asking members of the collective if they had any marked-up copies of early drafts: since the group had thriftily used discarded drafts as scrap paper, very few of them had been preserved. Eventually, I realized that the collective's last gift to me was this mark up of my own draft, peremptory and a little obsessive, delivered over in faith that the text that two or three writers had hashed out would be better than what any one writer could do. It was as close as I was going to get to a draft of an *Our Bodies, Ourselves* chapter. Without anyone's intending it, I had been inducted into the collective's writing process, and I was not at all ready for membership. As an activist in New Left and women's movement organizations, I had seen my writing stretched in all directions; as an academic, I was used to circulating drafts of memos, policy statements, and proposals for comments. I even prided myself on how little I minded making changes in these documents. But for me, scholarship was a domain of individual authorship; I was not at all prepared to accept collaboration, especially this late in the game, even from the people who had been most deeply involved in the organization I was writing about.

Distributed writing, or as my correspondents would have called it, "collective writing," required skills that had, for me, been long dormant: the ability to find alternate ways of saying things, to balance a sense of what had to be said with attention to what other writers wanted to say, to resist closing the text when I had done my own best work on it. It also required relinquishing other habits. I was used to struggling to represent the nuances of my own understanding, to taking full responsibility for my text and all that it said. For me, the coherence of the book from page to page and from chapter to chapter was an expression of my personal integrity. I had internalized Habermas's statement that for us, autonomy and responsibility are promised with our first sentences.[2] So I did not take up all the possibilities that a collaborative fact-checking might have offered. I corrected my errors; I reworked some passages; I deleted some sections and let others stand. As the work of revision proceeded, this seemed to make sense to members of the collective.

Some rhetoricians study the work of speakers and writers who figure on national and international stages: there is, for example, a large and lively literature on presidential rhetoric. But presidents are not concerned with defending their legacy against rhetoricians; this scholarship has little influence on the practice it analyses. Other rhetoricians recover the work of speakers and writers who were in danger of being lost to history, writers who did critical work in their own communities, unknown to the culture at large. Their subjects may feel vindicated by academic study and enjoy the process of recovery. But some of the most significant work we can do as rhetoricians concerns speakers and writers who are ready, willing, and able to talk back. That talk might be staged in scientific journals where work in rhetoric of science is reviewed, or in conferences where practicing physicians discuss their work with scholars in medical rhetoric, or in the disciplines, where work in the rhetoric of economics or political science is debated. Political groups like the Boston Women's Health Book Collective share this readiness to consider their own discursive practices, although they would almost surely deny that they are experts. Invested in their writing, they are open to conversations with rhetoricians—conversations that, for me, have been unruly and generative. The scholarship in rhetoric is, in a way, a huge babble of conversation among researchers and those they study: molecular biologists, women preachers, high-school teachers, insurance agents, accountants, and cancer patients. This talk will build a house of discourse where both expertise and democracy can be at home.

Reference Matter

Notes

Introduction

1. Boston Women's Health Collective, *Women and Their Bodies: A Course* (Boston, MA: Boston Women's Health Collective, 1970), 193.

2. Boston Women's Health Course Collective, *Our Bodies, Our Selves: A Course by and for Women* (Boston: New England Free Press, 1971).

3. Boston Women's Health Book Collective, *Our Bodies, Ourselves: A Book by and for Women* (New York: Simon and Schuster, 1973); Boston Women's Health Book Collective, *Our Bodies, Ourselves: A Book by and for Women*, 2d ed. (New York: Simon and Schuster, 1976); Boston Women's Health Book Collective, *Our Bodies, Ourselves* (New York: Simon and Schuster, 1979); Boston Women's Health Book Collective, *The New Our Bodies, Ourselves* (New York: Simon and Schuster, 1984); Boston Women's Health Book Collective, *The New Our Bodies, Ourselves*, 2d ed. (New York: Simon and Schuster, 1992); Boston Women's Health Book Collective, *Our Bodies, Ourselves for the New Century: A Book by and for Women*, newly revised and updated edition (New York: Simon and Schuster, 1998); Boston Women's Health Book Collective, *Our Bodies, Ourselves: A New Edition for a New Era*, 35th anniversary ed. (New York: Simon and Schuster, 2005).

4. Boston Women's Health Book Collective, "Our Bodies, Ourselves," Boston Women's Health Book Collective, http://www.ourbodiesourselves.org/default.asp (accessed December 4, 2007).

5. Sherwin Kaufman, *The Ageless Woman: Menopause, Hormones, and the Quest for Youth* (Englewood Cliffs, NJ: Prentice-Hall, 1967); Phyllis and Eberhard Kronhausen, *The Sexually Responsive Woman* (New York: Grove, 1964); David Rorvik, *Good Housekeeping Woman's Medical Guide* (New York: Good Housekeeping, 1974); Morris Fishbein, *The Handy Home Medical Adviser, and Concise Medical Encyclopedia* (1957; reprinted, Garden City, NY: Doubleday, 1963).

6. Donna Haraway, "The Virtual Speculum in the New World Order," in *Revisioning Women, Health and Healing: Feminist, Cultural and Technoscience Perspectives*, edited by Adele E. Clarke and Virginia L. Olesen (London: Routledge, 1999), 49–96.

7. Kathy Davis, *The Making of* Our Bodies, Ourselves: *How Feminism Travels Across Borders* (Durham, NC: Duke University Press, 2007).

8. I will refer to the group of women who wrote *Our Bodies, Ourselves* as the Boston

Women's Health Book Collective (BWHBC) or as "the collective," their most common ways of referring to themselves. Before the publication of the first book, the group was variously known as "the Doctor's Group" or "the group for finding out about our bodies," or "the Boston Women's Health Collective." The author of the first edition, *Women and Their Bodies*, is listed as the "Boston Women's Health Course Collective." After 1973, the writer of all subsequent editions is the "Boston Women's Health Book Collective."

9. Jürgen Habermas, *Structural Transformation of the Public Sphere: An Inquiry into a Category of Bourgeois Society*, trans. Thomas Burger (Cambridge, MA: MIT Press, 1991). For a fuller account of public sphere theory, see Chapter 1.

10. Michael Warner, *Publics and Counterpublics* (New York: Zone, 2002).

11. Boston Women's Health Course Collective, *Our Bodies, Our Selves: A Course by and for Women*, 137.

12. Publishing decisions are recounted in detail in the collective minutes, Boston Women's Health Book Collective (BWHBC) Records 1972–97, Schlesinger Library, Radcliffe Institute, Harvard University, MC 503, box 1, folder 13.

13. BWHBC Records, 1972–97, Schlesinger Library, Radcliffe Institute, Harvard University, MC 503, box 102, folder 4, Letter from Norma Swenson to "Ms. Charolotte," January 1972.

14. Boston Women's Health Course Collective, *Our Bodies, Our Selves: A Course by and for Women* (1971), 138.

15. Lucy Candib, interview with author, December 2006.

16. Paula Doress-Worters, interview with author, October 2002.

17. Judith Norsigian, interview with author, November 2002; Norma Swenson, interview with author, December 2006.

18. "The founders of the BWHBC were all college educated, but a significant number of us were from working-class backgrounds and were the first in our families to attend college," Judy Norsigian and others, "The Boston Women's Health Book Collective and *Our Bodies, Ourselves*," *Journal of the American Medical Women's Association* 54, no. 1 (Winter 1999): 35–39, 36.

19. Blanche Linden-Ward and Carol Hurd Green, *American Women in the 1960s: Changing the Future* (New York: Twayne, 1993), 73.

20. Judy Herman, "History of the Somerville Women's Health Project," Gene Bishop Papers, Schlesinger Collection, Radcliffe Institute, Harvard University, 90–M52, folder 1, page 46.

21. Roxanne Dunbar-Ortiz, *Outlaw Woman: A Memoir of the War Years, 1960–75* (San Francisco: City Lights, 2001).

22. Winifred Breines, *The Trouble Between Us: An Uneasy History of White and Black Women in the Feminist Movement* (New York: Oxford, 2006).

23. Margie Stamberg, "Women's Meeting Held in Boston," *Guardian* 21, no. 34 (May 24, 1969): 9.

24. For the politico/feminist split, see Alice Echols, *Daring to Be Bad: Radical Feminism in America, 1967–1975* (Minneapolis: University of Minnesota Press, 1989).

25. Wini Breines, "What's Love Got to Do with It? White Women, Black Women, and Feminism in the Movement Years," *Signs* 27, no. 4 (Summer 2002): 1095–133.

26. A Bread and Roses membership list includes five members of the collective, seven additional authors or coauthors of chapters in *Our Bodies, Ourselves*, and fifteen more women who were listed on the acknowledgments page of the book between 1970 and 1976. The membership list is in the Frances Ansley Papers, Schlesinger Library, Radcliffe Institute, Harvard University, 90–M-127, folder 1.

27. See mimeographed newsletters, *On Our Way* (1971–72), of the Cambridge Women's Center, which include announcements and plans for the Women's School. Courses on Women and Their (or Our) Bodies were offered regularly in 1971 and 1972. These newsletters are held at the Northeastern University Women's History Archives, Women's Education Center, M47, carton 2.

28. "Some goals: to be relevant to women's concerns; to be conversant with conventional wisdom; to produce a uniquely OBOS feminist perspective," from a Memo to Writers for Revised *Our Bodies, Ourselves*, September 17, 1981, BWHBC Records, 1972–79, MC 503, box 106, folder 1.

29. Deborah Brandt, *Literacy in American Lives* (New York: Cambridge University Press, 2001).

30. For representative work on authorship and collaboration, see Lisa Ede and Andrea Lunsford, *Singular Texts/Plural Authors: Perspectives on Collaborative Writing* (Carbondale: Southern Illinois University Press, 1990); Lisa Ede and Andrea Lunsford, "Collaboration and Concepts of Authorship," *PMLA* 116, no. 2 (March 2001): 354–69; and also Christine Saxton, "The Collective Voice as Cultural Voice," *Cinema Journal* 26, no. 1 (1986): 19–30; David Sanders and Ian Hunter, "Lessons from the 'Literatory': How to Historicize Authorship," *Critical Inquiry* 17, no. 3 (Spring 1991): 479–509; Edward Shanken, "Tele-Agency: Telematics, Telerobotics, and the Art of Meaning," *Art Journal* 59, no. 2 (Summer 2000): 64–77; Michael North, "Authorship and Autography," *PMLA* 116, no. 5 (October 2001): 1377–85; and M. Thomas Inge, "Collaboration and Concepts of Authorship," *PMLA* 116, no. 3 (May 2001): 354–69.

31. Gerard A. Hauser, *Vernacular Voices: The Rhetoric of Publics and Public Spheres* (Columbia: University of South Carolina Press, 1999); Rosa A. Eberly, *Citizen Critics: Literary Public Spheres* (Urbana: University of Illinois Press, 2000). Judy Z. Segal, *Health and the Rhetoric of Medicine* (Carbondale: Southern Illinois University Press, 2005).

Chapter 1

1. Deborah Brandt, *Literacy in American Lives* (Cambridge: Cambridge University Press, 2001), 19. For an alternate view of literacy sponsorship, see Eli Goldblatt, *"Round My Way": Authority and Double-Consciousness in Three Urban High School Writers* (Pittsburgh, PA: University of Pittsburgh Press, 1995).

2. Blanche Linden-Ward and Carol Hurd Green, *American Women in the 1960s: Changing the Future* (New York: Twayne, 1993).

3. For the publications associated with these events, see United Nations, Department of Economic and Social Affairs, *Civic and Political Education of Women* (New York: United Nations, 1964); United States President's Commission on the Status of Women Committee on Education, *Report of the Committee on Education to the President's Commission on the Status of Women* (Washington, DC: The Commission, 1964); Statewide

Conference on the Changing Status of Women, *Proceedings* (Columbus: Ohio State University, 1965); Itasca Conference on the Continuing Education of Women, *Education and a Woman's Life: Proceedings* (Washington, DC: American Council on Education, 1963); Leo Muller and others, eds., *New Horizons for College Women* (Washington, DC: Public Affairs Press, 1960), which includes papers from the Mississippi State College for Women symposium; University of Michigan Center for Continuing Education of Women, *New Careers in Community Service* (Ann Arbor: Center for Continuing Education of Women, University of Michigan, 1968); Southern Methodist University Women's Committee for the Sesquicentennial Year, *The Education of Women for Social and Political Leadership* (Dallas, TX: Southern Methodist University Press, 1967); and Ann Firon Scott, "Education and the Contemporary Woman," in *The Knowledge Most Worth Having*, ed. Wayne Booth (Chicago: University of Chicago Press, 1967), 141–50.

4. Linden-Ward and Green, 101.

5. Ibid., 93.

6. Study Group on Women's Education, Lucy Candib Papers, 1966–70, Schlesinger Library, Radcliffe Institute, Harvard University, 89–M89, box 11, folder 6.

7. Bibring Report, Mary Bunting Smith Papers, Schlesinger Library, Radcliffe College, Harvard University, RG, Series 4, box 33, folder 508.

8. Study Group on Women's Education, Minutes 1/10/66, 1.

9. Ibid., 2.

10. Study Group on Women's Education, Minutes, 2/28/66, 1.

11. Study Group on Women's Education, Minutes, 4/11/66, 4.

12. Norma Swenson, interview with author, December 2006.

13. Ruth Bell Alexander, interview with author, October 2002.

14. Wendy Coppedge Sanford, *Theater as Metaphor in Hamlet* (Cambridge, MA: Harvard University Press, 1967).

15. Boston Women's Health Book Collective, Board of Directors' Minutes, January 7, 1974, BWHC Records, Schlesinger Collection, Radcliffe Institute, Harvard University, MC 503, box 1, folder 17.

16. Judith Norsigian, interview with author, November 2002; Norma Swenson, interview with Sara Rimer, in the *New York Times*, 1998, Boston Women's Health Book Collective Papers, Schlesinger Collection, Harvard University, MC 503, box 1, folder 9.

17. The relationship of the New Left to the counterculture is a complex historical question, explored in such works as *Imagine Nation: The American Counterculture of the 1960s and 70s*, ed. Peter Braunstein and Michael Doyle (New York: Routledge, 2002). In this book, I will use "counterculture" to refer to a broad cultural movement of the 1960s, dominated by young people, and "New Left" to refer to the political organizations agitating for an end to racism, the Vietnam War, and economic exploitation during that period.

18. Two accessible anthologies of New Left writing are Judith Clavir Albert and Stewart Edward Albert, *The Sixties Papers: Documents of a Rebellious Decade* (New York: Praeger, 1984); and Ann Charters, *The Portable Sixties Reader* (New York: Penguin, 2003). For accounts of the New Left by participants, see Todd Gitlin, *The Sixties: Years of Hope, Days of Rage* (New York: Bantam, 1987); Tom Hayden, *Reunion: A Memoir* (New

York: Random House, 1988); and Jim Miller, *"Democracy Is in the Streets": From Port Huron to the Siege of Chicago* (New York: Simon and Schuster, 1987). Memoirs of the 1960s are both widely available and deeply frustrating; see Susan Stern, *With the Weathermen: The Personal Journal of a Revolutionary Woman*, ed. Laura Browder (New York: Doubleday, 1975; reprinted, New Brunswick, NJ: Rutgers University Press, 2007); and William Ayers, *Fugitive Days: A Memoir* (Boston: Beacon, 2001). For the scholarly history of the 1960s and 1970s, see David Farber, ed., *The Sixties: From Memory to History* (Chapel Hill: University of North Carolina Press, 1994); Beth Bailey and David Farber, eds., *America in the Seventies* (Lawrence: University of Kansas Press, 2004). For a recent comprehensive account, see Mark Lytle, *America's Uncivil Wars: The Sixties Era from Elvis to the Fall of Richard Nixon* (New York: Oxford University Press, 2006).

19. Braunstein and Doyle, xiv; Abe Peck, *Uncovering the Sixties: The Life and Times of the Underground Press* (New York: Pantheon, 1985), 267.

20. Thorne Dryer and Victoria Smith, "The Movement and the New Media," originally published by the Liberation News Service, March 1, 1969; available online at the Austin *Rag* Web site, http://www.nuevoanden.com/rag/newmedia.html (accessed August 2007).

21. Stern, 115.

22. Walter Bowart and Allen Katzman, "Sgt. Pepper's Political Club and Band," *The East Village Other*, July 1, 1967; reprinted in Jesse Kornbluth, *Notes from the New Underground* (New York: Viking, 1968), 189–97.

23. *Rag* 1, no. 3 (October 24, 1966), available online at the Austin *Rag* Web site, www.nuevoanden.com/rag/010319661024 (accessed February 2009).

24. Anonymous, "'Man Tends, God Mends,'" *Old Mole* 8 (February 21–March 7, 1969): 11.

25. V. T. Ronay, "Oakland Induction Center: Tuesday, October 17, 1967," *Avatar*, November 1967, reprinted in Kornbluth, 286–90.

26. Kornbluth, 290.

27. Ibid., 287–88.

28. Christopher Tillan, "Cooking Column," *Old Mole* 11 (April 11–24, [1969]): 14.

29. "To Allen Ginsburg by Liza Williams," *The Oracle of Southern California* (March 1967): 200. In Jerry Hopkins, *The Hippie Papers: Notes from the Underground Press* (New York: New American Library, 1968), 134.

30. San Francisco *Oracle*, January 1967, in Hopkins, 11.

31. *Old Mole* 12 (Special Issue) (April 22–May 9, 1969): 11–12.

32. Ibid., 5.

33. For the SNCC report, "Mississippi Power Structure," see the *Freedom School Curriculum: Mississippi Freedom Summer, 1964*, ed. Kathy Emery, Sylvia Braselmann, and Linda Gold, available at educationanddemocracy.org/FSCfiles (Education and Democracy Web site, Kathy Emery). For a detailed discussion of power-structure research reports, see Susan Wells, "Photo-Offset Printing and the Alternative Press in the Sixties and Seventies: Practices and Genres," in *Rhetorics and Technologies: Papers from the 20th Penn State Conference on Rhetoric and Composition*, ed. Stuart Selber (Columbia: University of South Carolina Press, forthcoming). For the relationship between SNCC and ERAP, see SNCC, The Student Nonviolent Coordinating Committee Papers, 1959–72

(Sanford, NC: Microfilming Corporation of America, 1982), Reel 67, File 339, Page 0746. The original papers are at the King Library and Archives, the Martin Luther King Jr. Center for Nonviolent Social Change, Atlanta, Georgia.

34. In the *Freedom School Curriculum*, students are asked to identify "groups of men who make the myths, who profit from them like the farmer and businessman who pay the police and give them their orders, who make the laws and decide what laws they want, who make the decisions about who gets paid and how much they get, about who votes and who doesn't vote, about what is taught in schools and what gets printed in the newspapers."

35. Helen Shapiro, "NACLA Reminiscences: An Oral History," *NACLA Report* 15, no. 5 (September 1981): 46–56, 48.

36. William Domhoff, *Who Rules America?* (New York: Prentice-Hall, 1967); *Who Rules Columbia?* (New York: NACLA, 1967), available online at the UT Watch Web site, http://www.utwatch.org/archives/whorulescolumbia.html (accessed February 2009).

37. See, for example, Eliahu Salpeter, *Who Rules Israel?* (New York: Harper and Row, 1973); Leonard Ruchelman, *Who Rules the Police?* (New York: New York University Press, 1973); and Victor Wood, *Who Rules the A.P.A?: A Study of the Backgrounds of Leaders of the American Psychological Association* ([Arcata, CA]).

38. A.R.G. [Africa Research Group] and *Old Mole, How Harvard Rules: Being a Total Critique of Harvard University, Including: New Liberated Documents, Government Research, the Educational Process Exposed, Strike Posters, & a Free Power Chart* ([Cambridge, MA: 1969]).

39. Daniel Schechter, "From a Closed Filing Cabinet: The Life and Times of the Africa Research Group," *Issue: A Journal of Opinion* 6, no. 23 (Summer–Autumn 1976): 41–48, 43.

40. "How Harvard Rules," *The Harvard Crimson*, 5/7/1969; available online at http://www.thecrimson.com/article.aspx?ref=210032 (accessed May 2008).

41. For the early program of Science for the People, projecting "exposés and power structure research" as an organizational priority, see Bill Zimmerman, Len Radinsky, Mel Rothenberg, and Bart Meyers, "Towards a Science for the People," (1972), http://ist-socrates.berkeley.edu/schwrtz/SftP/Towards.html (accessed May 2008).

The current incarnation of Health/PAC, an interactive Web site, credits the groups' formation to Robb Rulage's study of plans to privatize the New York City municipal hospitals. This study, published as *New York City's Municipal Hospitals: A Policy Review* (Washington, DC: Institute for Policy Studies, 1967), was excerpted in the first issue of the *Health/PAC Bulletin*, which appeared monthly from 1968 to 1993. See the group's Web site at http://www.healthpaconline.net/

42. *How Harvard Rules*, foldout inserted chart.

43. *How Harvard Rules*, 1.

44. "Who Rules Harvard?" verso of chart inserted in *How Harvard Rules*.

45. Boston Women's Health Collective, *Women and Their Bodies: A Course* (Boston, MA: Boston Women's Health Collective, 1970), 3.

46. Ibid., 14.

47. Ibid., 10.

48. For contemporaneous histories of the women's movement, see Jo Freeman,

The Women's Liberation Movement: Its Aims, Structures, and Ideas (Pittsburgh, PA: Know, 1971); and Judith Hole and Ellen Levine, *Rebirth of Feminism* (New York: Quadrangle, 1971). For a convenient collection of documents, see Rosalyn Baxandall and Linda Gordon, eds., *Dear Sisters: Dispatches from the Women's Liberation Movement* (New York: Basic, 2000). Memoirs are collected in Rachel Blau DuPlessis and Ann Snitow, eds., *The Feminist Memoir Project* (New York: Three Rivers Press, 1998). For good general accounts, see Kimberly Springer, *Living for the Revolution: Black Feminist Organizations, 1968–80* (Durham, NC: Duke University Press, 2005); and Ruth Rosen, *The World Split Open: How the Modern Women's Movement Changed America* (New York: Penguin, 2000).

49. Kathryn Thoms Flannery, *Feminist Literacies, 1968–75* (Urbana: University of Illinois Press, 2005).

50. Ginny Z. Berson, "The Furies: Goddesses of Vengeance," in *Voices from the Underground*, ed. Ken Wachsberger, vol. I, *Insider Histories of the Vietnam Era Underground Press* (Tempe, AZ: MICA Press, 1993), 313–24, 314.

51. Sara Evans, *Personal Politics: The Roots of Women's Liberation in the Civil Rights Movement and the New Left* (New York: Vintage, 1979).

52. Ruth Bell Alexander, interview with author, October 2002.

53. Paula Doress-Worters and Vilunya Diskin, interview with author, October 2002.

54. Jane Pincus, interview with Sara Rimer, *New York Times*, 1998, BWHBC Records, Schlesinger Library, Radcliffe Institute, Harvard University, MC 503, box 1, folder 9.

55. Anonymous, "How to Start Your Own Consciousness-Raising Group," leaflet, 1971; in CWLU History Project, Historical Archive, Consciousness, http://www.cwluherstory.com/CWLUArchive/conscious.html (accessed January 18, 2009).

56. Doress-Worters/Diskin interview.

57. Elizabeth Lindsey, "Reexamining Gender and Sexual Orientation: Revisioning the Representation of Queer and Trans People in the 2005 Edition of *Our Bodies, Ourselves*," *NWSA Journal* 17 (2005): 184–89.

58. Women of the New University Conference and others, *How Harvard Rules Women* (Cambridge, MA: 1970).

59. *Ibid.*, 7.

60. *Ibid.*, 1.

61. Ann Popkin, "Bread and Roses: An Early Moment in the Development of Socialist-Feminism" (dissertation, Brandeis University, Department of Sociology, 1976).

62. Nancy Shaw, "Working on Women," Frances Ansley Papers, 90–M127, Schlesinger Library, Radcliffe Institute, Harvard University, box 1, folder 3, page 1.

63. Ibid., 3.

64. Meredith Tax, "Working Notes on Labour, Leisure, Recuperation, Play and Sex," Frances Ansley Papers, 90–M127, Schlesinger Library, Radcliffe Institute, Harvard University, box 1, folder 1.

65. Letter from Shierry, Wini Breines papers, 87–M17, Schlesinger Library, Radcliffe Institute, Harvard University, folder 2.

66. Draft chapters of *Our Bodies, Ourselves* are filed with Bread and Roses open

letters in the Frances Ansley Papers, 90–M127, Schlesinger Library, Radcliffe Institute, Harvard University, box 1, folder 1.

67. Nancy Miriam Hawley, "Women and Control of Their Bodies," Frances Ansley Papers, Schlesinger Library, Radcliffe Institute, Harvard University, 90–M127, box 1, folder 3. This paper can also be found in the Schlesinger Library, Radcliffe Institute, Harvard University collections of two other Bread and Roses veterans, the Wini Breines papers, 89–MI7, and the Gene Bishop papers, 90–M52.

68. Ibid., 1.

69. Ibid., 2.

70. Letter from Nancy Hawley and Marya Levinson, Wini Breines papers, Schlesinger Library, Radcliffe Institute, Harvard University, 89–MI7, folder 2.

71. Ibid., 1.

72. Ibid., 3.

73. Gene Bishop papers, Schlesinger Library, Radcliffe Institute, Harvard University, 90–M52, folder 6.

74. Valentine sticker, Frances Ansley Papers, Schlesinger Library, Radcliffe Institute, Harvard University, 90–M127, box 1.

75. Massachusetts Coalition for Occupational Safety and Health and the Boston Women's Health Book Collective, *Our Jobs, Our Health: a Woman's Guide to Occupational Health and Safety* (Watertown, MA: Boston Women's Health Book Collective and Massachusetts Coalition for Occupational Safety and Health, 1983).

76. "Women Must Control Own Medical Destiny," *Big Mama Rag* 2, no. 7 (May 1974): 7–11, 7.

77. Chris Hobbs, "Our Bodies Ourselves," *off our backs* 3, no. 8 (May 1973): 29.

78. Karen Kahn, interview with author, October 2002.

79. Kirkpatrick Sale, "The New Left: What's Left?" *WIN* (1) (June 21, 1973): 4–11.

80. Elinor Langer, "Notes for Next Time: A Memoir of the 1960s," *Working Papers for a New Society* 1, no. 3 (Fall 1973): 48–84.

81. Ibid., 48.

82. Ibid., 49.

83. Ibid., 50.

84. Ibid., 83.

85. Lucy Candib, interview with author, April 2007.

86. Lucy Candib, *Medicine and the Family: A Feminist Perspective* (New York: Basic Books, 1995), xiv.

87. *The Red Nucleus,* Lucy Candib Papers, Schlesinger Collection, Radcliffe Institute, Harvard University, 89–M89, box 2.

88. *The Red Nucleus* [1969], no. 3, page 1. Lucy Candib Papers, Schlesinger Library, Radcliffe Institute, Harvard University, 89–M89, box 2.

89. Wini Breines, "What's Love Got to Do with It? White Women, Black Women, and Feminism in the Movement Years," *Signs: Journal of Women in Culture and Society* 27, no. 4 (Summer 2002): 1095–113.

90. Lucy Candib, interview with author, April 2007.

91. Boston Women's Health Collective, *Women and Their Bodies* (1970), 6–8.

92. Ibid., 6.

93. Ibid.

94. Ibid., 7.

95. Lucy Candib, interview with author, April 2007.

96. Lucy Candib, "How Medicine Tried to Make a Man Out of Me (and Failed, Finally)," in *Women in Medical Education: an Anthology of Experience*, ed. Delese Wear (Albany: State University of New York Press, 1996), 135–44.

97. Lucy Candib, interview with author, April 2007.

98. Nancy Miriam Hawley, interview with author, April 2007.

99. Ibid.

100. Ibid.

101. Ibid.

102. Boston Women's Health Book Collective, *The New Our Bodies, Ourselves* (New York: Simon and Schuster, 1984), 73.

103. Jürgen Habermas, *Between Facts and Norms: Contributions to a Discourse Theory of Law and Democracy* (Cambridge, MA: MIT Press, 1996), 176–86.

104. Boston Women's Health Book Collective, *The New Our Bodies, Ourselves*, 73.

105. Ibid.

106. Ibid., 74.

107. Ibid., 75.

108. Ibid., v.

109. Jürgen Habermas, *Structural Transformation of the Public Sphere: An Inquiry into a Category of Bourgeois Society*, trans. Thomas Burger (Cambridge, MA: MIT Press, 1991), 29.

110. Sandra Morgen, *Into Our Own Hands: The Women's Health Movement in the United States, 1969–1990* (New Brunswick, NJ: Rutgers University Press, 2002), 146.

111. The use of *Our Bodies, Ourselves* by women's groups is one gauge of such activity. In a phone call to the group in October 1973, their editor Alice Mayhew estimated that five hundred clinics had requested low-cost copies of the book (Board of Directors' minutes, October 1973, BWHBC Records, Schlesinger Library, Radcliffe Institute, Harvard University, MC 503, box 1, folder 17). A memo from Ruth Bell, 1974, lists fifty-three groups who had requested discounted copies of *Our Bodies, Ourselves* directly from the collective since publication in the summer of 1973. (Bell memo, BWHBC papers, Schlesinger Library, Radcliffe Institute, Harvard University, MC 503, box 1, folder 16).

112. Habermas, *Structural Transformation*; Geoff Eley, "Nations, Publics, and Political Cultures," in *Habermas and the Public Sphere*, ed. Craig Calhoun (Cambridge, MA: MIT Press, 1992), 300–23; and Mary Ryan, "Gender and Public Access: Women's Politics in Nineteenth-Century America," in Calhoun, 259–88.

113. Michael Warner, *Publics and Counterpublics* (New York: Zone, 2002), 68–69.

114. Norbert Elias, *Power and Civility* (New York: Oxford, 1982). An example of the relation between privacy and propriety is the scandal of the *rémontrances* in pre-revolutionary France. When the outraged groups published their complaints against government actions, or *rémontrances*, aristocrats objected because publication—not

complaining—was considered subversive, ill bred, British. It was acceptable to remonstrate with the king, to advise him or to plead for justice, but publication of those complaints implied that judgment, reason, and even power were distributed among potential readers rather than being concentrated in the Crown. (See Keith Michael Baker, "Public Opinion as Political Invention," in *Inventing the French Revolution* [Cambridge: Cambridge University Press, 1990], 245.) For discussions of the relation between women and publicity in the French Revolution, a critical issue in historians' discussions about gender and the public sphere, see Joan Landes, *Women and the Public Sphere in the Age of the French Revolution* (Ithaca, NY: Cornell University Press, 1988); Keith Baker's reply in "Defining the Public Sphere in Eighteenth Century France: Variations on a Theme by Habermas," in *Habermas and the Public Sphere*, ed. Craig Calhoun (Cambridge, MA: MIT Press, 1992), 181–212; and Sarah Maza, "Women, the Bourgeoisie, and the Public Sphere: Response to Daniel Gordon and David Bell," *French Historical Studies* 17, no. 4 (Autumn 1992): 935–50.

115. Joan Ditzion, interview with author, July 2006; Jane Pincus, interview with author, October 2006.

116. Harold Mah, "Phantasies of the Public Sphere: Rethinking the Habermas of Historians," *The Journal of Modern History* 72, no. 1 (March 2000): 155.

117. Ibid., 155.

118. Todd Gitlin, *The Sixties: Years of Hope, Days of Rage* (New York: Bantam, 1987), 397.

119. Baker, 10.

120. Boston Women's Health Book Collective, *The New Our Bodies, Ourselves* (1984), xxiv.

121. Robin Morgan, *Sisterhood Is Powerful: An Anthology of Writings from the Women's Liberation Movement* (New York: Random House, 1970), xxxvi.

Chapter 2

1. Michel Foucault, "What Is an Author?" *Language, Counter-memory, Practice*, ed. Donald F. Bouchard, trans. Donald F. Bouchard and Sherry Simon (Ithaca, NY: Cornell University Press, 1977), 113–38, 128.

2. Norma Swenson, interview with author, December 2007.

3. See Introduction, note 30. Most relevant to this context is the work of Christine Saxton on collective authorship in film, "The Collective Voice as Cultural Voice," *Cinema Journal* 26, no. 1 (1986): 19–30; and of David Sanders and Ian Hunter on the history of authorship, "Lessons from the 'Literatory': How to Historicize Authorship," *Critical Inquiry* 17, no. 3 (Spring 1991): 479–509. The essays by Michael North, "Authorship and Autography," *PMLA* 116, no. 5 (October 2001): 1377–85, and M. Thomas Inge, "Collaboration and Concepts of Authorship," *PMLA* 116, no. 3 (May 2001): 354–69, are also relevant.

4. BWHBC Board of Directors' Minutes, Boston Women's Health Book Collective Records, 1972–97, Schlesinger Library, Radcliffe Institute, Harvard University, MC 503, box 1, folder 17.

5. Nancy Miriam Hawley, interview with author, April 2007.

6. The exhibition "La plissure du texte," an experiment in distributed authorship, was jointly mounted by eleven artists from various countries at the Musée d'Art Moderne de la Ville de Paris in 1983. An account of the exhibit can be found in Carl Eugene Loeffler and Roy Ascott, "Chronology and Working Survey of Select Telecommunications Activity," *Leonardo Music Journal* 24, no. 2 (1991): 235–40, 237.

7. Sarah Robbins, "Distributed Authorship: A Feminist Case-Study Framework for Studying Intellectual Property," *College English* 66, no. 2 (November 2003): 155–71, 160.

8. Wendy Coppedge Sanford, "Working Together, Growing Together: A Brief History of the Boston Women's Health Collective," *Heresies* 2, no. 3 (1970): 83–92.

9. Students for a Democratic Society, "The Port Huron Statement," in *The Sixties Papers: Documents of a Rebellious Decade*, ed. Judith Albert and Steward Albert (New York: Praeger, 1984), 176–96, 177.

10. See the rules of The Feminists, issued August 22, 1969: "In order to make efficient use of all opportunities for writing and speaking, in order to develop members who are experienced in these areas, members who are experienced in them are urged to withdraw their names from a lot assigning those tasks. Also those members, experienced or inexperienced, who have once drawn a lot to write or speak must withdraw their names until all members have had a turn" ("The Feminists: A Political Organization to Annihilate Sex Roles," originally published in *Notes from the Second Year* [1969] in *Radical Feminism*, ed. Anne Koedt, Ellen Levin, and Anita Rapone [New York: Quadrangle Books, 1973], 372).

11. Boston Women's Health Collective, *Women and Their Bodies: A Course* (Boston, MA: Boston Women's Health Collective, 1970), 4.

12. Wendy Sanford used the "worlds inside my head" phrase to explain why she was not a writer (Sanford, interview with author, October 2002); Vilunya Diskin characterized herself as a "people person" who "does not love writing" (interview with author, October 2002). Many members of the collective did not consider themselves writers because writing did not come easily to them.

13. Nancy Miriam Hawley, interview with author, April 2007.

14. Paula Doress[-Worters] and Diana Siegal, "Summary of Writers' Meeting," BWHBC Records, 1972–97, Schlesinger Library, Radcliffe Institute, Harvard University, MC 503, box 45, folder 11.

15. Boston Women's Health Book Collective, *The New Our Bodies, Ourselves* (New York: Simon and Schuster, 1984), 6.

16. Vilunya Diskin and Paula Doress-Worters, interview with author, October 2002.

17. Jürgen Habermas, *The Structural Transformation of the Public Sphere: An Inquiry into a Category of Bourgeois Society*, trans. Thomas Burger (Cambridge, MA: MIT Press, 1991).

18. Jane Pincus, interview with author, October 2006.

19. "Notes from a Meeting on Revision," November 12, 1981, BWHBC Records, 1972–97, MC 503, box 107, folder 21.

20. Letter to Wendy Sanford, November 3, 1981, BWHBC Records, 1972–97, MC 503, box 107, folder 21.

21. Judith Norsigian, interview with author, November 2002.

22. Letter from Wendy [Sanford] Coppedge and Miriam [Nancy] Hawley, November 25, 1981, BWHBC Records, 1971–97, MC 503, box 107, folder 21.

23. Judith Norsigian, interview with author, November 2002.

24. For "Wandering Through the Food Maze," see BWHBC Records, 1972–97, MC 503, box 36, folder 12; for recruiting "lay women" from the food class as readers, see BWHBC Records, 1972–97, MC 503, box 110, folder 10.

25. "Invitation to Come to Discussion Groups," September 1981, BWHBC Records, 1972–79, MC 503, box 110, folder 22.

26. "1979—Members of the Boston Women's Health Book Collective Speaking Engagements/Hearings/Media Appearances (excluding Parenting Group events)," BWHBC Records, 1972–97, MC 503, box 149, folder 9.

27. Memo from Paula re: Sexuality unit, July 1, 1981, BWHBC Records, 1972–97, MC 503, box 110, folder 22.

28. Kathy Davis, *The Making of Our Bodies, Ourselves: How Feminism Travels Across Borders* (Durham, NC: Duke University Press, 2007); Wendy Kline, "'Please Include this in Your Book': Readers Respond to *Our Bodies, Ourselves,*" *Bulletin of the History of Medicine* 79 (2005): 81–110. My discussion of conization is drawn from Kline's article.

29. Boston Women's Health Book Collective, *The New Our Bodies, Ourselves,* 488.

30. Letter from James Selkin to Judith Norsigian, February 4, 1975, BWHBC Records, 1972–97, MC 503, box 104, folder 4.

31. Boston Women's Health Book Collective, Memo, October 2008.

32. For a biography of Zola and a bibliography of his work, see Gareth Williams, "Irving Kenneth Zola (1935–1994): An Appreciation," *Sociology of Health and Illness* 18, no. 1 (1996): 107–25.

33. Memo to Writers for Revised *Our Bodies, Ourselves,* September 17, 1981. (Unsigned report of conversations among Norma Swenson, Judith Norsigian, and Nancy Miriam Hawley, BWHBC Records, 1972–97, MC 503, box 106, folder 1.)

34. Irving Kenneth Zola, "Bringing Our Bodies and Ourselves Back In: Reflections on a Past, Present, and Future 'Medical Sociology,'" *Journal of Health and Social Behavior* 32, no. 1 (March 1991): 1–16; Irving Kenneth Zola, "Shifting Boundaries: Doing Social Science in the 1990s—A Personal Odyssey," *Sociological Forum* 10, no. 1 (March 1995): 5–19. An example of Zola's work connecting the collective to scholars in critical social sciences was the panel on *Our Bodies, Ourselves* at the 1994 meeting of the Eastern Sociological Society. Participants included Emily Martin, Nancy Mills, and Robbie Pfeufer Kahn. Judith Norsigian and Paula Doress-Worters showed slides illustrating the collective's history. Eastern Sociological Society, March 1994, Baltimore, "Our Bodies, Ourselves session," Judith Norsigian, private videotape collection.

35. Letter to the Boston Women's Health Book Collective from Susan Bell, December 6, 1978, BWHBC Records, 1972–97, MC 503, box 2, folder 2.

36. Susan Bell, "Translating Science to the People: Updating the *New Our Bodies, Ourselves,*" *Women's Studies International Forum* 17, no. 1 (1994): 9–18.

37. Ibid., 14.

38. Bell cites Donna Haraway, "Situated Knowledges: The Science Question in Feminism and the Privilege of Partial Perspective," *Feminist Studies* 14 (1988): 575–99;

but this position is usually associated with Haraway's later *Primate Visions: Gender, Race, and Nature in the World of Modern Science* (New York and London: Routledge, 1989).

39. Memo to Writers for Revised *Our Bodies, Ourselves*, September 17, 1981, BWHBC Records, 1972–97, MC 503, box 106, folder 1.

40. Ibid.

41. Jane Pincus, interview with author, October 2006.

42. Memo to Writers for Revised *Our Bodies, Ourselves*, September 17, 1981, BWHBC Records, 1972–97, MC 503, box 106, folder 1.

43. BWHBC Board of Directors' Minutes, April 1979, BWHBC Records, 1972–97, MC 503, box 1, folder 13.

44. Information from this sketch is drawn from the following sources: Jane Pincus, personal interview with writer, October 2006; Jane Pincus, "Our Bodies, Ourselves: Liberating Minds and Bodies [Interview with Chelsea Whitaker]," http://www.doingoralhistory.org/project_archive/2004/Papers/PDFs/C-Whit.pdf (accessed May 2008); and Kathy Huffhines, "Scenes from a Marriage: Ed Presents Ed," review of *Scenes from a Marriage*, *Cambridge Express*, November 21, 1981, BWHBC Records, MC 503, box 45, folder 14.

45. Jane Pincus, interview with author, October 2006.

46. Ibid.

47. Ibid.

48. Ibid.

49. Ibid.

50. Ibid.

51. Jane Pincus, letter to author, November 2008.

52. Ibid.

53. See Anthony Smith, *The Body* (New York: Walker and Company, 1968); "Calendar of Pregnancy," 112–17; and compare *Women and Their Bodies*, "Appendix: 1 Growth of the embryo-fetus from week to week," 118–20.

54. Boston Women's Health Book Collective, *The New Our Bodies, Ourselves* (1984), v.

55. Jane Pincus, interview with author, October 2006.

56. Michel Odent, *Birth Reborn*, trans. Jane Pincus and Juliette Levin (New York: Pantheon, 1984).

57. This information is drawn from a collection of her own materials that Pincus generously shared with me in October 2006. For Sloane, see *Biology of Women* (New York: Wiley, 1980).

58. Robbie Pfeufer Kahn is mentioned on the acknowledgments pages of all copies of *Our Bodies, Ourselves* from 1984. Her *Bearing Meaning: The Language of Birth* (Urbana: University of Illinois Press, 1995) includes a long chapter on *Our Bodies, Ourselves* and acknowledges collaborations with the collective and particularly with Jane Pincus. Becky Sarah is acknowledged in *Our Bodies, Ourselves* beginning in 1984 and specially thanked for the 1984 chapters on pregnancy and childbirth.

59. Davis, *Making of Our Bodies*.

60. BWHBC Board of Directors' Minutes, April 14, 1974, BWHBC Records, 1972–97, MC 503, box 1, folder 16.

61. ALAS members believed that their work in the collective influenced the text of *Our Bodies, Ourselves* (see Ester Shapiro's quotation of Muñoz Lopez, below). This may well be true, but the index of editions from 1984 and 1992 show sparse and per- functory mentions of Latina health concerns. Even the 1998 edition, which was a real step forward in diversity, includes only fifteen such items in the index.

62. Ester Shapiro, "Because Words Are Not Enough: Latina Re-Visionings of Transnational Collaborations Using Health Promotion for Gender Justice and Social Change," *NWSA Journal* 17, no. 1 (Spring 2005): 141–72.

63. Ibid., 147.

64. For a full account of Spanish translations, see Davis, chaps. 2 and 6.

65. Zobeida Bonilla, *"Our Bodies, Ourselves* Goes Latina," *The Network News*, May/ June 2002, 5.

66. Shapiro, 161.

67. BWHBC Board of Directors' Minutes, BWHBC Records, 1972–97, Schlesinger Library, Radcliffe Institute, Harvard University, box 1, folder 13.

68. Boston Women's Health Book Collective, Memo, October 2008. Document provided by the collective.

69. These letters were formerly held with the Cambridge Women's Center Papers at Northeastern University, Boston. They were transferred to the Schlesinger and are cur- rently held as part of the BWHBC Records, 1972–97, MC 503, boxes 159 and 160.

70. BWHBC Board of Directors' Minutes, BWHBC Records, 1972–97, MC 503, box 1, folder 16.

71. Wendy Sanford, revision correspondence, BWHBC Records, 1972–97, MC 503, box 104, folder 4.

72. Boston Women's Health Book Collective, *Our Bodies, Ourselves: A Book by and for Women* (New York: Simon and Schuster, 1973), 72–73.

73. Boston Women's Health Book Collective, *Our Bodies, Ourselves: A Book by and for Women*, 2d ed. (New York: Simon and Schuster, 1976), 96.

74. Norma Swenson, "Proposed Draft Proposal to S&S RE: Our Revision," BWHBC Records, 1972–97, MC 503, box 107, folder 20.

75. Boston Women's Health Book Collective, *The New Our Bodies, Ourselves* (1984), 141.

76. Combahee River Collective, "Combahee River Collective Statement," in *All the Women Are White, All the Blacks Are Men, but Some of Us Are Brave: Black Women's Studies*, ed. Gloria Hull, Patricia Bell-Scott, and Barbara Smith (Old Westbury, NY: Feminist Press, 1982), 13–22, 16.

77. Boston Women's Health Book Collective, *Our Bodies, Ourselves* (1973), 1.

78. According the U.S. census, 104,707 of the 641,071 inhabitants of Boston in 1971 were African American (16.3 percent); in Cambridge, where many collective members lived, African Americans were 6.6 percent of the population. The Hispanic population was 2.8 percent in Boston and 1.9 percent in Cambridge. See Bureau of the Census, Selected Historical Decennial Census Population and Housing Counts, at http://www .census.gov/population/www/censusdata/hiscendata.html (accessed February 2008).

79. Kimberly Springer, *Living for the Revolution: Black Feminist Organizations, 1968–1980* (Durham, NC: Duke University Press, 2005).

80. Combahee River Collective, "Combahee River Collective Statement," 13–22, 13.

81. Wini Breines, "What's Love Got to Do With It? White Women, Black Women, and Feminism in the Movement Years," *Signs* 27, no. 4 (Summer 2002): 1095–133, 1109.

82. Sandra Morgen, *Into our Own Hands: The Women's Health Movement in the United States, 1969–1990* (New Brunswick, NJ: Rutgers University Press, 2002).

83. Audre Lourde, *Zami: A New Spelling of My Name* (Berkeley, CA: Cross Press, 1982), 226.

84. Stephen Simurda, "Byllye Avery: Guardian of Black Women's Health," *American Health* (March 1993); for the 1975 conference, see Avery's preface to the 1998 *Our Bodies, Ourselves.*

85. Morgen, chap. 3.

86. Martha Scherzwer, "Byllye Avery and the National Black Women's Health Project," *The Network News* May–June 1995, 1, 4, 64.

87. BWHBC Records, 1972–97, MC 503, box 1, folder 8.

88. Francesca Polletta, *It Was Like a Fever: Storytelling in Protest and Politics* (Chicago: University of Chicago Press, 2006).

89. Boston Women's Health Book Collective, *Women and Their Bodies: A Course* (1970), 106.

90. Ibid.

91. Ibid.

92. Boston Women's Health Book Collective, *The New Our Bodies, Ourselves* (1984), 298.

93. Ibid., 300.

94. Ibid., xiii.

95. Boston Women's Health Book Collective, *Our Bodies, Ourselves for the New Century* (1998), 23.

96. Elizabeth Grosz, "Sexual Difference and the Problem of Essentialism," *Inscriptions* 5 (1989), www.ucsc.edu/DivWeb/CultStudies/PUBS/Inscriptions/vol_5 (accessed August 2007).

97. See Satya Mohanty, *Literary Theory and the Claims of History* (Ithaca, NY: Cornell University Press, 1997).

98. Spivak herself has repudiated the widespread use of strategic essentialism: "I don't go with the strategic uses of essentialism anymore. I'm much more interested in seeing the differences among these so-called essences in various cultural inscriptions. . . . The question of female agency is dependent upon constitutions. Constitutions are extremely historical things that are produced quite often by the dismantling of a colony or an empire, and, therefore, in the constitution, the mark of the former masters is still present . . . and yet, the possibility of female agency is written in that discourse" (Sara Danius, Stefan Jonsson, and Gayatri Chakravorty Spivak, "An Interview with Gayatri Chakravorty Spivak," *boundary 2* 20, no. 2 [Summer 1993]: 24–50, 36).

99. Judith Butler, "Discussion ('The Identity in Question')," *October* 61 (Summer 1992): 108–20, 108.

100. Linda Martin Alcoff, "Who's Afraid of Identity Politics," in *Reclaiming Identity: Realist Theory and the Predicament of Post-Modernism,* ed. Paula Moya and Michael

Hames-Garcia (Berkeley: University of California Press, 2000); available at www.alcoff .com/content/afraidid.html (accessed February 4, 2009).

Chapter 3

1. Joan Ditzion, interview with author, July 2007.

2. "Metalepsis," in Gideon O. Burton, *Silvae Rhetoricae*. http://www.byu.edu/ rhetoric (accessed December 2008).

3. Gérard Genette, *Narrative Discourse*, trans. J. E. Lewin (Ithaca, NY: Cornell University Press, 1980), 235.

4. Roger Jauneau, *Small Printing Houses and Modern Technology* (Paris: UNESCO Press, 1981), 15.

5. Nancy Miriam Hawley, interview with author, April 2007.

6. Nancy Miriam Hawley, interview with author, April 2007; Jane Pincus, interview with author, October 2007.

7. Boston Women's Health Collective, *Women and Their Bodies: A Course* (Boston, MA: Boston Women's Health Collective, 1970), 1.

8. Ruth Bell, interview with author, November 2002.

9. Vilunya Diskin and Paula Doress-Worters, interview with author, October 2002.

10. Jane Pincus, interview with author, October 2007.

11. Judith Norsigian, interview with author, November 2002.

12. Board of Directors Minutes, January 7, 1974, Boston Women's Health Book Collective Records, 1972–97, Schlesinger Library, Radcliffe Institute, Harvard University, MC 503, box 1, folder 16.

13. Summary of Publishing History, *Our Bodies, Ourselves*, 1996. BWHBC Records, Schlesinger Library, Radcliffe Institute, Harvard University, MC 503, box 1, folder 8.

14. Boston Women's Health Collective, *Women and Their Bodies* (1970), 60.

15. Ibid., 108.

16. Ibid., 133.

17. Boston Women's Health Collective, *Women and Their Bodies* (1970), 4.

18. Ibid., 9.

19. Ibid., 16.

20. Ibid., 18.

21. Ruth Bell Alexander, interview with author, November 2002.

22. Boston Women's Health Book Collective, *Our Bodies, Ourselves: A Book by and for Women*, 2d ed. (New York: Simon and Schuster, 1976), 222.

23. Ibid., 311.

24. Ibid., 296.

25. Boston Women's Health Book Collective, *The New Our Bodies, Ourselves* (New York: Simon and Schuster, 1984), 9.

26. Sandra Morgen, *Into Our Own Hands: The Women's Health Movement in the United States, 1969–80* (New Brunswick, NJ: Rutgers University Press, 2002), 1–75.

27. Nancy Miriam Hawley, interview with author, April 2007.

28. Boston Women's Health Book Collective, *Our Bodies, Ourselves: A Book by and for Women* (New York: Simon and Schuster, 1973), 110.

29. Boston Women's Health Book Collective, *Our Bodies, Ourselves: A Book by and for Women* (1976), 355.

30. For the "typical case," see Kathryn Montgomery Hunter, *Doctors' Stories: The Narrative Structure of Medical Knowledge* (Princeton, NJ: Princeton University Press, 1991), chap. 1.

31. For some of the surprisingly rich literature on chiasmus, see S. Budick, "Chiasmus and the Making of Literary Tradition: The Case of Wordsworth and 'The Days of Dryden and Pope,'" *ELH* 60, no. 4 (1993): 961–87; Jonathan Xavier Inda, "Foreign Bodies: Migrants, Parasites, and the Pathological Nation," *Discourse* 22, no. 3 (Fall 2000): 46–62; Jeffrey Nealon, "Maxima Immoralia? Speed and Slowness in Adorno's *Minima Moralia*," *Theory and Event* 4, no. 3 (2000); and Cecilia Sjoholm, "Crossing Lovers: Luce Irigaray's *Elemental Passions*," *Hypatia* 15, no. 3 (2000): 92–112.

32. The literature on chiasmus in biblical studies is daunting. For the merest taste, see Elie Assis, "Chiasmus in Biblical Narrative: Rhetoric of Characterization," *Prooftexts* 22 (2002): 273–304.

33. Martin Luther King Jr., "Beyond Vietnam" (address delivered to the Clergy and Laymen Concerned About Vietnam, Riverside Church, April 4, 1967); available online at Martin Luther King Jr. Papers Project, http://www.stanford.edu/group/King/publications/speeches/Beyond_Vietnam.pdf (accessed January 8, 2009).

34. New University Conference, *How Harvard Rules Women* (n.p.: n.p., 1970), 7.

35. Women's Health Ring, "Women and Health," leaflet and wall poster, Gene Bishop Papers, Schlesinger Library, Radcliffe Institute, Harvard University, 90–M62, folder 6.

36. Boston Women's Health Book Collective, *The New Our Bodies, Ourselves* (1984), 447.

37. Laura Tanner, *Intimate Violence: Reading Rape and Torture in Twentieth-Century Fiction* (Bloomington: Indiana University Press, 1980).

38. The untitled document appears in the Frances Ansley papers, Schlesinger Library, Radcliffe Institute, Harvard University, 90–M127, box 1, folder 3. Ansley was a member of Bread and Roses and an early collaborator with the collective.

39. Boston Women's Health Collective, *Women and Their Bodies* (1970), 19.

40. Alexander Lowen, *Love and Orgasm* (New York: New American Library, 1967).

41. Boston Women's Health Collective, *Women and their Bodies* (1970), 27.

42. Ibid., 29.

43. Ibid., 35.

44. Ibid., 12–13.

45. Boston Women's Health Book Collective, *Our Bodies, Ourselves; a Book by and for Women* (1973), 18.

46. Ibid.

47. Ibid., 53.

48. Boston Women's Health Book Collective, *Our Bodies, Ourselves* (1976), 47.

49. Ibid., 48.

50. Ibid.

51. Boston Women's Health Book Collective, *The New Our Bodies, Ourselves* (1984), 177.

52. Ibid., 51.

53. Boston Women's Health Collective, *Women and their Bodies* (1970), 28.

54. W.H. Masters and V.E. Johnson, *Human Sexual Response* (Toronto and New York: Bantam Books, 1966).

55. Boston Women's Health Collective, *Women and Their Bodies* (1970), 28.

56. Anne Koedt, "The Myth of the Vaginal Orgasm," first published 1968, in Rosalyn Baxandall and Linda Gordon, eds., *Dear Sisters: Dispatches from the Women's Liberation Movement* (New York: Basic Books, 2000), 160.

57. Nancy Mann, "Fucked-Up in America," Wini Breines Papers, Schlesinger Library, Radcliffe Institute, Harvard University, 89–M17, folder 2.

58. Various writers, Notes on OBOS Proposal, October 6, 1980, BWHBC Papers, Schlesinger Library, Radcliffe Institute, Harvard University, MC 503, box 107, folder 20.

59. Norma Swenson, "Proposed Draft Proposal to S&S Re: Our Revision," BWHBC Records, Schlesinger Library, Radcliffe College, Harvard University, MC 503, box 107, folder 20.

60. Norma Swenson, "Relationships Question and Suggested Outline/Notes: Responses from Norma," August 1981, BWHBC Records, Schlesinger Library, Radcliffe Institute, Harvard University, MC 503, box 110, folder 20.

61. Norma Swenson, letter to the BWHBC, April 1980, BWHBC Records, Schlesinger Library, Radcliffe Institute, Harvard University, MC 503, box 107, folder 20.

62. See this typical comment, on Samuel Beckett's use of metalepsis: "The reading process has thus become implicated in, and the reader swept up into, the violent and unending process of subjectification and subjugation" (Debra Malina, *Breaking the Frame: Metalepsis and the Construction of the Subject* [Columbus: Ohio State University Press, 2002], 55). Malina's study has been extremely useful.

63. Boston Women's Health Book Collective. *The New Our Bodies, Ourselves* (1984), 166.

64. Ibid., 180.

65. Wendy Sanford, "The Spice of Life: A Review of *Heresies* "Sex Issue," typed manuscript for *Heresies* 3, no. 4 (Spring 1981), BWHBC Papers, Schlesinger Library, Radcliffe Institute, Harvard University, MC 503, box 110, folder 22.

66. Ibid., 2.

67. Boston Women's Health Book Collective, *The New Our Bodies, Ourselves* (1984), 182.

68. Ibid., 176.

69. Morgen, 181.

70. C. W. Cooke, MD, and S. Dworkin, *The Ms. Guide to a Woman's Health* (New York: Doubleday, 1979); Beth Richardson Gutcheon, *Abortion: A Woman's Guide* (New York: Abelard-Schuman, 1975).

71. Kirsten Grimsted and Susan Rennie, *The New Woman's Survival Sourcebook* (New York: Alfred A. Knopf, 1975).

72. Deborah Chase, *The Medically-Based No-Nonsense Beauty Book* (New York: Alfred A. Knopf, 1974).

73. Jackie King, interview with author, September 2002.

74. Boston Women's Health Book Collective. *The New Our Bodies, Ourselves* (1984), 43.

75. Ibid., 52.

76. Rosi Braidotti, *Metamorphoses: Towards a Materialist Theory of Becoming* (Cambridge: Polity Press, 2002), 57.

77. Daniel Heller-Roazen, *Echolalias: On the Forgetting of Language* (New York: Zone, 2005).

78. Jane Pincus, Letter to the Boston Women's Health Book Collective Board, February 1992, BWHBC Records, Schlesinger Library, Radcliffe Institute, Harvard University, MC 503, box 4, folder 2.

79. Heller-Roazen, 51.

80. Ibid., 74–75.

81. Michael Warner, *Publics and Counterpublics* (New York: Zone, 2002), 130.

Chapter 4

1. For a selection of these studies, see Susan Bordo, *Unbearable Weight: Feminism, Western Culture, and the Body* (Berkeley: University of California Press, 1993); Caroline Bynum, *Fragmentation and Redemption: Essays on Gender and the Human Body in Medieval Religion* (New York: Zone, 1993); Elizabeth Grosz, *Space, Time, and Perversion* (New York: Routledge, 1995); Elizabeth Grosz, *Volatile Bodies: Toward a Corporeal Feminism* (Bloomington: Indiana University Press, 1994); Thomas Laqueur, *Making Sex: Body and Gender from the Greeks to Freud* (Cambridge, MA: Harvard University Press, 1990); Mary M. Lay, Laura J. Gurak, Clare Gravon, and Cynthia Myntti, *Body Talk: Rhetoric, Technology, Reproduction* (Madison: University of Wisconsin Press, 2000); Christopher Lawrence and Steven Shapin, eds., *Science Incarnate: Historical Embodiments of Natural Knowledge* (Chicago: University of Chicago Press, 1990); Linda Birke, *Feminism and the Biological Body* (Rutgers, NJ: Rutgers University Press, 1999); Vera Kalitzkus and Peter Twohig, eds., *Bordering Biomedicine* (New York: Rodopi, 2006); and Stacy Alaimo and Susan Hekman, eds., *Material Feminisms* (Bloomington: Indiana University Press, 2008).

2. For studies of anatomy as a cultural practice, see Londa Schiebinger, *Nature's Body: Gender in the Making of Modern Science* (Boston: Beacon, 1993); Mimi Cazort, Monique Kornell, K. B. Roberts, and National Gallery of Canada, *The Ingenious Machine of Nature: Four Centuries of Art and Anatomy* (Ottawa: National Gallery of Canada), 1996; Michael Sappol, *Dream Anatomy* (Washington, DC: National Library of Medicine, 2006); Barbara Maria Stafford, *Body Criticism: Imaging the Unseen in Enlightenment Art and Medicine* (Cambridge, MA: MIT Press, 1991). For historical investigations of embodiment and psychoanalysis, as well as critical reflections on representations of the body, see Dianne F. Sadoff, *Sciences of the Flesh: Representing Body and Subject in Psychoanalysis* (Stanford, CA: Stanford University Press, 1998). For critical reflections on representations of the body, see Judith Butler, *Bodies that Matter: On the Discursive Limits of 'Sex'*

(London: Routledge, 1993); Judith Butler, *Gender Trouble: Feminism and the Subversion of Identity* (London: Routledge: 1990); Elizabeth Grosz, *Space, Time, and Perversion: Essays on the Politics of Bodies* (New York: Routledge, 1994); Iris Marion Young, *"Throwing Like a Girl" and Other Essays: Studies in Feminist Philosophy*, ed. Cheshire Calhoun (New York: Oxford University Press, 2005); and Anne Fausto-Sterling, *Sexing the Body: Gender Politics and the Construction of Sexuality* (New York: Basic Books, 2000). For collections of representative essays, see Janet Price and Margrit Shildrick, *Feminist Theory and the Body: A Reader* (New York: Routledge, 1999); and Gail Weis Haber and Honi Fern, *Perspectives on Embodiment: The Intersections of Nature and Culture* (New York: Routledge, 1999).

3. Paula Doress-Worters, interview with author, October 2002.

4. Joan Ditzion, interview with author, July 2007.

5. Lisa Jean Moore and Adele E. Clarke, "Clitoral Conventions and Transgressions: Graphic Representations in Anatomy Texts, c. 1900–1991," *Feminist Studies* 21, no. 2 (Summer 1995): 255–301, 255.

6. Grosz, 36–37.

7. Paula Doress-Worters, interview with author, October 2002.

8. Boston Women's Health Book Collective, *Our Bodies, Ourselves: A Book by and for Women*, 2d ed. (New York: Simon and Schuster, 1976), 15.

9. For performances of the It's All Right to Be a Women Theater, see Charlotte Rea, "Women's Theatre Groups," *The Drama Review: TDR* 16, no. 2 (1972): 79–89.

10. Paula Doress-Worters, interview with author, October 2002.

11. Bernadette Wegenstein, "Getting Under the Skin, Or, How Faces Have Become Obsolete," *Configurations* 10, no. 2 (2002): 221–60.

12. Boston Women's Health Book Collective, *Our Bodies, Ourselves: A Book by and for Women* (New York: Simon and Schuster, 1973).

13. Boston Women's Health Book Collective, *The New Our Bodies, Ourselves* (New York: Simon and Schuster, 1984), 46.

14. Ibid., 204–5.

15. Boston Women's Health Book Collective, *The New Our Bodies, Ourselves* (1984), 47.

16. Ibid., 43.

17. Boston Women's Health Course Collective, *Our Bodies, Our Selves; a Course by and for Women* (Boston: New England Free Press, 1971), 4.

18. Boston Women's Health Book Collective, *Our Bodies, Ourselves: A Book by and for Women* (1976), 41.

19. Shere Hite, *The Hite Report: A Nationwide Study of Female Sexuality* (New York: Macmillan, 1976).

20. Boston Women's Health Book Collective, *The New Our Bodies, Ourselves* (1984), 169.

21. Jacques Lacan, "Some Reflections on the Ego," *International Journal of Psychoanalysis* 34 (1953): 11–17.

22. Boston Women's Health Course Collective, *Our Bodies, Our Selves* (1971), 4.

23. Jane Pincus, interview with author, October 2006.

24. Meredith Tax, "Woman and Her Mind: The Story of Everyday Life," in *Radical Feminism*, ed. Anne Koedt, Ellen Levine, and Anita Rapone (New York: Quadrangle

Books, 1973), 23–35, 25.

25. Simone de Beauvoir, *The Second Sex* (1952; reprinted, New York: Random House, 1989).

26. Chicago Liberation School for Women, "Courses, Spring 1973," in Rosalyn Baxandall and Linda Gordon, eds., *Dear Sisters: Dispatches from the Women's Liberation Movement* (New York: Basic Books, 2000), 246–47, 246.

27. De Beauvoir, 358.

28. Ibid., 29.

29. Boston Women's Health Course Collective, *Our Bodies, Our Selves* (1971), 4.

30. Nancy Miriam Hawley, interview with author, April 2007.

31. Jane Pincus, interview with author, October 2006.

32. Boston Women's Health Course Collective. *Our Bodies, Our Selves: A Course by and for Women* (1971), 4.

33. Ibid., 8.

34. Ibid., 6.

35. Ibid.

36. Ibid., 7, caption for pictures of male and female fetal organs.

37. Ibid., 7.

38. Ibid., 13.

39. Ibid., 15–36.

40. Ibid., 28.

41. For second-wave feminist interest in androgyny, see Alice Echols, *Shaky Ground: The 60s and Its Aftershocks* (New York: Columbia University Press, 2002), 106–8.

42. Boston Women's Health Course Collective, *Our Bodies, Our Selves: A Course by and for Women* (1971), 8.

43. Donna Haraway, "The Virtual Speculum in the New World Order," in *Revisioning Women, Health and Healing: Feminist, Cultural and Technoscience Perspectives*, ed. Adele E. Clarke and Virginia L. Olesen (New York: Routledge, 1998), 49–96, 67.

44. Kathy Davis, *How Feminism Travels Across Borders: The Making of* Our Bodies, Ourselves (Durham, NC: Duke University Press, 2007), chap. 4.

45. Carolyn Merchant, *The Death of Nature: Women, Ecology, and the Scientific Revolution* (New York: HarperCollins, 1980).

46. Donna Haraway, Modest_Witness@Second_Millennium.*FemaleMan_Meets_OncoMouse: Feminism and Technoscience* (New York: Routledge, 1997).

47. Boston Women's Health Book Collective, *Our Bodies, Ourselves: A Book by and for Women* (1976), 25.

48. Boston Women's Health Book Collective, *Our Bodies, Ourselves; a Book by and for Women* (1973), 14.

49. Ibid.

50. Ibid., 15.

51. Ibid.

52. Ibid., 15–16.

53. Wendy Sanford, interview with author, October 2002.

54. Boston Women's Health Book Collective, *Our Bodies, Ourselves: A Book by and for Women* (1976), 27.

55. Boston Women's Health Book Collective, *Our Bodies, Ourselves: A Book by and for Women* (1973), 2–3.

56. Jacques Lacan, "Feminine Sexuality in Psychoanalytic Doctrine," in *Feminine Sexuality*, ed. Juliet Mitchell and Jacqueline Rose (New York: W. W. Norton, 1982), 123–36, 124.

57. For the significance of reafference, see Jennifer Ruth Hosek and Walter J. Freeman, "Osmetic Ontogenesis, or Olfaction Becomes You: The Neurodynamic Intentional Self and Its Affinities with the Foucaultian/Butlerian Subject," *Configurations* 9 (2001): 509–42.

58. Robin Morgan, "Goodbye to All That," in *Dear Sisters: Dispatches from the Women's Liberation Movement*, ed. Rosalyn Baxandall and Linda Gordon (New York: Basic Books, 2000), 53–57; Naomi Weisstein, "Psychology Constructs the Female," in *Radical Feminism*, ed. Anne Koedt, Ellen Levine, and Anita Rapone (New York: Quadrangle, 1973), 165–77.

59. Karl Marx and Eleanor Marx Aveling, *Value, Price and Profit* (New York: International, 1969); *The Economic and Philosophic Manuscripts of 1844* (New York: International, 1964).

60. Karl Marx, *The Economic and Philosophic Manuscripts of 1844* (New York: International Publishers, 1964), 109.

61. Ibid.

62. Lucy Candib Papers, 1966–1970, Schlesinger Library, Radcliffe Institute, Harvard University, box 1.

63. "Private Property and Communism," in Marx, *Economic and Philosophic Manuscripts of 1844*, 139.

64. Shulamith Firestone, *The Dialectic of Sex* (New York: Morrow, 1970).

65. Ibid., 41.

66. Tax, 29.

67. Ibid., 31–32.

68. Shulamith Firestone and Anne Koedt, eds., *Notes from the Second Year of Women's Liberation: Major Writings of the Radical Feminists* (New York: Radical Feminism, 1970), 10–12; Anne Koedt, Ellen Levine, and Anita Rapone, eds., *Radical Feminism* (New York: Quadrangle Books, 1973), 23–36.

69. Judith Butler, *The Psychic Life of Power: Theories in Subjection* (Stanford, CA: Stanford University Press, 1997), 3.

70. Boston Women's Health Book Collective, *Our Bodies, Ourselves: A Book by and for Women* (1976), 39.

71. Boston Women's Health Book Collective, *Our Bodies, Ourselves: A Book by and for Women* (1973), 13.

72. Ibid., 83.

73. Boston Women's Health Book Collective, *Our Bodies, Ourselves for the New Century: A Book by and for Women*, newly revised and updated ed. (New York: Simon and Schuster, 1998), 40.

74. Boston Women's Health Book Collective, *Our Bodies, Ourselves: A Book by and for Women* (1973), 24.

75. Ibid.

76. "Sexuality" chapter, draft manuscript, Frances Ansley papers, Schlesinger Library, Radcliffe Institute, Harvard University, box 1, folder 3.

77. Boston Women's Health Book Collective, *Our Bodies, Ourselves: A Book by and for Women* (1973), 8.

78. Ibid., 9.

79. Ibid., 10.

80. Ibid., 2.

81. Boston Women's Health Book Collective, *Our Bodies, Ourselves: A Book by and for Women*, (1976), 216.

82. Boston Women's Health Book Collective, *The New Our Bodies, Ourselves* (1984), 339; italics in original.

83. Ibid.

84. Ibid., 341.

85. Ibid., 334.

86. Ibid.

87. Ibid., 335.

88. Ibid., 329.

89. Ibid.

90. Grosz, 13.

91. Ibid., 36.

Chapter 5

1. "Who Is Your Doctor?" Jane Pincus, personal papers.

2. *Boston Women's Liberation Newsletter* 1, no. 4 (November 18, 1969), Frances Ansley Papers, Schlesinger Library, Radcliffe Institute, Harvard University.

3. Vilunya Diskin and Paula Doress-Worters, interview with author, Boston, October 17, 2002.

4. Boston Women's Health Collective, *Women and Their Bodies: A Course* (Boston: Boston Women's Health Collective, 1970), 9.

5. Ibid., 9–10.

6. Wendy Coppedge Sanford, interview with author, October 2002.

7. Lucy Candib, interview with author, April 2007.

8. For a full discussion of this position in feminism, see Sandra Harding, *Whose Science? Whose Knowledge? Thinking from Women's Lives* (Ithaca, NY: Cornell University Press, 1991).

9. Boston Women's Health Book Collective, *Our Bodies, Ourselves: A Book by and for Women* (New York: Simon and Schuster, 1973), 333.

10. Ibid.

11. Boston Women's Health Book Collective, *The New Our Bodies, Ourselves* (New York: Simon and Schuster, 1984), 558.

12. Ibid., 557.

13. Ibid., 3.

14. Giorgio Agamben, *Homo Sacer: Sovereign Power and Bare Life*, trans. Daniel Heller-Roazen (Stanford, CA: Stanford University Press, 1998), 8.

15. Michael Moon and Cathy N. Davidson, eds., *Subjects and Citizens: Nation, Race, and Gender from Oroonoko to Anita Hill* (Durham, NC: Duke University Press, 1995), 529; Mary Poovey, *Making a Social Body: British Cultural Formation, 1830–1864* (Chicago: University of Chicago Press, 1995), 255; Dianne F. Sadoff, *Sciences of the Flesh: Representing Body and Subject in Psychoanalysis* (Stanford, CA: Stanford University Press, 1998), 343.

16. Worthington Hooker, *Physician and Patient; Or, a Practical View of the Mutual Duties, Relations, and Interests of the Medical Profession and the Community* (reprint of the 1849 ed.; New York: Arno, 1972), 443.

17. Charles D. Meigs, *Females and their Diseases* (Philadelphia, PA: Blanchard and Lea, 1848), 413.

18. Better Homes and Gardens Child Care and Training Department, *Better Homes and Gardens Baby Book: A Handbook for Mothers; from Prenatal Care to Child's Sixth Year* (Des Moines, Iowa: Meredith Publishing Company, 1946), 19. Other editions were published in 1943, 1951, and 1963; the 1963 edition was a best seller. For the popularity of the book, see Walter Boek, Marvin Sussman, and Alfred Yankauer, "Social Class and Child Care Practices," *Marriage and Family Living* 20, no. 4 (November 1958): 326–33, 330.

19. Ibid., 20.

20. Ibid., 48.

21. Ibid., 87.

22. Ibid., 7.

23. Jane E. Brody, "A New Birth Pill Cuts Side Effects: Contraceptive Developed by Concern on Coast Does Not Interfere with Ovulation," *New York Times*, January 20, 1966.

24. For the Sunday magazine article on birth control, see Lawrence Lader, "Three Men Who Made a Revolution," *The New York Times*, April 10, 1966, sec. Sunday Magazine; for the account of birth control in the 1970 *Our Bodies, Ourselves*, see 66–67.

25. Takey Crist and Lana Starnes, "Student Printing Presses Bring Birth Control Story to Colleges," *Family Planning Perspectives* 4, no. 1 (January 1972): 60–61.

26. Ellen Willis, "Birth Control Pill." *Mademoiselle*, January 1961, 54.

27. Boston Women's Health Collective, *Women and Their Bodies* (1970), 5.

28. Ibid.

29. Ibid., 60.

30. Ibid., 61.

31. Boston Women's Health Book Collective, Records, 1972–97, Schlesinger Library, Radcliffe Institute, Harvard University, Minutes (October 21, 1974), BWHBC, MC 503, box 1, folder 16.

32. Boston Women's Health Collective, *Women and Their Bodies* (1970), 286.

33. Ibid., 70.

34. "Meeting with Jenny, Beth, Myla, and Becky," handwritten notes, Jane Pincus, private papers.

35. Elizabeth Grosz, *Space, Time, and Perversion: Essays on the Politics of Bodies* (New York: Routledge, 1995), 33.

36. Ibid.

37. M.A.K. Halliday and J. R. Martin, *Writing Science: Literacy and Discursive Power* (Pittsburgh, PA: University of Pittsburgh Press, 1993); J. R. Martin and Robert Veel, eds., *Reading Science: Cultural and Functional Perspectives on Discourses of Science* (London: Routledge, 1998).

38. M.A.K. Halliday, "The Construction of Knowledge and Value in the Grammar of Scientific Discourse: Charles Darwin's the Origin of the Species," in *Writing Science: Literacy and Discursive Power*, ed. M.A.K. Halliday and J. R. Martin (Pittsburgh, PA: University of Pittsburgh Press, 1993), 86–105, 87.

39. M.A.K. Halliday, "Things and Relations: Regrammaticising Experience as Technical Knowledge," in *Reading Science: Critical and Functional Perspectives on Discourses of Science*, ed. J. R. Martin and R. Veel (London: Routledge, 1998), 184–235, 222.

40. Jay Lemke, "Multiplying Meaning: Visual and Verbal Semiotics in Scientific Text," in *Reading Science*, ed. J. R. Martin and R. Veel (London: Routledge, 1998), 87.

41. Ibid., 116.

42. Ibid.

43. Ibid., 123.

44. Boston Women's Health Course Collective, *Our Bodies, Our Selves: A Course by and for Women* (1971), 4.

45. Boston Women's Health Book Collective, *Our Bodies, Ourselves: A Book by and for Women* (1973), 31.

46. Ethel Sloane, *Biology of Women* (New York: Wiley, 1980).

47. Ibid., vi.

48. Ibid., 289.

49. Ibid.

50. "Biology of Women," handwritten document, Jane Pincus, private papers.

51. Boston Women's Health Book Collective, *The New Our Bodies, Ourselves* (1984), 332.

52. Ibid.

53. Ibid.

54. Cynthia W. Cooke, MD, and Susan Dworkin, *The Ms. Guide to a Woman's Health* (New York: Berkley Books, 1981), 199.

55. Draft, "Introduction to Childbearing," Jane Pincus, personal papers.

56. Draft, Proposed Outline for Childbearing Sections, October 15, 1981, Jane Pincus, personal papers.

57. Boston Women's Health Book Collective, *The New Our Bodies, Ourselves* (1984), 367.

58. Interviews, January 1982, Jane Pincus, personal papers.

59. Summer conversations, Jane Pincus, personal papers.

60. Ibid.

61. Notes from conversations, Jane Pincus, personal papers.

62. Draft, Childbearing chapter, Jane Pincus, personal papers.

63. Ibid.

64. Boston Women's Health Book Collective, *The New Our Bodies, Ourselves* (1984), 390.

65. Ibid.

66. Cooke and Dworkin, 154.

67. Ibid., 164.

68. Ibid., 165.

69. Ibid., 170.

70. Boston Women's Health Book Collective, *The New Our Bodies, Ourselves* (1984), 365.

71. Ibid., 369.

72. Ibid., 371.

73. Ibid., 374.

74. Ibid.

75. Ibid., 386.

76. Ibid., 379.

77. Ibid., 383.

78. Emily Martin, *The Woman in the Body: A Cultural Analysis of Reproduction* (Boston: Beacon, 1987).

79. Susan Bell, "Translating Science to the People: Updating *The New Our Bodies, Ourselves*," *Women's Studies International Forum* 17, no. 1 (1994): 9–18, 11.

80. *Our Bodies, Ourselves* (1984), 220.

81. Ibid.

82. Cooke and Dworkin, 36.

83. Boston Women's Health Book Collective, *The New Our Bodies, Ourselves* (1984), 222.

84. Ibid., 221.

85. Ibid., 225.

86. McGill Students' Society, *Birth Control Handbook* (Montreal: Students' Society of McGill University, 1969).

87. Judith Rooks, "The Feminist Health Book," *Family Planning Perspectives* 17, no. 5 (1985), 238 and 241, 238.

88. Boston Women's Health Book Collective, *The New Our Bodies, Ourselves* (1984), 557.

89. Ibid., 559.

90. Ibid., 225.

91. Ibid., 246.

92. Ibid., 234, 230

93. Ibid., 227, 236, 242.

94. Boston Women's Health Book Collective, Records, Schlesinger Library, Radcliffe Institute, Harvard University, Minutes (October 30, 1980, and November 4, 1980), BWHBC, MC 503, box 3, folder 3.

95. Ibid.

96. Norma Swenson, telephone interview with author, December 2006.

97. Ibid.

98. Boston Women's Health Book Collective, Records, Schlesinger Library, Radcliffe Institute, Harvard University, Minutes (October 30, 1980), BWHBC, MC 503, box 3, folder 3.

99. Pamela Berger, Nancy Miriam Hawley, and Jane Pincus, "Health and Healing: Alternatives to Medical Care," draft typescript, Pamela Berger, private papers.

100. Ibid., 9.

101. Ibid., 21.

102. Ibid., 24.

103. Boston Women's Health Book Collective, *The New Our Bodies, Ourselves* (1984), 4.

104. Pamela Berger, Nancy Miriam Hawley, and Jane Pincus, "Health and Healing: Alternatives to Medical Care," draft typescript, Pamela Berger, private papers, 13.

Postscript

1. Boston Women's Health Book Collective. Minutes, Schlesinger Library, Radcliffe Institute, Harvard University, MC 503, box 3, folder 13.

2. Jürgen Habermas, *Knowledge and Human Interests*, trans. J. Shapiro (Boston: Beacon, 1971), 341.

Bibliography

Archives and Collections

Frances Ansley Papers. Schlesinger Library, Radcliffe Institute, Harvard University.

Pamela C. Berger, private papers.

Gene Bishop Papers. Schlesinger Library, Radcliffe Institute, Harvard University.

Wini Breines Papers. Schlesinger Library, Radcliffe Institute, Harvard University.

Boston Women's Health Book Collective Records, 1972–97. Schlesinger Library, Radcliffe Institute, Harvard University.

Lucy Candib Papers. Schlesinger Library, Radcliffe Institute, Harvard University.

Northeastern University Women's History Archives. Women's Education Center.

Jane Pincus, private papers.

Mary Bunting Smith Papers. Schlesinger Library, Radcliffe Institute, Harvard University.

SNCC. *The Student Nonviolent Coordinating Committee Papers, 1959–1972.* Sanford, NC: Microfilming Corporation of America, 1982. Original papers at the King Library and Archives, The Martin Luther King Jr. Center for Nonviolent Social Change, Atlanta, Georgia.

Works Cited

A. R. G. [Africa Research Group] and *Old Mole. How Harvard Rules: Being a Total Critique of Harvard University, Including: New Liberated Documents, Government Research, the Educational Process Exposed, Strike Posters, & a Free Power Chart.* Cambridge, MA: 1969.

Agamben, Giorgio. *Homo Sacer: Sovereign Power and Bare Life.* Translated by Daniel Heller-Roazen. Stanford, CA: Stanford University Press, 1998.

Alaimo, Stacy, and Susan J. Hekman. *Material Feminisms.* Bloomington: Indiana University Press, 2008.

Albert, Judith Clavir, and Stewart Edward Albert. *The Sixties Papers: Documents of a Rebellious Decade.* New York: Praeger, 1984.

Alcoff, Linda Martin. "Who's Afraid of Identity Politics?" In *Reclaiming Identity: Realist Theory and the Predicament of Post-Modernism,* ed. Paula Moya and Michael Hames-Garcia. Berkeley: University of California Press, 2000.

Anonymous. "How Harvard Rules" [review of *How Harvard Rules*]. *The Harvard Crimson,* May 7, 1969. http://www.theharvardcrimson.com/article.aspx?ref=210032. Accessed May 2008.

Anonymous. "How to Start Your Own Consciousness-Raising Group." Original publication in *Black Maria* (Chicago); reprinted as Chicago Women's Liberation Union leaflet, 1971. Available online at CWLU History Project, Historical Archive, Consciousness. http://www.cwluherstory.com/CWLUArchive/conscious.html. Accessed May 2008.

Anonymous [five workers at Mt. Auburn Hospital, Cambridge, MA]. "Man Tends, God Mends." *Old Mole: A Radical Biweekly* 8 (February 21–March 7, 1969): 11.

Anonymous. "Women Must Control Own Medical Destiny." *Big Mama Rag* 2, no. 7 (May 1974): 7–11.

Assis, Elie. "Chiasmus in Biblical Narrative: Rhetoric of Characterization." *Prooftexts* 22, no. 3 (Fall 2002): 270–82.

Ayers, William. *Fugitive Days: A Memoir.* Boston: Beacon Press, 2001.

Bailey, Beth L., and David R. Farber. *America in the Seventies.* Lawrence: University Press of Kansas, 2004.

Baker, Keith Michael. "Defining the Public Sphere in Eighteenth Century France: Variations on a Theme by Habermas." In *Habermas and the Public Sphere,* ed. Craig Calhoun, 181–212. Cambridge, MA: MIT Press, 1992.

———. *Inventing the French Revolution.* Cambridge: Cambridge University Press, 1990.

Baxandall, Rosalyn, and Linda Gordon, eds. *Dear Sisters: Dispatches from the Women's Liberation Movement.* New York: Basic, 2000.

Beauvoir, Simone de. *The Second Sex.* 1952. New York: Random House, 1989.

Bell, Susan. "Translating Science to the People: Updating *The New Our Bodies, Ourselves.*" *Women's Studies International Forum* 17, no. 1 (1994): 9–18; 9.

Berson, Ginny Z. "The Furies: Goddesses of Vengeance." In *Voices from the Underground,* vol. I, *Insider Histories of the Vietnam Era Underground Press,* ed. Ken Wachsberger, 313–24. Tempe, AZ: MICA Press, 1993.

Better Homes and Gardens Child Care and Training Department. *Better Homes and Gardens Baby Book: A Handbook for Mothers; from Prenatal Care to Child's Sixth Year.* Des Moines, IA: Meredith Publishing Company, 1946.

Birke, Lynda I. A. *Feminism and the Biological Body.* Edinburgh: Edinburgh University Press, 1999.

Boek, Walter, Marvin Sussman, and Alfred Yankauer. "Social Class and Child Care Practices." *Marriage and Family Living* 20, no. 4 (November 1958): 326–33.

Bonilla, Zobeida. *"Our Bodies, Ourselves* Goes Latina." *The Network News*, May/June 2002, 5.

Bordo, Susan. *Unbearable Weight: Feminism, Western Culture, and the Body.* Berkeley: University of California Press, 1993.

Boston Women's Health Book Collective. *The New Our Bodies, Ourselves.* New York: Simon and Schuster, 1992.

——. *The New Our Bodies, Ourselves.* New York: Simon and Schuster, 1984.

——. "Our Bodies, Ourselves." Boston Women's Health Book Collective. http://www.ourbodiesourselves.org/default.asp. Accessed December 4, 2007–December 12, 2008.

——. *Our Bodies, Ourselves.* New York: Simon and Schuster, 1979.

——. *Our Bodies, Ourselves: A Book by and for Women.* New York: Simon and Schuster, 1973.

——. *Our Bodies, Ourselves: A Book by and for Women.* 2d ed. New York: Simon and Schuster, 1976.

——. *Our Bodies, Ourselves: A New Edition for a New Era.* 35th anniversary ed. New York: Simon & Schuster, 2005.

——. *Our Bodies, Ourselves for the New Century: A Book by and for Women.* Newly rev. and updated ed. New York: Simon & Schuster, 1998.

Boston Women's Health Collective. *Women and Their Bodies: A Course.* Boston: Boston Women's Health Collective, 1970.

Boston Women's Health Course Collective. *Our Bodies, Our Selves: A Course by and for Women.* Boston: New England Free Press, 1971.

Bowart, Art, and Allen Katzman. "Sgt. Pepper's Political Club and Band." In *Notes from the New Underground*, ed. Jesse Kornbluth, 189–97. New York: Viking, 1968.

Braidotti, Rosi. *Metamorphoses: Towards a Materialist Theory of Becoming.* Cambridge and Malden, MA: Polity; Blackwell, 2002.

Brandt, Deborah. *Literacy in American Lives.* New York: Cambridge University Press, 2001.

Braunstein, Peter, and Michael William Doyle. *Imagine Nation: The American Counterculture of the 1960s and 70s.* New York: Routledge, 2002.

Breines, Winifred. *The Trouble Between Us: An Uneasy History of White and Black Women in the Feminist Movement.* Oxford: Oxford University Press, 2006.

——. "What's Love Got to Do with It? White Women, Black Women, and Feminism in the Movement Years." *Signs: Journal of Women in Culture and Society* 27, no. 4 (Summer 2002): 1095–133.

Brody, Jane E. "A New Birth Pill Cuts Side Effects: Contraceptive Developed by Concern on Coast Does Not Interfere with Ovulation." *New York Times*, January 20, 1966.

Budick, Sanford. "Chiasmus and the Making of Literary Tradition: The Case of Wordsworth and 'The Days of Dryden and Pope.'" *ELH* 60, no. 4 (Winter 1993): 961–87.

Bureau of the Census, Selected Historical Decennial Census Population and Housing Counts, http://www.census.gov/population/www/censusdata/hiscendata.html. Accessed February 2008.

Burton, Gideon O. "Metalepsis." *Silvae Rhetoricae.* http://rhetoric.byu.edu. Accessed December 12, 2008.

Butler, Judith. *Bodies that Matter: On the Discursive Limits of 'Sex'.* London: Routledge, 1993.

———. "Discussion ('The Identity in Question')." *October* 61 (Summer 1992): 108–20.

———. *Gender Trouble: Feminism and the Subversion of Identity.* London: Routledge, 1990.

———. *The Psychic Life of Power: Theories in Subjection.* Stanford, CA: Stanford University Press, 1997.

Bynum, Caroline Walker. *Fragmentation and Redemption: Essays on Gender and the Human Body in Medieval Religion.* New York and Cambridge, MA: Zone Books, 1991.

Calhoun, Craig J. *Habermas and the Public Sphere: Studies in Contemporary German Social Thought.* Cambridge, MA: MIT Press, 1992.

Candib, Lucy. "How Medicine Tried to Make a Man Out of Me (and Failed, Finally)." In *Women in Medical Education: An Anthology of Experience,* ed. Delese Wear, 135–44. Albany: State University of New York Press, 1996.

———. *Medicine and the Family: A Feminist Perspective.* New York: Basic Books, 1995.

Cazort, Mimi, Monique Kornell, and K. B. Roberts. *The Ingenious Machine of Nature: Four Centuries of Art and Anatomy.* Ottawa: National Gallery of Canada, 1996.

Charters, Ann, ed. *The Portable Sixties Reader.* Penguin Classics. New York: Penguin Books, 2003.

Chase, Deborah. *The Medically-Based No-Nonsense Beauty Book.* New York: Alfred A. Knopf, 1974.

Chicago Liberation School for Women. "Courses, Spring 1973." In *Dear Sisters: Dispatches from the Women's Liberation Movement,* ed. Rosalyn Baxandall and Linda Gordon, 246. New York: Basic Books, 2000.

Combahee River Collective. "Combahee River Collective Statement." In *All the Women Are White, All the Blacks Are Men, but Some of Us Are Brave: Black Women's Studies,* ed. Gloria Hull, Patricia Bell-Scott, and Barbara Smith, 13–22. Old Westbury, NY: Feminist Press, 1982.

Cooke, Cynthia W., MD, and Susan Dworkin. *The Ms. Guide to a Woman's Health.* New York: Berkley Books, 1981.

Crist, Takey, and Lana Starnes. "Student Printing Presses Bring Birth Control Story to Colleges." *Family Planning Perspectives* 4, no. 1 (1972): 60–61.

Danius, Sara, Stefan Jonsson, and Gayatri Chakravorty Spivak. "An Interview with Gayatri Chakravorty Spivak." *Boundary 2* 20, no. 2 (Summer 1993): 24–50.

Davis, Kathy. *The Making of Our Bodies, Ourselves: How Feminism Travels Across Borders*. Durham, NC: Duke University Press, 2007.

Domhoff, William. *Who Rules America?* New York: Prentice-Hall, 1967.

Doress-Worters, Paula B., Diana Laskin Siegal, Midlife and Older Women Book Project, and Boston Women's Health Book Collective. *Ourselves, Growing Older: Women Aging with Knowledge and Power*. New York: Simon and Schuster, 1987.

Dryer, Thorne, and Victoria Smith. "The Movement and the New Media." *Liberation News Service*, March 1, 1969. http://www.nuevoanden.com/rag/newmedia.html. Accessed August 2007.

Dunbar-Ortiz, Roxanne. *Outlaw Woman: A Memoir of the War Years, 1960–75*. San Francisco: City Lights, 2001.

DuPlessis, Rachel Blau, and Ann Barr Snitow. *The Feminist Memoir Project: Voices from Women's Liberation*. 1st ed. New York: Three Rivers Press, 1998.

Eberly, Rosa A. *Citizen Critics: Literary Public Spheres*. The History of Communication. Urbana: University of Illinois Press, 2000.

Echols, Alice. *Daring to Be Bad: Radical Feminism in America, 1967–1975*. American Culture. Minneapolis: University of Minnesota Press, 1989.

———. *Shaky Ground: The '60s and Its Aftershocks*. New York: Columbia University Press, 2002.

Ede, Lisa, and Andrea Lunsford. "Collaboration and Concepts of Authorship." *PMLA* 116, no. 2 (March 2001): 354–69.

———. *Singular Texts/Plural Authors: Perspectives on Collaborative Writing*. Carbondale: Southern Illinois University Press, 1990.

Eley, Geoff. "Nations, Publics, and Political Cultures." In *Habermas and the Public Sphere*, ed. Craig Calhoun, 300–23. Cambridge, MA: MIT Press, 1992.

Elias, Norbert. *Power and Civility: The Civilizing Process [Wandlungen der Gesellschaft]*. Vol. 2. New York: Pantheon Books, 1982.

Emery, Kathy, Sylvia Braselman, and Linda Gold, eds. *Freedom School Curriculum: Mississippi Freedom Summer, 1964*. Education and Democracy Web site, http://www.educationanddemocracy.org/ED_FSC.html. Accessed May 9, 2008.

Evans, Sara. *Personal Politics: The Roots of Women's Liberation in the Civil Rights Movement and the New Left*. New York: Vintage, 1979.

Farber, David R. *The Sixties: From Memory to History*. Chapel Hill: University of North Carolina Press, 1994.

Fausto-Sterling, Anne. *Sexing the Body: Gender Politics and the Construction of Sexuality*. New York: Basic Books, 2000.

Feminists, The. "The Feminists: A Political Organization to Annihilate Sex Roles." Originally published in *Notes from the Second Year: Women's Liberation*, ed. Shulamith Firestone with Anne Koedt. New York: Radical Feminism, 1970. Reprinted in *Women's Liberation: Major Writings of the Radical Feminists*, ed. Anne Koedt, Ellen Levine, and Anita Rapone, 368–78. New York: Quadrangle, 1973.

Firestone, Shulamith. *The Dialectic of Sex: The Case for Feminist Revolution*. New York: Morrow, 1970.

Fishbein, Morris. *The Handy Home Medical Adviser, and Concise Medical Encyclopedia*. Garden City, NY: Doubleday, 1957.

Flannery, Kathryn T. *Feminist Literacies, 1968–75*. Urbana: University of Illinois Press, 2005.

Foucault, Michel. "What Is an Author?" In *Language, Counter-memory, Practice*, ed. Donald F. Bouchard, trans. D. F. Bouchard and Sherry Simon, 113–38. Ithaca, NY: Cornell University Press, 1977.

Freeman, Jo. *The Women's Liberation Movement: Its Aims, Structures, and Ideas*. Pittsburgh, PA: Know, 1971.

Genette, Gérard. *Narrative Discourse: An Essay in Method [Discours du récit]*. Ithaca, NY: Cornell University Press, 1980.

Gitlin, Todd. *The Sixties: Years of Hope, Days of Rage*. Toronto and New York: Bantam Books, 1987.

Goldblatt, Eli. *Round My Way: Authority and Double-Consciousness in Three Urban High School Writers*. Pittsburgh, PA: University of Pittsburgh Press, 1995.

Grimsted, Kristen, and Susan Rennie. *The New Woman's Survival Sourcebook*. New York: Alfred A. Knopf, 1975.

Grosz, Elizabeth. "Sexual Difference and the Problem of Essentialism." *Inscriptions* 5, (1989). www.ucsc.edu/DivWeb/CultStudies/PUBS/Inscriptions/vol_5. Accessed August 2007.

———. *Space, Time, and Perversion: Essays on the Politics of Bodies*. New York: Routledge, 1995.

———. *Volatile Bodies: Toward a Corporeal Feminism*. Bloomington: Indiana University Press, 1994.

Gutcheon, Beth Richardson. *Abortion: A Woman's Guide*. New York: Abelard-Schuman, 1975.

Haber, Gail Weis, and Honi Fern. *Perspectives on Embodiment: The Intersections of Nature and Culture*. New York: Routledge, 1999.

Habermas, Jürgen. *Between Facts and Norms: Contributions to a Discourse Theory of Law and Democracy*. Translated by William Rehg. Cambrdige, MA: MIT Press, 1996.

———. *Knowledge and Human Interests*. Translated by J. Shapiro. Boston: Beacon, 1971.

———. *The Structural Transformation of the Public Sphere: An Inquiry into a Category of Bourgeois Society*. Translated by Thomas Burger with Frederick Lawrence. Cambridge, MA: MIT Press, 1991.

Halliday, M.A.K. "The Construction of Knowledge and Value in the Grammar of Scientific Discourse: Charles Darwin's *The Origin of the Species*." In *Writing Science: Literacy and Discursive Power*, ed M.A.K. Halliday and J. R. Martin, 86–105. Pittsburgh, PA: University of Pittsburgh Press, 1993.

———. "Things and Relations: Regrammaticising Experience as Technical Knowledge." In *Reading Science: Critical and Functional Perspectives on Discourses of Science*, ed. J. R. Martin and Robert Veel, 184–235. London: Routledge, 1998.

Haraway, Donna. *Modest_Witness@Second_Millennium.FemaleMan_Meets_OncoMouse: Feminism and Technoscience*. New York: Routledge, 1997.

———. *Primate Visions: Gender, Race, and Nature in the World of Modern Science*. New York and London: Routledge, 1989.

———. "Situated Knowledges: The Science Question in Feminism and the Privilege of Partial Perspective." *Feminist Studies* 14 (1988): 575–99.

———. "The Virtual Speculum in the New World Order." In *Revisioning Women, Health and Healing: Feminist, Cultural, and Technoscience Perspectives*, ed. Adele E. Clarke and Virginia L. Olesen, 49–96. New York: Routledge, 1998.

Harding, Sandra. *Whose Science? Whose Knowledge? Thinking from Women's Lives*. Ithaca, NY: Cornell University Press, 1991.

Hauser, Gerard A. *Vernacular Voices: The Rhetoric of Publics and Public Spheres*. Columbia: University of South Carolina Press, 1999.

Hayden, Tom. *Reunion: A Memoir*. New York: Random House, 1988.

Heller-Roazen, Daniel. *Echolalias: On the Forgetting of Language*. New York: Zone Books, 2004.

Hite, Shere. *The Hite Report: A Nationwide Study of Female Sexuality*. New York: McMillan, 1976.

Hobbs, Chris. *"Our Bodies Ourselves"* [review]. *off our backs* 3, no. 8 (May 1973): 29.

Hole, Judith, and Ellen Levine. *Rebirth of Feminism*. New York: Quadrangle Books, 1971.

Hooker, Worthington. *Physician and Patient; or, A Practical View of the Mutual Duties, Relations, and Interests of the Medical Profession and the Community*. Reprint of the 1849 ed. New York: Arno, 1972.

Hopkins, Jerry, ed. *The Hippie Papers: Notes from the Underground Press*. New York: New American Library, 1968.

Hosek, Jennifer Ruth, and Walter J. Freeman. "Osmetic Ontogenesis, Or Olfaction Becomes You: The Neurodynamic Intentional Self and Its Affinities with the Foucaultian/Butlerian Subject." *Configurations* 9 (2001): 509–42.

Huffhines, Kathy. "Scenes from a Marriage: Ed Presents Ed." *Cambridge Express*, November 21, 1981, 12.

Hume, Jan, and Kathryn Baetens. "Speed, Rhythm, Movement: A Dialogue on K. Hume's Article 'Narrative Speed.'" *Narrative* 14, no. 3 (October 2006): 349–55, 349.

Hunter, Kathryn Montgomery. *Doctors' Stories: The Narrative Structure of Medical Knowledge*. Princeton, NJ: Princeton University Press, 1991.

Inda, Jonathan Xavier. "Foreign Bodies: Migrants, Parasites, and the Pathological Nation." *Discourse* 22, no. 3 (Fall 2000): 46–62.

Inge, M. Thomas. "Collaboration and Concepts of Authorship." *PMLA* 116, no. 3 (May 2001): 354–69.

Itasca Conference on the Continuing Education of Women. *Education and a Woman's Life. Proceedings.* Washington, DC: American Council on Education, 1963.

Kahn, Robbie Pfeufer. *Bearing Meaning: the Language of Birth.* Urbana: University of Illinois Press, 1995.

Kalitzkus, Vera, and Peter Twohig. *Bordering Biomedicine.* Amsterdam and New York: Rodopi, 2006.

Kaufman, Sherwin. *The Ageless Woman: Menopause, Hormones, and the Quest for Youth.* Englewood Cliffs, NJ: Prentice-Hall, 1967.

King, Martin L. "Beyond Vietnam." Address Delivered to the Clergy and Laymen Concerned about Vietnam, Riverside Church, New York, April 4, 1967. Martin Luther King Jr. Papers Project, http://www.stanford.edu/group/King/publications/speeches/Beyond_Vietnam.pdf. Accessed July 2007.

Kline, Wendy. "'Please Include this in Your Book': Readers Respond to *Our Bodies, Ourselves.*" *Bulletin of the History of Medicine* 79 (2005): 81–110.

Koedt, Anne. "The Myth of the Vaginal Orgasm." In *Dear Sisters: Dispatches from the Women's Liberation Movement,* ed. Rosalyn Baxandall and Linda Gordon, 158–63. New York: Basic Books, 2000.

Koedt, Anne, Ellen Levine, and Anita Rapone, eds. *Radical Feminism.* New York: Quadrangle Books, 1973.

Kronhausen, Phyllis, and Eberhard Kronhausen. *The Sexually Responsive Woman.* New York: Grove Press, 1964.

Lacan, Jacques. "Feminine Sexuality in Psychoanalytic Doctrine." In *Feminine Sexuality,* ed. Juliet Mitchell and Jacqueline Rose, 123–36. New York: W. W. Norton, 1982.

———. "Some Reflections on the Ego." *International Journal of Psychoanalysis* 34 (1953): 11–17.

Lader, Lawrence. "Three Men Who Made a Revolution." *New York Times,* April 10, 1966, Sunday Magazine, 181–85.

Landes, Joan B. *Women and the Public Sphere in the Age of the French Revolution.* Ithaca, NY: Cornell University Press, 1988.

Langer, Elinor. "Notes for Next Time: A Memoir of the 1960s." *Working Papers for a New Society* 1, no. 3 (Fall 1973): 48–84.

Laqueur, Thomas Walter. *Making Sex: Body and Gender from the Greeks to Freud.* Cambridge, MA: Harvard University Press, 1990.

Lawrence, Christopher, and Steven Shapin, eds. *Science Incarnate: Historical Embodiments of Natural Knowledge.* Chicago: University of Chicago Press, 1998.

Lay, Mary M., Laura J. Gurak, Clare Gravon, and Cynthia Myntti. *Body Talk: Rhetoric, Technology, Reproduction.* Madison: University of Wisconsin Press, 2000.

Lemke, Jay. "Multiplying Meaning: Visual and Verbal Semiotics in Scientific Text." In *Reading Science*, ed. J. R. Martin and R. Veel. London: Routledge, 1998.

Linden-Ward, Blanche, and Carol Hurd Green. *American Women in the 1960s: Changing the Future*. American Women in the Twentieth Century. New York: Twayne, 1993.

Lindsey, Elizabeth Sarah. "Reexamining Gender and Sexual Orientation: Revisioning the Representation of Queer and Trans People in the 2005 Edition of *Our Bodies, Ourselves*." *NWSA Journal* 17, no. 1 (Spring 2005): 184–89.

Loeffler, Carl Eugene, and Roy Ascott. "Chronology and Working Survey of Select Telecommunications Activity." *Leonardo Music Journal* 24, no. 2 (1991): 235–40.

Lourde, Audre. *Zami: A New Spelling of My Name*. Berkeley, CA: Cross Press, 1982.

Lowen, Alexander. *Love and Orgasm*. New York: New American Library, 1967.

Lytle, Mark H. *America's Uncivil Wars: The Sixties Era from Elvis to the Fall of Richard Nixon*. New York: Oxford University Press, 2006.

Mah, Harold. "Phantasies of the Public Sphere: Rethinking the Habermas of Historians." *The Journal of Modern History* 72, no. 1, New Work on the Old Regime and the French Revolution: A Special Issue in Honor of Francois Furet (March 2000): 153–82.

Malina, Debra. *Breaking the Frame: Metalepsis and the Construction of the Subject*. Theory and Interpretation of Narrative. Edited by James Phelan and Peter Rabinowitz. Columbus: Ohio State University Press, 2002.

Martin, Emily. *The Woman in the Body: A Cultural Analysis of Reproduction*. Boston: Beacon, 1987.

Martin, J. R., and Robert Veel, eds. *Reading Science: Cultural and Functional Perspectives on Discourses of Science*. London: Routledge, 1998.

Marx, Karl. *The Economic and Philosophic Manuscripts of 1844*. Translated by Martin Milligan, edited by Dirk Struik. New York: International, 1964.

Marx, Karl, and Eleanor Marx Aveling. *Value, Price and Profit*. Little Marx Library. New York: International, 1969.

Massachusetts Coalition for Occupational Safety and Health and the Boston Women's Health Book Collective. *Our Jobs, Our Health: A Woman's Guide to Occupational Health and Safety*. Watertown, MA: Boston Women's Health Book Collective and Massachusetts Coalition for Occupational Safety and Health, 1983.

Masters, William H., Virginia E. Johnson, and Reproductive Biology Research Foundation. *Human Sexual Response*. 1st ed. Boston: Little, Brown, 1966.

Maza, Sarah. "Women, the Bourgeoisie, and the Public Sphere: Response to Daniel Gordon and David Bell." *French Historical Studies* 17, no. 4 (Autumn 1992): 935–50.

McGill Students' Society. *Birth Control Handbook*. Montreal: Students' Society of McGill University, 1969.

Meigs, Charles D. *Females and their Diseases*. Philadelphia, PA: Blanchard and Lea, 1848.

Merchant, Carolyn. *The Death of Nature: Women, Ecology, and the Scientific Revolution.* New York: HarperCollins, 1980.

Miller, Jim. *"Democracy Is in the Streets": From Port Huron to the Siege of Chicago.* New York: Simon and Schuster, 1987.

Mohanty, Satya. *Literary Theory and the Claims of History.* Ithaca, NY: Cornell University Press, 1997.

Moon, Michael, and Cathy N. Davidson, eds. *Subjects and Citizens: Nation, Race, and Gender from Oroonoko to Anita Hill.* Durham, NC: Duke University Press, 1995.

Moore, Lisa Jean, and Adele E. Clarke. "Clitoral Conventions and Transgressions: Graphic Representations in Anatomy Texts, c. 1900–1991." *Feminist Studies* 21, no. 2 (Summer 1995): 255–301.

Morgan, Robin. "Goodbye to All That." In *Dear Sisters: Dispatches from the Women's Liberation Movement*, ed. Rosalyn Baxandall and Linda Gordon, 53–57. New York: Basic Books, 2003.

———. *Sisterhood Is Powerful: An Anthology of Writings from the Women's Liberation Movement.* New York: Random House, 1970.

Morgen, Sandra. *Into Our Own Hands: The Women's Health Movement in the United States, 1969–1990.* New Brunswick, NJ: Rutgers University Press, 2002.

Muller, Leo, and others, eds. *New Horizons for College Women.* Washington, DC: Public Affairs Press, 1960.

NACLA [North American Congress on Latin America]. *Who Rules Columbia?* New York: NACLA, 1967.

Nealon, Jeffrey. "Maxima Immoralia? Speed and Slowness in Adorno's *Minima Moralia*." *Theory and Event* 4, no. 3 (2000).

Norsigian, Judith, and others. "The Boston Women's Health Book Collective and *Our Bodies, Ourselves*." *Journal of the American Medical Women's Association* 54, no. 1 (Winter 1999): 35–39.

North, Michael. "Authorship and Autography." *PMLA* 116, no. 5 (October 2001): 1377–85.

Odent, Michel. *Birth Reborn.* Translated by Jane Pincus and Juliette Levin. New York: Pantheon, 1984.

Peck, Abe. *Uncovering the Sixties: The Life and Times of the Underground Press.* New York: Citadel Press, 1991.

Pincus, Jane. "Our Bodies, Ourselves: Liberating Minds and Bodies." Interview with Chelsea Whitaker, February 2004. http://www.doingoralhistory.org/project_ archive/2004/Papers/PDFs/C-Whit.pdf. Accessed May 2008.

Polletta, Francesca. *It Was Like a Fever: Storytelling in Protest and Politics.* Chicago: University of Chicago Press, 2006.

Poovey, Mary. *Making a Social Body: British Cultural Formation, 1830–1864.* Chicago: University of Chicago Press, 1995.

Popkin, Ann. "Bread and Roses: An Early Moment in the Development of Socialist-Feminism." PhD diss., Brandeis University, Department of Sociology, 1976.

Price, Janet, and Margrit Shildrick, eds. *Feminist Theory and the Body: A Reader*. New York: Routledge, 1999.

Rag, vol. 1, available online at the Austin *Rag* Web site, www.nuevoanden.com/rag/010319661024. Accessed February 14, 2009.

Rea, Charlotte. "Women's Theatre Groups." *The Drama Review: TDR* 16, no. 2 (1972): 79–89.

Robbins, Sarah. "Distributed Authorship: A Feminist Case-Study Framework for Studying Intellectual Property." *College English* 66, no. 2 (November 2003): 155–71.

Ronay, V. T. "Oakland Induction Center: Tuesday, October 17, 1967." In *Notes from the New Underground: An Anthology*, ed. Jesse Kornbluth, 286–90. New York: Viking Press, 1968.

Rooks, Judith. "The Feminist Health Book" [review of *Our Bodies, Ourselves*]. *Family Planning Perspectives* 17, no. 5 (1985): 238–41.

Rorvik, David. *Good Housekeeping Woman's Medical Guide*. New York: Good Housekeeping, 1974.

Rosen, Ruth. *The World Split Open: How the Modern Women's Movement Changed America*. New York: Penguin, 2000.

Ruchelman, Leonard I., ed. *Who Rules the Police?* New York: New York University Press, 1973.

Ryan, Mary. "Gender and Public Access: Women's Politics in Nineteenth-Century America." In *Habermas and the Public Sphere*, ed. Craig Calhoun, 259–88. Cambridge, MA: MIT Press, 1992.

Sadoff, Dianne F. *Sciences of the Flesh: Representing Body and Subject in Psychoanalysis*. Stanford, CA: Stanford University Press, 1998.

Sale, Kirkpatrick. "The New Left: What's Left?" *WIN* 9, no. 18 (June 21, 1973): 4–11.

Salpeter, Eliahu, and Yuval Elitzur. *Who Rules Israel?* New York: Harper & Row, 1973.

Sanders, David, and Ian Hunter. "Lessons from the 'Literatory': How to Historicize Authorship." *Critical Inquiry* 17, no. 3 (Spring 1991): 479–509.

Sanford, Wendy Coppedge. *Theater as Metaphor in Hamlet*. The LeBaron Russell Briggs Prize Honors Essays in English. Vol. 1967. Cambridge, MA: Harvard University Press, 1967.

———. "Working Together, Growing Together: A Brief History of the Boston Women's Health Collective." *Heresies* 2, no. 3 (1970): 83–92.

Sappol, Michael. *Dream Anatomy*. Washington, DC: National Library of Medicine, 2006.

Saxton, Christine. "The Collective Voice as Cultural Voice." *Cinema Journal* 26, no. 1 (1986): 19–30.

Schechter, Daniel. "From a Closed Filing Cabinet: The Life and Times of the Africa Research Group." *Issue: A Journal of Opinion* 6, no. 23 (Summer–Autumn 1976): 41–48.

Scherzwer, Martha. "Byllye Avery and the National Black Women's Health Project." *Network News* (May–June 1995): 1, 4, 6.

Schiebinger, Londa. *Nature's Body: Gender in the Making of Modern Science.* Boston: Beacon, 1993.

Scott, Ann Firon. "Education and the Contemporary Woman." In *The Knowledge Most Worth Having*, ed. Wayne Booth, 141–50. Chicago: University of Chicago Press, 1967.

Segal, Judy Z. *Health and the Rhetoric of Medicine.* Carbondale: Southern Illinois University Press, 2005.

Shanken, Edward. "Tele-Agency: Telematics, Telerobotics, and the Art of Meaning." *Art Journal* 59, no. 2 (Summer 2000): 64–77.

Shapiro, Ester. "Because Words Are Not Enough: Latina Re-Visionings of Transnational Collaborations Using Health Promotion for Gender Justice and Social Change." *NWSA Journal* 17, no. 1 (Spring 2005): 141–72.

Shapiro, Helen. "NACLA Reminiscences: An Oral History." *NACLA Report* 15, no. 5 (September 1981): 46–56.

Simurda, Stephen. "Byllye Avery: Guardian of Black Women's Health." *American Health* (March 1993).

Sjoholm, Cecilia. "Crossing Lovers: Luce Irigaray's Elemental Passions." *Hypatia* 15, no. 3 (Summer 2000): 92.

Sloane, Ethel. *Biology of Women.* New York: Wiley, 1980.

Smith, Anthony. *The Body.* New York: Walker and Company, 1968.

Southern Methodist University Women's Committee for the Sesquicentennial Year. *The Education of Women for Social and Political Leadership.* Dallas, TX: Southern Methodist University Press, 1967.

Springer, Kimberly. *Living for the Revolution: Black Feminist Organizations, 1968–1980.* Durham, NC: Duke University Press, 2005.

Stafford, Barbara Maria. *Body Criticism: Imaging the Unseen in Enlightenment Art and Medicine.* Cambridge, MA: MIT Press, 1991.

Stamberg, Margie. "Women's Meeting Held in Boston." *Guardian* 21, no. 34 (May 24, 1969): 9.

Statewide Conference on the Changing Status of Women. *Proceedings.* Columbus: Ohio State University, 1965.

Stern, Susan. *With the Weathermen: The Personal Journal of a Revolutionary Woman.* New York: Doubleday, 1975.

Students for a Democratic Society. "The Port Huron Statement." In *The Sixties Papers: Documents of a Rebellious Decade*, ed. Judith Albert and Stewart Albert, 176–96. New York: Praeger, 1984.

Tanner, Laura E. *Intimate Violence: Reading Rape and Torture in Twentieth-Century Fiction.* Bloomington: Indiana University Press, 1994.

Tax, Meredith. "Woman and Her Mind: The Story of Everyday Life." In *Radical Feminism,* ed. Anne Koedt, Ellen Levine, and Anita Rapone, 23–35. New York: Quadrangle Books, 1973.

Tillan, Christopher. "Cooking Column." *Old Mole: A Radical Biweekly* no. 11 (April 11–24, 1969): 14.

United Nations, Department of Economic and Social Affairs. *Civic and Political Education of Women.* New York: United Nations, 1964.

United States President's Commission on the Status of Women, Committee on Education. *Report of the Committee on Education to the President's Commission on the Status of Women.* Washington, DC: The Commission, 1964.

University of Michigan Center for Continuing Education of Women. *New Careers in Community Service.* Ann Arbor: Center for Continuing Education of Women, University of Michigan, 1968.

Warner, Michael. *Publics and Counterpublics.* New York: Zone, 2002.

Wegenstein, Bernadette. "Getting Under the Skin; or, How Faces Have Become Obsolete." *Configurations* 10, no. 2 (2002): 221–60.

Weisstein, Naomi. "Psychology Constructs the Female." In *Radical Feminism,* ed. Anne Koedt, Ellen Levine, and Anita Rapone, 165–77. New York: Quadrangle, 1973.

Wells, Susan. "Photo-Offset Printing and the Alternative Press in the Sixties and Seventies: Practices and Genres." In *Rhetorics and Technologies: New Directions in Communication,* ed. Stuart Selber. Columbia: University of South Carolina Press, 2010.

Williams, Gareth. "Irving Kenneth Zola (1935–1994): An Appreciation." *Sociology of Health and Illness* 18, no. 1 (1996): 107–25.

Williams, Liza. "To Allen Ginsberg by Liza Williams." Originally published in *The Oracle of Southern California* (Los Angeles), March 1967, 200; reprinted in *The Hippie Papers: Notes from the Underground Press,* ed. Jerry Hopkins, 134–35. New York: New American Library, 1968.

Willis, Ellen. "Birth Control Pill." *Mademoiselle,* January 1961, 54.

Women of the New University Conference and others. *How Harvard Rules Women.* Cambridge, MA: n.p., 1970.

Wood, Victor. *Who Rules the A.P.A.?: A Study of the Backgrounds of Leaders of the American Psychological Association.* MA thesis, Humbolt State University, Arcata, CA, 1973.

Young, Iris Marion. *"Throwing Like a Girl" and Other Essays: Studies in Feminist Philosophy.* New York: Oxford University Press, 2005.

Zimmerman, Bill, Len Radinsky, Mel Rothenberg, and Bart Meyers. "Towards a Science for the People." 1972. http://socrates.berkeley.edu/schwrtz/SftP/Towards.html. Accessed May 2008.

Zola, Irving Kenneth. "Bringing Our Bodies and Ourselves Back In: Reflections on a Past, Present, and Future 'Medical Sociology.'" *Journal of Health and Social Behavior* 32, no. 1 (March 1991): 1–16.

————. "Shifting Boundaries: Doing Social Science in the 1990s—A Personal Odyssey." *Sociological Forum* 10, no. 1 (March 1995): 5–19.

Index